WHAT YOUR MOTHER COULDN'T TELL YOU & YOUR FATHER DIDN'T KNOW

WHAT YOUR MOTHER COULDN'T TELL YOU & YOUR FATHER DIDN'T KNOW **JOHN GRAY**

A PRACTICAL GUIDE TO IMPROVING COMMUNICATION BETWEEN THE SEXES

VERMILION
LONDON

First published 1994

3 5 7 9 10 8 6 4 2

First published in the United Kingdom in 1995 by Vermilion
an imprint of Ebury Press
Random House UK Ltd
Random House
20 Vauxhall Bridge Road
London SW1V 2SA

Random House, South Africa (Pty) Limited
PO Box 337, Bergvlei, South Africa

Random House UK Limited Reg. No. 954009

A CIP catalogue record for this book is available from the British Library.

ISBN 0 09 180653 4

Designed by Alma Hochhauser Orenstein
Printed and bound in Great Britain by
Mackays of Chatham PLC, Chatham, Kent

Papers used by Vermilion are natural, recyclable products made from wood grown in sustainable forests.

This book is dedicated with
deepest love and gratitude
to my parents
David and Virginia Gray

Their undying love, trust, and encouragement
continues to surround and support me in my journey
as a teacher, husband, and father.

CONTENTS

ACKNOWLEDGMENTS

I thank my wife, Bonnie, for once again sharing the journey of developing a book with me. I thank her for her continued patience and support in helping me be successful as a loving mate and father to our children. I also thank her for allowing me to share our stories and especially for continuing to expand my understanding and ability to honor the female perspective. Her insightful suggestions and comments have provided an important and necessary balance.

I thank our three daughters, Shannon, Juliet, and Lauren, for their love and admiration. The joy of being a parent helps immensely to offset the pressures of a very busy lifestyle. I thank them for their warmth, wisdom, and appreciation of what I do. Particularly I want to thank Lauren for painting the sign in my office: "Please Daddy, finish the book! Hooray!!!"

I thank my father, David Gray, for attending my seminars on relationships. His support and belief in me and my work was and still is immensely helpful. His candid sharing of his successes and failures in his relationships helped me to understand the differences between our generations. Although he didn't know the skills for growing in intimacy, he did his best, and from that I learned that I could make mistakes and still be worthy of love. He is remembered by many as a loving, charming, and generous man.

I thank my mother, Virginia Gray, for the many intelligent and fun conversations we have had on how women and men in her generation behaved and reacted in relationships. Times have certainly changed. I thank her for allowing me to share stories from her marriage and for her persistent accepting and embracing love that surrounds and supports me in everything I do.

I thank all my five brothers and sister for our long discussions into the night at holiday get-togethers. I thank my oldest brother, David, and his wife, Doris, for their keen insight and their appreciation of my new and creative ideas as well as their challenges. I thank my brother William and his wife, Edwina, for sharing with me the more traditional perspectives. I thank my brother Robert once again for his brilliant and spiritual ideas that fundamentally support everything I talk about. I thank my brother Tom for his continued encouragement and pride in my success. I thank him for the many personal conversations when he has shared his insights about men and women. I thank my sister, Virginia, for her openness and loving interest in my life and her candid and discerning understanding of herself as a woman. I thank my deceased younger brother, Jimmy, for his special love and generous spirit. His memory and spirit continue to touch my heart and support me through my most difficult times.

I thank Lucille Brixey for her special and loving support of me since I was six years old. She was always there for me and still is. In her store in Houston, the Aquarian Age Bookshelf, she has displayed my books out front for over ten years. I thank her for always believing in me.

I thank my agent, Patti Breitman, for her helpful assistance, brilliant creativity, and enthusiasm that have guided this book from its conception to its completion. She is a special angel in my life. I thank Carole Bidnick, who connected Patti and me together for the beginning of our first project, *Men Are from Mars, Women Are from Venus*.

I thank Susan Moldow for her wit and editorial clarity, and although she only worked on this book at the beginning, her savvy comments directed and molded its unfoldment. I thank Nancy Peske for her persistent editorial expertise and creativity throughout the whole process. I thank Carolyn Fireside for her editorial contributions. I thank Jack McKeown for his interest and committed support of this project since its beginning and for the support of the entire staff at HarperCollins for their continued responsiveness to my needs.

I thank Michael Nagarian and his wife, Susan, for the successful organization of so many seminars. I thank Michael for the many extra hours of creative planning plus the important and insightful feedback he has given to me in developing and testing this material. I thank the many different promoters and organizers who have put their hearts and souls into producing and supporting seminars for me to teach and develop the material in this book: Elly and Ian Coren in Santa Cruz; Ellis and Consuelo Goldfrit in Santa Cruz; Sandee Mac in Houston; Richi and Debra Mudd in Honolulu; Garry Francell of Heart Seminars in Honolulu; Bill and Judy Elbring of *Life Partners* in San Francisco; David Farlow and Julie Ricksacker in San Diego; David and Marci Obstfeld in Detroit; Fred Kleiner and Mary Wright in Washington, D.C.; Clark and Dotti Bartells in Seattle; Earlene and Jim Carillo in Las Vegas; Bart and Merril Berens in L.A.; Grace Merrick of the Dallas Unity Church.

I thank Richard Cohn and Cindy Black and the staff at Beyond Words Publishing for their continued support in promoting and publishing my book *Men, Women and Relationships*, which gave birth to the ideas in this book.

I thank John Vestman at Studio One Recording for his expert audio recordings of my seminars. I thank Dave Morton and the staff of Cassette Express for their continued appreciation of this material and their quality service. I thank Bonnie Solow for her competence and gentle support in producing the audio version of this book as well as the staff of HarperAudio.

I thank Ramy El-Batrawi of Genesis Nuborn Associates and his wife, Ronda, for the successful creation and ongoing production of television infomercials making available audio and video presentations of my seminars.

I thank my executive assistant, Ariana Husband, for her hard work, devotion, and efficient managing of my schedule and office.

I thank my chiropractor, Terry Safford, for the incredible support he provided twice a week during the most intensive six months of this project. I thank Raymond Himmel for his many acupuncture sessions at the end of this project that miraculously healed me of dizziness and exhaustion. I thank Renee Swisko for her amazing and powerful healing sessions with me and the rest of my family.

I thank my friends and associates for their open, honest, and supportive sharing of ideas and feedback: Clifford McGuire, Jim Kennedy and Anna Everest, John and Bonnie Grey, Reggie and Andrea Henkart, Lee and Joyce Shapiro, Marcia Sutton, Gabriel Grunfeld, Harold Bloomfield and Sirah Vettese, Jordan Paul, Lenny Eiger, Charles Wood, Jacques Earley, Chris Johns, Mike Bosch and Doug Aarons.

I thank Oprah Winfrey for her warm and personal support and the opportunity to share freely my ideas on her show before 30 million viewers.

I thank the thousands of participants of my relationship seminars who shared their stories and encouraged me to write this book. Their positive and loving support, along with the thousands of calls and letters I have received from readers, continues to support me in developing and validating the principles of this book.

Particularly for the enormous success of my previous books, I wish to thank the millions of readers who not only have shared my books with others but continue to benefit from these ideas in their lives and relationships.

I give thanks to God for the opportunity to make a difference in this world and the simple but effective wisdom that comes to me and is presented in this book.

WHAT YOUR MOTHER COULDN'T TELL YOU & YOUR FATHER DIDN'T KNOW

INTRODUCTION

Away from home for the weekend, I was getting ready for bed when someone knocked on my hotel door. It was a participant in the seminar I was teaching. I had noticed her many times during my presentation and found her very attractive. There was strong physical chemistry.

As she silently entered the room, she looked straight into my eyes and without saying a word unzipped her skirt and let it drop to the floor. My jaw dropped along with it.

"I want you," she whispered. My mind went blank. I didn't know what to say. My body rejoiced, but my mind began to panic: after all, I was happily married, and I dearly loved my wife.

My uninvited guest continued to undress, and while my mind was trying to get a grip on the situation, every cell in my body was saying yes. Still, I somehow managed to stand my ground and hold back.

Without missing a beat, she moved toward me and began to unbutton my shirt. Time seemed to stand still, and nothing existed except the explosive passion of the moment. At the first physical contact, I felt an electric shock shoot through my entire body. In the next moment, I remembered my wife and pulled back.

I said, "Excuse me, but I am married. I can't do this."

As if the scene had been perfectly choreographed she confidently responded, "It's OK, I'll never tell."

I politely explained, "My wife has little antennas. She knows everything, and this would only hurt her and our relationship. I think you'd better go."

She just smiled and said, "But don't you want me to stay?"

Although I was a believer in monogamy, I found myself suddenly beginning to reconsider. My mind flooded with rationalizations. How, for instance, could something that felt so good be bad? Why couldn't I be a loving husband at home and also have a little extra pleasure on the side?

Finally, after much discussion and emotional struggle I asked her to leave. I was able to restrain myself because I knew having an affair would hurt my wife. Although I felt I had done the right thing, I could not sleep.

For hours my thoughts continued to churn. I had resisted temptation, but my mind began to question if monogamy was really necessary. I could not understand why having sex with a willing partner was wrong. I thought maybe monogamy was an outdated tradition and should be "overcome." After all, a loving marriage should not be a prison. People should be free to do what they want. Why couldn't I do what my body wanted to do?

On the other hand, I certainly didn't want to do anything that would hurt my wife. I myself had been betrayed in a past relationship, and I knew how it felt. The last thing in the world I wanted was to cause her pain, and I certainly wouldn't want her to betray me. Maybe monogamy really was important and I just didn't understand why.

Tossing and turning in bed, I considered the pros and cons of having an affair. My body was saying do it, my heart was saying don't do it, and my mind was trying to figure out a way for both to be happy.

Before falling asleep I finally concluded that if I could assure Bonnie of my undying love for her, then maybe it wouldn't hurt her if I had occasional discreet affairs. I reasoned that as long as the affairs were brief and recreational, then possibly there would be no negative emotional repercussions. Thinking this was a good solution, I decided to share with her my new ideas when I returned home.

I was excited to see Bonnie, and almost immediately we

enjoyed great passionate, loving sex. Afterward I told her the story of what had happened on my trip. She was crushed.

She asked, "Do you love the woman?"

I explained that my attraction to this woman was only physical. Feeling completely rejected, she asked me if I still loved *her*. I tenderly said that I loved her more than anyone in my life.

She asked what the other woman looked like and who she was. I answered all her questions, assuring her that we had done no more than talk. Taking Bonnie gently in my arms, I apologized for hurting her.

After some time, I proceeded to share with her my new thoughts and feelings about monogamy. Although I was hoping she wouldn't mind if I had discreet little affairs, her response not only changed my mind, but it changed my life forever.

I began this memorable conversation by saying, "I didn't do anything with this woman because I would never want to betray you. But I would also very much like to have your permission to have an affair. It doesn't mean I don't love you. It would just be for fun. And I promise to be very discreet and do it only when I am out of town."

Before I could finish, Bonnie began to weep, but distressed as she was, she spoke to me with astonishing strength and clarity. I will always remember her words because they affected me so deeply.

She said, "John, I would never want to tell you what you can do. You don't need me to be your mother, nor do I want to be. All I can tell you is my experience. I am already trying so hard to be open and give you the trust you deserve. I don't want to give up on loving you. I want to grow in love and trust for you."

With tears running down her cheeks she continued, "I have been left before. If I thought you were possibly having affairs when you left to teach your seminars, I would begin to close up. I would always be comparing myself and trying to measure up. I would never feel good enough."

Then, after a long pause, she said, "I don't know whether it is right or wrong. All I know is that it would be too difficult for me to stay open."

In that instant, my mind became crystal clear, my rationalizations melted away, and my heart was filled with an even deeper, more committed love for my wife. I was so grateful that Bonnie could share her feelings with me in such a magnificent way. I was able to listen without becoming defensive; there was no criticism, blame, or judgment in her words; I felt no need to justify myself. I was able to hear her legitimate need, think about her words, and respond freely.

In that moment, I knew that Bonnie loved me and truly wanted me to be happy. I also knew that regardless of whether an affair was morally right or wrong, she needed monogamy as a requirement for growing in love. She needed to feel special in order to love me in an open, receptive, and responsive way. And that "specialness" was based on the security of monogamy.

Like many men (and some women), I had imagined that having an occasional "fling" would make no major impact on my marriage. I was wrong. I hadn't appreciated the sacredness of sex or that monogamy, and not just love, is the cornerstone of lasting happiness, passion, and intimacy. If Bonnie and I had not shared our feelings that night, I would never have understood that.

And why should I have been expected to understand in the first place? My father didn't understand any more than his father did, and my mother would never have felt entitled to tell him about her need to feel special, certainly not with the strength and clarity Bonnie exhibited. My mother's attitudes were forged in another time, and her strength was of a different kind.

In the fifties, when I was growing up, my father secretly confessed to my mother that he was having an affair. What had probably started out as a moment of passion gradually became more serious, and he asked my mother for a divorce.

My mother loved my father and was deeply hurt. Instead of sharing her tender feelings and thereby showing him how much she loved and needed him, she became strong, and in the most loving way she knew said, "If that's what you want, then I will give you a divorce. Let's think about it for a month, and then you decide."

Fate intervened when, a week later, my mother discovered that she was pregnant with their seventh child. With this new responsibility, my father decided not to leave her and the family. My mother was very happy, and nothing more was said about his "other interests." For several years he continued to have affairs in other cities, but they never talked about it.

Though they never divorced, this was a major turning point in their relationship. They continued to love and support each other as husband and wife, but something was missing. The loving romance and playfulness of love slowly began to disappear.

When I became an adult I eventually heard the rumors of my dad's affairs and asked him about it. His response was "What you don't know can't hurt you." As I persisted in asking more questions, that is all he would tell me.

I realized that this was the way he had justified his affairs. He didn't want to hurt my mother and had rationalized that if he was discreet, she wouldn't be hurt.

To some extent he was right. My mother seemed to be OK with his affairs and never broached the subject or asked him to stop. What neither of them knew was that without monogamy they would eventually snuff out the delicate and tender feelings of affection that attracted them to each other. Like many couples, they mistakenly assumed that it was natural to lose physical attraction and passion after years of marriage.

After my father's death, Mom and I came across a snapshot of him with one of his mistresses. When my mother saw it, tears came to her eyes, tears that were not shed when he was alive. I knew why she was crying.

I could feel her pain at seeing him so open and free with another woman, seeing in his eyes the sparkle they had once shared but which had gradually disappeared from their relationship.

I also felt the personal pain of never having seen my dad so happy. He'd been a loving father, but often moody, angry, or depressed. In this picture, in his secret world, he was charming, helpful, and happy. This was the father I'd longed to know and be like.

When I asked my mother why she thought he had felt the need to stray, she answered, "Your father and I loved each other very much. But as the years passed I became a mother, and your father wanted a wife." I was amazed by how she was so accepting of his infidelity. She told me, "I admired your father for staying. It was a great sacrifice on his part. He had strong desires, but he didn't desert us."

On that day I could finally understand why he had betrayed her: he had stopped being romantically attracted to her and just didn't know what to do about it. He didn't know how to share the responsibilities of a family and also be romantic. He didn't know how to bring back the passion and joy in their relationship. If he had known, he would not have given up and strayed.

I also realized that my mother had done the best she could. She knew too well how to be a loving mother, but was not adept at the art of keeping romance alive. She was following in the footsteps of her mother and her mother's mother. It was, after all, a different world then, with different rules.

In the days of my mother's youth, with the depression followed by World War II, survival was more important than romantic and emotional needs. People just didn't reveal their inner feelings: my mother was too busy raising six and, later, seven children to explore her feelings. Even if she had, she would never have considered sharing her heartaches with Dad, and she wouldn't have known how to unburden herself without making him feel controlled or defensive.

When my father decided not to leave, she was enormously relieved that the family would stay intact. Like her female ancestors, she put the good of her family ahead of her personal needs. My father also put aside his personal needs and honored his commitment to the family by staying married but, like his male ancestors, continued discreetly to have affairs on the side. And, despite everything, my mother assured me that they loved each other very much, and in many ways grew closer through the years.

While my mother's and father's story is common to many people of our parents' and grandparents' generations, we men and women of today want, expect, and require more from our relationships. At a time when the whole basis for marriage has dramatically altered, we no longer mate for survival and protection but for love, romance, and emotional fulfillment. Now, many of the rules and strategies our parents used to keep their marriages together have become ineffective and even counterproductive.

Unfortunately, it could be said that we all have Ph.D.'s in conducting relationships that are just *like* our parents', since we lived with them for eighteen years or more and unconsciously learned how to behave and react from them. For this simple reason, childhood experience heavily influences the quality of our relationships in later life. Look at how close, without even knowing it, I had come to reenacting my father's behavior. But look, too, at the enormous difference in the way Bonnie and I reacted to and dealt with it. That's what this book is about.

You see, even if our parents dearly loved us, and did everything they could to be examples of strength and love, they could not teach us what they did not know. They could not give us solutions to problems that did not exist in their lifetimes. We, their heirs, are pioneers in a new frontier, facing new problems that require new strategies. We not only have to master new relationship skills but must also shoulder the additional burden of unlearning what we learned from our parents. And what are these new lessons and rules? What do we, the men and women of today, need in order to feel fulfilled?

Women today no longer primarily need men to provide and protect on a physical level. They want men to provide on an emotional level as well. Men today also want more than homemakers and mothers for their children. They want women to nurture their emotional needs but not mother them or treat them like children.

I'm not saying that our parents didn't want emotional support; it was just not their primary expectation. It was basically enough for Mom if Dad worked and provided. It was enough for Dad if Mom managed the house and kids and didn't constantly nag him.

But what was good enough for our parents isn't good enough for us. We are no longer willing to make such enormous personal sacrifices. We demand and deserve lasting happiness, intimacy, and passion with a single partner. If we don't get it, we are prepared to sacrifice the marriage; personal fulfillment is suddenly more important than the family unit.

Recent national statistics reveal that an astronomical average of two out of four marriages end in divorce, and the rate is rising.

(In California, the figure is three out of four.) Over 50 percent of America's schoolchildren come from broken homes, while over 30 percent of babies are born out of wedlock. Domestic violence, crime, drug addiction, and the use of psychological medication are at an all-time high. Without doubt, the breakdown of the family is largely responsible for such alarming statistics.

These new problems raise critical questions. Are we to turn back the clock and deny our personal needs and suddenly make the family more important? Could this be the answer? Are we to serve our sentence and simply endure a marriage that is not emotionally satisfying for the sake of others? While these strategies have worked to ensure our survival in the past, they are not options when our priority is personal fulfillment.

In most cases, the solution is not divorce nor is it self-sacrifice. Instead, the answer lies in learning how to create relationships and marriages that support our personal fulfillment. This is not only possible, but necessary. Divorce has been the only solution for many because they just didn't know what else to do.

Our parents simply could not teach us how to have relationships that fulfill our emotional and romantic needs. Without the knowledge of how to get our emotional needs fulfilled, the reality of marriage has, for many, become an emotional prison. However, with the new knowledge of how to fulfill our emotional needs and create lasting passion and happiness, marriage and family are no longer obstacles but can again be the means to fulfilling our personal needs.

There is nothing bad or narcissistic about wanting more than our parents did. The truth is that times have changed, and our values have changed with them. The new problems we face are not symptoms of failure but are the successful result of the evolution of our society.

Now that civilization, to a great extent, ensures our physical survival and security, it also provides us with the physical freedom to be ourselves and achieve all that we can. To men and women of our parents' generation, that freedom seems an undreamed-of luxury. No longer motivated by basic drives but by higher needs, we expect more from ourselves and life. As a result, we look to our relationships for the emotional support to help us be *all* we can.

In this generational movement toward wholeness, women are developing the masculine side of their natures and men are moving toward acknowledging their feminine sides. Women want to be more than mothers and homemakers; they want to make a difference in the world outside the home. Men also aspire to be more than warriors and work machines; they want affectionate and loving relationships in the home, more time for recreation, and greater participation in child rearing.

The age-old distinction between male and female roles has suddenly blurred, creating confusion and frustration. At this time of transition, it's hard to get the emotional support we need from our partners. After all, it's taken thousands of years to overcome the challenges and hardships of physical survival; we are only just beginning to learn the rudiments of getting our emotional needs fulfilled.

While statistics reveal that millions of couples are facing the possibility of breakup, *What Your Mother Couldn't Tell You and Your Father Didn't Know* demonstrates clearly and simply why relationship problems are inevitable and offers a host of practical insights and suggestions for developing advanced skills to ensure more loving and fulfilling unions.

For those of you in a great relationship, these skills will make it even better. You'll learn how to smooth the rough edges, iron things out, and bring back the passion of the first few years together. In fact, literally thousands of couples attending my relationship seminars have been delighted to discover a greater mutual passion than they ever felt before. And, in addition to making a good relationship better, these advanced skills ensure that your marriage will continue to grow in love.

If you are single, this book will be a revelation. It will give you hope that you can have better relationships. It will allow you to view past mistakes without feeling guilty or bad. It will make it easier to forgive those who have hurt or disappointed you. By clearly seeing others' mistakes with the new awareness that they just didn't know better, layers of resentment will be released. This newfound openness will lighten your heart's burden and allow you to draw into your life the perfect person for you. In addition, you will learn new skills so that you won't unknowingly turn off this special person or create unnecessary problems.

If you are presently experiencing problems in a relationship, this book will reassure you that you're not alone. In many cases, you'll discover that there is nothing wrong with you or your partner. It is simply that your parents didn't, and couldn't, teach you the necessary skills for making a relationship work.

Over and over, I've witnessed couples on the verge of divorce miraculously fall in love again. Through discovering and recognizing their mistakes, they do not feel so powerless and hopeless. Their hearts open up again. Understanding their parts of the problem lets them release their blame and begin practicing new skills. As they quickly get results, their relationships are truly transformed.

After twenty-three years of marriage, Linda and Daryl were ready to give up and sign their divorce papers. Like so many couples, they didn't really want to split up but weren't getting what they needed from each other and knew of no alternative to divorce. All they knew was that staying in the relationship was like choosing to die emotionally. But, after they learned advanced relationship skills, everything changed!

What Linda learned: "I always thought my husband just didn't love me or care enough when he didn't do the things I expected. I felt hopeless, like I would never get what I wanted. When I tried to talk about making things better, he just resisted, and things got worse. Now I know that he was just doing what his father did. I discovered that he really did want to make me happy but just didn't understand me. By learning how to approach him differently, I find he has suddenly become a different person. He listens to me, and I appreciate him greatly. Not only am I happy, but he is too."

What Daryl learned: "So many times I just didn't know what she wanted. When she would talk, no matter what I said it seemed to make matters worse. When I tried to explain myself, she would just get more upset. Now I understand that she basically just wanted to be heard. I have learned to say less and listen more, and it actually works. She is so happy these days that I just want to do more for her. It is kind of embarrassing, but I suddenly feel alive again and I didn't even know I was dying."

To save their marriage, Daryl and Linda had simply to acquire relationship skills their parents couldn't teach them. Daryl learned the importance of responding to Linda's feelings. Linda learned the secrets of keeping a man happy. As a team they quickly improved their relationship by making *small* but crucial adjustments in their attitudes.

Only after these minor changes are made can the big shifts in the relationship take place. The secret to the effectiveness of the techniques I share is that they do not require radical sacrifice of who we are.

For example, to expect a man who doesn't talk much to suddenly open up and share is unrealistic. However, with a little encouragement, the same man can easily focus his energies on learning to be a better listener. When approached in this manner, behavioral change is possible regardless of what we learned from our parents. Instead of focusing on what we can't or don't do, this book focuses on what we can do and how to do it.

Many of the participants in my relationship seminars report amazing results even if their partners couldn't or, in some cases, wouldn't come to the sessions. By learning from their own mistakes and developing new skills for relating, the participants were able to generate dramatic and positive changes on their own.

The same thinking applies to this book. Your partner does not have to read it for you to improve your relationship. The skills I share deal with how you can begin today to get more of what you deserve in all your relationships. Certainly, change will happen faster if your partner does read it. But even if he or she is not interested, the secret of success lies in your learning and using its principles.

So how do women convince their partners to read my books? Men, after all, are very particular about the way in which they are approached. If you hand them the book and say "You need this," it creates more resistance. But if you open the book to sections that describe men and ask your mate if what is written is really true, he may suddenly become interested.

This strategy works for two reasons. First of all, men like to be experts, and you'll be approaching him as an expert on the male perspective. Second, when he hears parts of this book, he will quickly realize that it is not against men nor does it try to change them. It is 100 percent "male-friendly."

In fact, women are generally amazed by the equal attendance of men at my seminars. They can't believe that they're seeing lots of males actually listening, nodding their heads in agreement, even laughing. I repeatedly point out that men are just as interested in improving relationships, but require practical strategies that don't ask them to become feminine.

Since the enormous success of my previous best-seller, *Men Are from Mars, Women Are from Venus,* thousands of relationships have improved. In the first year, my office heard from over fifteen thousand readers saying that "the book" had saved their relationships. In some of the calls or letters, readers had more questions, practical questions like "What should I do when . . . " or "What does it mean when . . . " or "How do I get him to . . . " or "What should I say when . . . " or "When do I . . . ?" This book is also a response to those questions.

What Your Mother Couldn't Tell You and Your Father Didn't Know answers the questions that our parents could not. It points us in a new direction. It promises and delivers the necessary information for creating and sustaining loving and mutually fulfilling relationships. It offers a new seed that, when planted and watered, will grow into a relationship that is not only loving but easy.

I offer this book as a collection of jewels, pearls of wisdom and practical gems from which I have personally benefited. I sincerely hope that they work for you as they continue to work for me and the thousands of participants in my seminars. May you always grow in love and continue to share your special gifts.

JOHN GRAY, Ph.D.
November 22, 1993
California

CHAPTER 1

What Your Mother Couldn't Tell You and Your Father Didn't Know

Once upon a time, untold ages ago, men and women were peaceful partners in a hostile and dangerous world. A woman felt loved and respected because each day her mate went out and risked his life to provide for her. She didn't expect him to be sensitive or nurturing. Good communication skills were not a part of his job description. As long as he was a good hunter and could find his way home, relationship skills were not required for a mate to be desirable. As providers, men felt loved and appreciated by women. While surviving was difficult, relationships were comparatively easy.

Men and women existed in different spheres. They greatly depended on each other in order to survive. Food, sex, children, shelter, and security motivated them to work together because the fulfillment of these basic needs required specific roles and skills. Men assumed the role of provider and protector while women specialized in nurturing and homemaking.

It was a natural separation. Biology had determined that a woman gives birth and hence feels a great responsibility for raising children and creating a home. The man honored and respected her role by agreeing to take such dangerous assignments as venturing into the wild to hunt, or standing guard to protect her and their young. Although men would often be out for days in the freezing cold or blazing sun before making a kill, they were proud of these sacrifices because they greatly honored the female, the life giver. And because a man and woman's interdependent partnership provided the basics of survival and security, it automatically generated mutual respect and appreciation.

While the men were out hunting, the women would sustain life at home. Women greatly valued the opportunity to love and nurture their children and maintain domestic harmony without having also to provide and protect. A man's assistance in making life safer, easier, and more comfortable caused him to be a hero in her eyes. As long as both partners fulfilled their basic tasks, men and women felt quite content emotionally. Century after century, the challenges of survival remained paramount, and the division of labor between men and women remained fundamentally the same.

Now, though, life has changed dramatically. Since we are no longer utterly dependent on each other for security and survival, the rules and strategies of our ancestors have become outdated. For the first time in recorded history, we look to each other primarily for love and romance, not survival and security. Happiness, intimacy, and lasting passion are now requirements for fulfilling relationships.

To succeed in today's relationships, we must learn new lessons that our ancestors and parents simply could not teach us. What your mother couldn't tell you and your father didn't know is how to satisfy your partner's emotional needs without sacrificing your own personal fulfillment. This new agenda can be accomplished only through the practice of advanced relationship skills.

To succeed in today's relationships, we must learn
new lessons that our ancestors and parents
couldn't teach us.

Times Have Changed

The social and economic changes of the last forty years have
enormously affected the traditional male and female roles that
have been in place since the beginning of civilization. Women
leaving the home and entering the workforce has greatly diminished men's traditional value to women. Increasingly independent and self-sufficient, contemporary women no longer feel the
same need for men to provide for or protect them.

A modern woman charts her own destiny and pays her own
bills. When in danger she can pull out her Mace or call the
police. Most important, she now has much more control over
when to have children and how many she wants. Until the dis-
covery of the birth control pill, and the widespread availability
of contraceptives, women were utterly biologically determined
to have children and be dependent on men. No more.

We are just beginning to comprehend the changes in relationships that have resulted from the widespread use of birth
control and the following sexual revolution. We are living in a
time of dramatic transition and sexual tension.

In a sense, we could say that all men are out of work. They
no longer have the job they held for countless centuries. They
are no longer valued and appreciated as providers and protectors. Although they continue to do what they have always done,
it suddenly isn't enough to make their partners happy. Women
require something else, something more than their mothers did.

Men are out of work, and women are overworked.

In the same way that men are out of work, women are overworked. Not only are they mothers, nurturers, and homemakers, but now they are also providers and protectors. They are

no longer protected from the hard, harsh, and cold realities of the work world outside the home. How can a wife be expected to be relaxed, sensitive, and pleasing to her husband when an hour before she's had to fight a man for a cab? While women today no longer want to wait on a man at the end of a day, men still want what their fathers wanted—to be waited on.

Times have changed, and we have no choice but to change with them. A new job description is required for men in relationships. New skills must be learned if a man is to feel needed and appreciated by his mate. A new awareness is required of women if they are to continue working side by side with men, then come home to a loving and nurturing relationship. New skills are required to remain feminine and also be strong.

In this troubled time, if men and women are to succeed in supporting each other happily, new relationship skills are essential.

What We Didn't Learn

Our mothers could not teach their daughters how to share their feelings in a way that didn't make men defensive, or how to ask for support so that a man would respond favorably. They did not understand how to nurture a man without mothering him or giving too much. They did not know how to accommodate his wishes without sacrificing their own. They were experts at pleasing their men at their own expense.

In essence, our mothers could not teach their daughters how to be feminine and also powerful. They couldn't teach them how to support their partners and also get the emotional support that they deserved.

Our fathers could not teach their sons how to communicate with a woman without passively giving in or aggressively arguing. Men today have no role models for leading and directing the family in a way that respects and includes their partners' points of view. They do not know how to remain strong while providing emotional support.

Our fathers did not understand how to truly give the empathy and sympathy that women require today. They did not know the little things that a woman requires to be fulfilled. They did not know the importance of monogamy and making a woman feel special. Our fathers simply did not understand women, but without that understanding the contemporary male cannot develop the skills necessary to get the kind of support he now requires in his relationships.

Our parents couldn't teach us the advanced relationship skills necessary to make relationships thrive in the modern world. Just remembering this—that we could not learn these things from our families—is enough to soften your heart and forgive yourself and your partner for the mistakes you repeatedly make. This gentle wisdom brings hope again.

> We must not blame our parents for failing to teach us things about relationships that they could not know.

An Overview of Advanced Relationship Skills

Throughout this book I will discuss in great detail the relationship skills necessary to support our partners' new emotional needs while getting exactly what we need to be happy and enjoy lasting intimacy and passion. Even if some of the ideas laid out here seem familiar or old-fashioned, they are being presented in dramatically fresh and different ways.

For example, I advocate that a woman be pleasing to her man, which could be interpreted as sexist. However, within the context of an advanced relationship skill, it is anything but, because she is asked to please him by actively helping him to successfully please her. Instead of passively waiting on him like so many of our mothers did, she learns ways in which to get the support she needs.

In a sense, she is still required to help him, but with a new twist: she learns how to help him help her, how to support him in supporting her more, and how to accommodate him so that he will in turn accommodate her needs and wishes.

All of the skills presented require traditional female abilities, but with an additional new spin that ensures that she gets back what she needs.

Advanced relationship skills for a woman require traditional abilities, but with a new twist to ensure that she'll get back what she needs.

Men have always been asked to provide financial and physical support but now, for the first time in history, they are being asked to provide emotional support. To achieve this goal it is *not* necessary or advisable for them to become womanlike by opening up and sharing their feelings. The new man learns how to apply his ancient hunting skills—silently waiting and watching—to listening to a woman.

Men must learn to use their ancient hunting skills of silently watching and waiting when listening to their mates.

With the correct understanding, men can quickly become adept in this new skill by using abilities that have taken untold centuries to develop. Using his warrior skills, he will learn to protect himself constructively when a woman speaks. The new twist is that he learns to defend himself *without* attacking his partner.

Here is an overview of the major advanced relationship skills we will explore:

In chapter 2, "What Women Need Most and Men Really Want," we will explore the hidden reasons why men and women are dissatisfied in relationships. Women are overworked and need extra support when they get home, while men feel unappreciated because women want more. Suddenly, what men have done for centuries is not enough. Through understanding what women need most, men develop new skills to elicit the appreciation they deserve. With a new awareness of what men really want, women learn powerful new skills for getting the support they require.

In chapter 3, "A New Job Description for Relationships," we will explore how our changing gender roles have affected relationships. Formulas our parents used can be counterproductive today. Both men and women require a new job description for making relationships work. Men will understand what women really mean when they talk about problems, and women will comprehend what's going on inside a man's head when he is silent. With an enhanced understanding of men's and women's different needs for coping with stress, we will explore new avenues of mutual support so that both partners get what they want.

In chapter 4, "How Men and Women Are Different," we will explore how the two sexes react differently to stress and how they can best support each other. (Through understanding how our brains develop differently we gain tremendous insight into effectively using advanced relationship skills.) When a woman is upset, a man generally assumes that he must do more for her. By learning to *do* less and *listen* more, a man not only feels more energetic but, seeing that his mate is happier, feels less inner pressure to perform. Women also learn skills for motivating a man to give support without having to nag.

In chapter 5, "Masculine Skills for Listening Without Getting Upset," men learn how to avoid taking it personally or getting upset when a woman shares her feelings. Without an awareness of how to defend himself, a man may automatically get bent out of shape and feel blamed, criticized, or controlled. However, by using ancient warrior skills with a contemporary spin, he will find communication becoming easier and easier.

In chapter 6, "Feminine Skills for Talking So a Man Will Listen," women will learn the skills needed to assist their men in being successful listeners. By drawing on ancient nurturing skills and the unconditional love so natural to women, they will find themselves loving and caring for a mate without mothering him, while guaranteeing themselves the love and support they crave.

In chapter 7, "Men Speak 'Male' and Women Speak 'Female,'" we will explore how men and women speak different languages and need to learn advanced communication skills for avoiding conflict and increasing intimacy. Women learn how to successfully ask for what they want, and men learn how to more effectively fulfill a woman's need to feel heard.

In chapter 8, "Why Men Forget and Women Remember," we will explore the male tendency to forget to do things and/or procrastinate, along with the female inclination to bring up issues again and again. Through understanding this universal difference, it becomes much easier to recognize our partners' love for us and acknowledge that, even if misguidedly, they are trying to make us happy. Women will learn skills to help a man remember her needs, while men will learn how to help a woman forget and forgive.

In chapter 9, "What Happened to the Man I Love?," we will explore the natural changes that occur in a relationship over time and learn to cope with them so that love and intimacy continue to grow. Men will come to see how they unknowingly prevent a woman from feeling loved. Women will discover what happens to the man they love through the years, and how to bring out the best in him at any given moment.

In chapter 10, "Where Is the Woman I Fell For?," we will explore how women also change over the length of a relationship. They will become aware of the various ways they unknowingly push a man's love away. Men will discover new ways to rediscover in their mates the women they first fell in love with.

In chapter 11, "Men Are Still from Mars, Women Are Still from Venus," we will explore how over the passage of time, male partners may become more feminine and females more masculine. This emotional role reversal can create very predictable problems unless we carefully create balance within our own inner masculine and feminine aspects.

In chapter 12, "A Lifetime of Love and Passion," we will explore how monogamy and taking the time to nurture the male and female sides of our natures is the basis for lasting romance in a marriage. In addition, we will explore in detail the seven secrets of lasting intimacy and increasing passion.

In chapter 13, "Dance Steps for Lasting Intimacy," we will discuss the importance of partnership and service to a higher purpose. Together we will explore dance steps for lasting intimacy through creating a win/win partnership which not only contributes to a more passionate relationship, but to a better and more loving world.

In each chapter of *What Your Mother Couldn't Tell You and Your Father Didn't Know*, you will have the opportunity to learn relationship skills that, in most cases, your parents simply could not teach you.

Relationships Can Be Easy

Relationships become increasingly difficult when we expect too much of ourselves or our partners. In education theory it is commonly known that to learn something new, you must hear it (and/or apply it) two hundred times. If you are a genius, maybe a hundred and fifty. This means that it will take time to master new relationship skills.*

Occasionally forgetting what you have learned is perfectly normal; old patterns and reactions do come back to haunt us. Now, however, each time it will be different. You will understand your part of the problem instead of hopelessly blaming your partner or solely yourself. Changing for the better is sometimes hard work, but at each progressive step it will also become easier, more rewarding, and more fun. And, once learned, these skills will enrich all aspects of your life and your relationships.

Anticipating Setbacks

The most important relationship skill of all is anticipating temporary setbacks and thus acknowledging the necessity of repeat-

---

*Taking into account the importance of repetition to learn a new skill, throughout this book certain key elements have been purposely repeated.

edly relearning a lesson until it becomes second nature. This understanding gives us the hope to be patient and the forgiveness to be loving. It is imperative that we not expect our partners to always know what we need.

It is imperative that we do not expect our partners to always know instinctively what we need without our telling them.

Although it may at times seem overwhelming to consider all the new skills we have to learn, it is also very exciting. As you begin to practice them, the immediate and tangible results will give you continued cause for hope, encouragement, and support. With your very first step on this journey that your parents didn't take, your relationships can dramatically and immediately improve, and gradually, with more practice, keep on getting better.

Through learning these essential skills you can achieve in your relationships lasting passion, intimacy, and happiness. Passion does not have to dissipate, the happiness shared during the courting process does not have to fade, and intimacy can deepen into a source of increasing fulfillment. In the next chapter, we will explore what women need most, and men really want, if we are to experience lasting intimacy.

What Women Need Most and Men Really Want

The women who attend my relationship seminars are always amazed by the fact that half the audience is composed of men. They find it hard to believe, but men really are seeking ways to make women happy and are just as interested as women in improved relationships. The problem is that their traditional ways of doing so aren't getting through to the women.

If problems arise at home, the traditional male approach to solving them is to become more successful at work. If a relationship is troubled, a traditional man doesn't take a seminar or purchase a book on relationships; he takes a course or buys a book on business or success. Why? Because from time immemorial, a man could always make his partner happier by being a better provider.

In hunter/gatherer days, this arrangement worked out fine. It worked well enough even for our fathers. For us, however, it doesn't work at all. Today's wives do not leave husbands because they're not being provided for. They leave because they are emotionally and romantically unfulfilled. When a man does not understand a woman's new needs, it is inevitable that she will be unfulfilled. This increased dissatisfaction is also what turns men off. Husbands do not leave wives because they no longer love them, they leave because they can't make them happy. Generally speaking, a man gives up on a relationship when he feels powerless to succeed in fulfilling his partner. Such shared frustration is common because men simply do not understand women's needs any more than women understand what men really want or how to give it to them.

Men do not understand women's needs, and women do not understand what men really want or how to give it to them.

Through understanding how circumstances have changed for both sexes, we can begin to gain the insight and compassion necessary to begin to master new approaches to mutually supportive relationships.

Why Modern Women Are Unhappy

Modern women are overworked, overstressed, and commonly feel unsupported and overwhelmed with good reason: at no other time in history has so much been expected of them. At least five days a week, they put on a uniform and march into an eight-to-twelve-hour battle. When they come home, they feel the need to clean house, make dinner, do laundry, love and nurture the kids, and also be pleasing and happy as well as romantically receptive to their mates. It's just too much to ask of themselves, and it's making them feel split inside.

At work, women are required to think, talk, react, dress, and behave according to the traditional masculine rules of conduct. At home, they have to switch to being warm, giving, and feminine. It's no wonder women complain that they need a wife to greet them with love and tenderness at the end of the day.

Why Motherhood Is More Difficult

Even a contemporary stay-home mother has a more difficult job than her own mother did because, with most other mothers at work and her kids' playmates at day care, she lacks the traditional company and support of other women.

In the past, a woman was proud to say that she was a full-time wife and mother. Now she may even feel embarrassed when asked, "What do *you* do?" Isolated from the support of other women, she must go it alone, as the value of her commitment is largely unacknowledged by the world.

Still, while women now need more support than at any other time in history, men also miss the ego boost they traditionally received from their mates. Never before have relationships been so difficult for men.

At no time in history have relationships been as difficult for men as now.

Why Men Are Dissatisfied

Modern men feel underpaid, defeated, and unappreciated. Like women, they are experiencing the toll that a two-career marriage takes.

Years ago, when a man returned to a stay-home wife she could easily show him how much she appreciated his efforts and sacrifices. Happy to care for him because she wasn't stressed out, she asked relatively little in return. Now, abruptly, the home as a male comfort base is under siege.

Many men work just as hard as their forefathers, perhaps even harder, but still can't manage to be their family's sole support. Like his ancestors, a modern man with a working mate labors and sacrifices but may still find himself unable to provide what he wants. Deprived of the strong sense of self that being a sole provider would bring him, on a deep emotional (and sometimes unconscious) level he easily feels defeated when his partner seems unhappy or unfulfilled.

A Man's Primary Goal

When a man loves a woman, his primary goal is to make her happy. Through history, men have endured the competitive and hostile world of work because, at the end of the day, their struggles and efforts were justified by a woman's appreciation. In a very real sense, his mate's fulfillment was the reward that made a man's labor worthwhile.

Today, because women are overworked, they often and understandably feel unfulfilled. Now, at a long day's end, *both* she and her mate are looking for love and appreciation. "I work as hard as he does," she tells herself. "Why is it my responsibility to appreciate him?" Exhaustion now prevents her from giving her man the emotional support he knows he has earned.

If a man is not appreciated, he feels his work is meaningless; his wife's unhappiness confirms his defeat. To him, her unhappiness signals that he is a failure. "Why should I bother to do more?" he asks himself. "I'm unappreciated for what I do already." The harmful effects of this relatively new pattern are greatly underestimated by both women and men.

When a modern man returns home he generally faces defeat instead of victory. His partner's unhappiness signals that he is a failure.

What Makes Women Happy

Years ago, when most women were full-time homemakers, a woman enjoyed the support of other women throughout the day. She could break up her tasks and relax by talking and sharing while giving and receiving in the spirit of cooperation, not competition. She had the luxury of unstructured time to create beauty in her home, garden, and community. She cared for others and they cared for her.

This daily routine was conducive to nurturing her feminine spirit and the love in her heart. Her caring relationships gave meaning to her existence and supported her through life's inevitable crises.

Women were not expected to shoulder the double burden of nurturing relationships and providing for the family. Men were happy to provide, and able to be sole providers, leaving their partners free to perform their tasks while creating and sustaining loving relationships. In the competitive and hard-driving male-dominated workforce of today, this emphasis on relationships is greatly missing, and for the first time in history women are being forced to do without the support of being in a nurturing and feminine environment.

Imitation Men

One woman in my seminar expressed her feelings in this way: "I feel like an imitation man. Women in the workforce have no female role models for success. I don't know how a woman can be expected to be strong and assertive and feminine at the same time. I'm losing touch with who I really am." Like so many other women, she was dissatisfied because she felt that she couldn't be both herself and successful.

> **Without same-sex role models, women in the workplace experience frustration because they don't know how to be themselves *and* be successful.**

When women spend their days behaving in traditionally masculine roles, it is clearly tremendously difficult to remain feminine. Working on a very structured timetable, making decisions based primarily on the bottom line and not people's feelings, giving orders when there is no time to share the decision-making, calculating strategic moves to protect herself from attack, creating alliances based solely on profit margins and not on friendship, investing time and energy for personal gain rather than others' benefit, all contribute to the impoverishment of the feminine soul. Put simply, the world of work does nothing to nurture women's spirits, and is dramatically damaging the quality of their intimate relationships.

> The work world does nothing to nourish the female spirit and is dramatically affecting the quality of man/woman relationships.

Women at Work and at Home

Women are affected much more adversely than men by career stress, for the pressures of work outside the home have doubled their load. On the job, they give as much as men do, but when they get home, instinct takes over and they continue giving.

It is hard for a woman to come home, forget the problems of the day, and relax when her programming says, "Cook more, clean more, love more, share more, nurture more, give more, do more."

> In the office a woman is motivated to strive by a conscious need to survive, but at home her instincts drive her.

Think of it. Tasks which used to fill a woman's whole day must now be done in a few hours. Along with providing, there is just not enough time, support, or energy to fulfill her biological yearnings for a beautiful, peaceful home and a loving, harmonious, and healthy family. She feels overwhelmed by too much to do.

Whether these instincts come from biology or from watching and identifying with her mother while growing up, they can be very strong. Many times these pressures increase when a woman begins planning for children or has children. While these feelings and pressures are self-induced, they are based on modern physical realities that our mothers didn't have to deal with in their efforts to create a home and family. It is not only essential for women to learn new ways of coping, but for men to learn new ways to support their partners.

Men at Work and at Home

Through history, men could tolerate the stresses of the outside world because they would return home to a nurturing and loving woman. All day the male was goal-oriented, but come evening, he either relaxed, played, or was waited on with love. What he didn't have to do was continue working to win his partner's favor.

When a modern woman shares her feelings of having to do too much, a man generally hears it as blame for not doing enough or as an order to do more. Neither message is agreeable to his nature, which is telling him, "OK, you're home. Relax and reap the rewards of your labor."

For men, the home has traditionally been a vacation
spot. For women, it is a major hub of activity.

Giving Requires Receiving

Men are wired to give their all to work, then come home and receive. To a great extent women are built to give and receive at the same time. They love to give but need to be fueled simultaneously: when they give without receiving, they tend to give more and eventually feel overwhelmed, empty, and resentful.

It follows that a woman who spends her day in a competitive, masculine workplace does not get the emotional support she would if she were in a more feminine, nurturing environment. She gives and gives at her job but doesn't receive validation and support. She comes home burned out, but instead of relaxing, she continues to give.

This is an important difference between men and women. When a man is tired, he will generally have a strong tendency to forget his problems and rest and relax. If he is not getting the support he needs, then he will tend to stop giving more. If he gives at work without getting back, then particularly when he gets home he feels ready to relax and receive for a while, or at least take some time for himself.

On the other hand, when a woman feels unsupported, she feels responsible for doing more and begins to think of or worry about all the problems she doesn't have the energy to solve. The more overwhelmed she feels, the more difficult it is for her to relax and put off the chores that just can't be done, and really don't have to be done right away.

When she feels overwhelmed, it is difficult for her to determine what really needs to be done and what can wait. In some cases, the expectations her mother had about how a home should be kept instinctively come into play. The more overwhelmed or unsupported she feels, the more these instincts come up. In a subconscious way she may be trying to live up to the standards of housekeeping and entertaining that were appropriate back when every wife was a homemaker and had the time and energy to do it all.

Particularly when a working woman cannot afford outside help for chores at home, she may begin to feel that she is just not doing enough. Instinctively she feels that she has to do more, yet realistically she can't do it all. It is as though she is gripped by out-of-date social programming that expects her to do it all at home.

In some cases, just as a woman feels responsible for doing it all at home, a man is socially programmed to also feel that it is all her responsibility. Just as it is difficult for her to relax and do less, it is equally difficult for him to find the energy to help out. His programming is saying that his job is done when he returns home, while hers is saying that she has to do more. Understanding this pattern can bring more compassion between the sexes.

Scott and Salley

Scott works full-time to support his family, while Salley, his wife, works part-time while trying to be a mother and home-maker. When Scott returns home, he seems to ignore her unless she asks for something and then he seems to be a little irritated by her requests. Then, at dinner, when she distances herself from him, he doesn't understand why.

When asked about her feelings, she says, "I resent that he doesn't even ask me about my day or care about me. He doesn't even offer to help me. He sits on the couch while I do every-thing for him."

Scott says, "I sit on the couch to relax from my day. If I ask her about her day, all I hear is that she does too much and that I should do more. I need to relax when I get home. I don't need another boss. If she is doing too much, then she should just do less."

Salley says, "And you think I don't need to relax from my day? I can't relax. Someone has to make dinner, clean house, and take care of these kids. Why can't you do more or at least value what I do?"

Scott then looks at me and says, "See."

In that one word he means "See, this is why I don't listen to her when I get home. If I did, she would have me doing more and more. I can't open myself to that."

Like many couples, Salley resents the fact that her partner doesn't offer his help, while Scott is turned off because he gets the message that what he has done is not enough for her. On the one hand, she wants to feel seen, cared for, and supported, while on the other hand, he wants to feel acknowledged and appreciated for his work with the recognition that he earned the right to relax in his home. The solution to this problem is to first recognize that no one is wrong or to blame. Then, through applying advanced skills, the pattern can be changed.

However, Scott's suggesting that Salley do less is like telling a river to stop running: giving is an innate expression of the lov-ing female nature. What women today need most is not to curb their loving tendencies but to receive more nurturing in their relationships with men. But to expect Scott to suddenly have the energy to do more is equally unrealistic. It would be like telling a river to suddenly switch directions. As we have explored, a man is set up to relax and recuperate when he gets home, not to exert himself more. Traditionally, he leaves home to work and returns home to not work.

Through understanding what they both really need, however, a new solution can begin to emerge and come into focus. This solution must not require a man to suddenly do more or a woman to suddenly relax and do less. As we will see, men and women can learn new skills of communicating that require very little from men and provide a lot for women. Both partners can learn to practice new skills that really don't require more effort but result in the woman feeling emotionally supported and the man feeling appreciated.

As a woman feels more emotionally supported in the relationship it will directly assist her in finding a peaceful center within herself where she is not so driven to do more. She will gain a more relaxed perspective of what can or can't be done, and what really has to be done in light of her limited resources of time and energy. Likewise, as a man begins to feel more appreciated when he returns home, slowly but surely he will have more energy in the home as well. More important, however, he will immediately be able to give his partner the empathy and understanding that she needs to continue being able to give of herself.

> Contemporary women do not need to curb their loving impulses. They need more nurturing in their relationships with men.

Giving Freely Expresses the Female Side

Giving freely to others is a natural expression of the female side. For a woman, giving throughout the day and evening is not only instinctual but traditionally very rewarding; women have been doing it for centuries without feeling the emotional pressures and resentments that women feel today.

In hunter/gatherer times, when a woman had the opportunity to give freely to her neighbors, she rejoiced. By giving freely, without any expectation of return, she created deeper bonds of loyalty and friendship. This simple act of unconditional giving ensured that if in later life she needed their support she would have it. By giving freely whenever she could, she ensured that at her time of need others would be there for her. The best life insurance policy she could get on her husband was to give freely whenever she could.

Men Are Not Lazy and Women Are Not Servants

While visiting primitive villages relatively untouched by modern civilization, I was able to directly observe how men and women interacted differently. Women appeared very content to share and give all day long and on into the evening. They loved giving more. Even at dusk the women could be seen busily talking, sharing, cooking, cleaning, and washing together while managing their children. Meanwhile, the men were sitting in a circle, recuperating from the stress of their day by silently gazing into the fire, singing songs, telling stories and jokes, or playing games.

At a superficial glance when observing a group of women working at dusk and a group of men sitting silently in a circle, one could easily conclude that the men were lazy and that the women were servants. But by looking more closely you would see that the men greatly respected the women, and the women appreciated the men. The men served the women through men's work, and the women expressed their appreciation by waiting on men when they were home.

The women were happy to continue giving more because they were also receiving back from each other. The men sitting by the fire were not lazy but were coping with the stress of their work and wisely making a transition back into family life.

To understand this scene it is necessary to remember that these women working at dusk had not been doing "men's work" during the day. They, like their mothers, preferred "women's work" and didn't want to do "men's work." Likewise, the men preferred their work and didn't want to do women's work. It was a fair bargain. She was happy in her work, and he in his. Men were not regarded as lazy or women as servants, and both enjoyed mutual appreciation and respect.

Men's Work and Women's Work

The division of labor in a primitive tribe, as in our parents' generation, was much clearer and well defined. When men did men's work and women did women's work, women did not expect men to work much at home. They knew his work outside the home was more focused, risky, uncomfortable, and demanding. When he returned home, the woman appreciated his efforts and fully embraced his need to relax and rest before going back out. Women were happy to support men in this way.

When ancient men left on hunting trips, women were glad to stay home and safely nurture their families and friends. They were happy to do "feminine work" as long as they were not isolated and felt supported by friends. Women learned to depend on men as providers and protectors and nothing more. That was enough for them, and they didn't require anything else.

Women adapted in a very practical sense by doing everything in the home because it was never certain when the men would come home from a hunting trip. Women successfully satisfied this requirement by looking to each other for support. In modern times, this support for women is sorely missed and the result is burnout.

Why Women Burn Out

Today, while men are away working, women are also away working; modern women don't have the time, energy, or opportunity to support each other as their mothers did. A modern woman will give and give, but because she is not feeling supported, she commonly returns home feeling burned out.

In addition, when a woman is dependent not on a man but on her work to survive, her tendency to give freely is also restricted. If a women gives to make money, her support is not "freely offered." This manner of conditional giving further disconnects her from her femininity.

> Conditional giving further disconnects the
> wage-earning woman from her femininity.

In ways such as conditional giving, working women are required to be overly masculine. They are no longer supported in expressing their femaleness through mothering, working together in cooperative and nurturing relationships, gathering (shopping), and homemaking. This tipping of the balance toward their masculine aspect is rapidly creating female burnout and dissatisfaction throughout the modern world.

The women of ancient days didn't burn out because their work environment nurtured their female nature. Women today burn out because they are not being sufficiently nurtured in their jobs. Ultimately, it is not how much a woman does but the quality of her relationships and the support she receives that determine the difference between burnout and fulfillment.

> The difference between female burnout and
> fulfillment is determined not by how much a
> woman does at work but by the quality of the
> support she receives.

The Mother's Role

Traditionally, women felt proud of their biological roles, since mothering was highly honored, respected, and even considered sacred. In some cultures a woman was seen as being closer to God than a man, for she alone had been given the power to create life. Women were honored as the mothers, and men gladly became warriors, willing to risk their lives to provide for and protect the mothers of their children.

Going back to just my mother's generation it is easy to find women who felt very good about themselves as mothers. I remember once as an adult asking my mother if she had liked being a mother. Her immediate response was, "Well, John, I still am a mother, and I still love it. I feel so fortunate to have seven beautiful children."

I was surprised that she so strongly and proudly identified herself as a mother even after her children were grown. I felt fortunate that she hadn't had to go to work and had truly enjoyed being a full-time mom with a husband to support her.

Learning from the Wisdom of the Past

Most mothers today do not often have the luxury of full-time parenting. Having kids *and* having a job mandate a very difficult list of duties requiring new skills that your mother definitely could not have taught you. Without these strategies, the juggling of motherhood and career amounts to a tortuous trek through uncharted territory. Contemporary women considering motherhood are understandably hesitant.

While I am in no way suggesting that we turn back the clock and encourage women back into the kitchen, it is important that we understand what we have given up. As we stride forward on our quest for a new and better world for both women and men, we need to keep in mind the wisdom of the past and use it wherever applicable. Contained in that ancient wisdom are certain elements that are essential for female and male contentment. Through understanding them, we can more effectively map out fresh approaches to relating that fulfill our instincts while allowing us to move ahead to new goals and dreams.

We should never lose touch with the ancient truths
that have always enhanced female and male
fulfillment.

A Woman's Work Is Never Done

I remember a very telling conversation on the subject of contemporary motherhood. While I was signing books in a bookstore, three women and my wife were sharing stories about how difficult it is to be a mother today. When one woman disclosed that she was the mother of seven, another immediately gasped in admiration and sympathy.

"I only have two children," she said, "and I thought I had it bad. How do you do it?"

A third mother added, "I have only one child and that wears me out."

"I have three children," said my wife, "and I thought that was a lot. I can't imagine how you handle seven."

"Whether you have one, two, three, or seven kids, you give them everything you have," the mother of seven replied. "You only have so much to give, and every mother, no matter how many children she has, gives it all."

Suddenly the other three mothers realized that they were in effect doing the same job. They were each giving everything they had to give to mothering. They were following the ancient wisdom.

This insight completely changed my relationship with my wife. Before, when she complained about doing so much, I assumed she would never be happy until she learned to do less. Now I realized her doing too much was not the problem because she would always do all she could. Instead, I began to focus on finding ways to nurture her female side as she gave and gave. Not only was she happier, but because she felt so much more supported, she could indeed relax and do less.

Overgiving Is Not Dysfunctional

Giving too much becomes a problem only when a woman is not adept in getting back the nurturing support she needs to continue giving. Many popular books label women who give too much as "codependent" or dysfunctional when in many cases they are not.

They are just women following their healthy feminine instincts to give freely of themselves. This natural inclination to give unconditionally becomes problematic only when her business and personal relationships do not nurture her in return.

> Female giving becomes a problem only when a woman is primarily deprived of nurturing relationships that support her.

The more focused, responsible, competitive, and aggressive she is required to be at work, the more difficult it is for her to reconnect with the softness of her femininity when she gets home. In addition it is then more difficult for her to clearly feel her needs. Unlike a man, who more easily takes care of his own needs when the workday is over, she will return home and continue thinking about the needs of others.

When a modern woman gets home she generally doesn't have the energy her mother had for domestic work. Although she instinctively feels that she has to do more, she doesn't have the energy. This combination of feelings makes her feel suddenly exhausted.

It is one thing to feel tired, but it is completely different to feel tired and feel that you have to do more, more than you have the energy to do. Instead of looking forward to and enjoying some nice "downtime," a woman, to various degrees, is driven to do more and can't relax. This mixture creates the feeling of exhaustion and dissatisfaction with her life.

The Nurture Cure

If an exhausted woman is given a big dose of nurturing, I assure you that she will get a second wind and not only more effectively cope with her need to act but actually enjoy it. When a woman feels exhausted, it is because she is not nurturing her female side. When her female side is nurtured, she begins to feel supported, her body begins to function naturally, and the exhaustion magically lifts.

**When a woman's female side is nurtured, her body
begins to function naturally, and her exhaustion
magically lifts.**

This does not mean that women today don't need more help around the house. It is important that a man understand that modern women do require more support in the home. It is, however, also equally important that a woman understand that in some cases her expectations of what needs to be done in the home are unrealistic, given that they may be based on standards set by a generation of women who had more time for housework. While it is not fair to place those expectations on her male partner, it is also not fair for a man to ignore her legitimate need for more support.

While the resolution to this problem will be different in every unique situation, the ability to resolve this potential conflict is based on mutual understanding, patience, and compassion on both sides.

What a Man Can Do

Through allotting an extra twenty minutes three or four days a week, a man can do wonders to nurture a woman's female side. Not only will she be happier, but he will begin to get the appreciation and acceptance he needs when he gets home. No matter how overworked or exhausted she feels, he can, with a small amount of concentrated attention, focus his love and caring in ways that make a big difference.

However, unless he comprehends the importance of nurturing a woman's female side, he may mistakenly leave her alone or try to persuade her to do less. Neither approach works, and may actually alienate her.

Quite commonly he might say any of the following comments, thinking he is being helpful when he is really making matters much worse. These are a few examples:

He Mistakenly Says:	She Hears:
1. *He says:* "You take on too much."	1. *She hears:* "You don't leave enough time for me."
He really means: "You deserve more support."	She thinks: "He doesn't value all that I do and just wants more."
2. *He says:* "You shouldn't worry about that."	2. *She hears:* "What you are worried about is really not that important."
He really means: "I care about you and I am here to support you if the problem gets worse."	She thinks: "He doesn't care about what is important to me."
3. *He says:* "It's not that bad."	3. *She hears:* "You are once again making a mountain out of a molehill. You are an alarmist, overreacting to the problem."
He really means: "I trust that you will handle it. You are quite competent and capable, and I am sure that you will work it out. I believe in you."	She thinks: "He doesn't care about my feelings. I am not important to him."
4. *He says:* "You expect too much of yourself."	4. *She hears:* "You shouldn't be upset with yourself, you are always getting upset for no good reason."
He means: "I think you are wonderful, and you give so much of yourself to others. I appreciate what you do, and I think you deserve a	She thinks: "He doesn't understand what I am going through and why I feel so bad. Nobody understands what I am going through."

He Mistakenly Says:	She Hears:
lot more support than you get. I understand if you have less to give me today."	
5. *He says:* "If you are going to complain about it, then just don't do it."	5. *She hears:* "You are being too negative. Anybody else would be able to do it, but you can't."
He means: "I care about you, and I don't want you to do what you don't want to do. You already do so much, you deserve to relax more."	She thinks: "He thinks I only care about myself. He doesn't understand how much I do for others."
6. *He says:* "If you don't want to do it, then don't."	6. *She hears:* "A loving person would be happy to give more."
He means: "You already give so much, I don't expect you to do more. You deserve to have more of what you want."	She thinks: "He thinks that I am selfish and that I am not entitled to relax and give to myself."
7. *He says:* "You don't have to do so much."	7. *She hears:* "What you're doing is unnecessary and a waste of time."
He means: "What you do is already so supportive that I don't expect you to do more."	She thinks: "If he doesn't value what I do, I will never get the support I need in return."

Simply trying to understand what her feelings are and what she goes through with some empathy or sympathy, and not making any of the above comments, can have a tremendous nurturing effect on a woman's female side.

An overworked woman, with neither the time nor the opportunity to nurture her female side, may not even be aware of what she's missing; consequently, she may not know how to recapture her femininity. To do so, she needs a healthy dose of "relationship." Anything a man can do to nurture her female side will assist her in releasing her cares.

Through addressing this female side of her being, a man can respond compassionately and skillfully to a woman feeling exhausted and overwhelmed. Through clearly delineating her male and female aspects, he can effectively work at steering her toward "feeling like herself again."

A man can skillfully respond when a woman feels overwhelmed by addressing the female side of her being, which cries out for nurturing.

Why Talking Is So Important for Women

A woman can most successfully cope with the stress of experiencing nonnurturing relationships in the goal-oriented work world by coming home and experiencing a loving, caring, and cooperative relationship. The most important element of a nurturing relationship that she is generally missing at work is non-goal-oriented conversation. Through "talking" in a non-goal-oriented way, without having to get to the bottom line, without having to solve the problem, a woman is gradually released from the domination of her masculine side.

Talking in a nonlinear, unedited, emotional way is especially beneficial when her listener understands that by articulating her problems, she can put them aside.

> **A woman can forget the problems of the day by remembering them and talking about them.**

That a woman can forget the problems of her day by remembering them is a concept foreign to most men, who generally banish the problems of the day by not talking about them. To bring them up in conversation, a man would have to address himself to solving them.

A Perfect Fit

While it is important to men to *not* talk, it is equally important to women *to* talk. This apparent incompatibility is actually, we will find, a perfect fit.

When a woman needs to talk, it is really not necessary for a man to talk. In fact, if he talks too much, it can actually prevent her from opening up. When he thinks too much about what he is going to say, his mental focus shifts away from her.

Any man can learn to listen when he is approached in the right way. Telling a man "You never listen to me" or "We never talk, we should talk more!" is definitely taking the wrong tack. Such comments only make a man feel blamed, attacked, and defensive. Although he may wish to make his woman happy, a man needs to be approached in an appreciative and welcoming manner.

> **Any man can learn to listen if he is approached in an appreciative, welcoming manner.**

How to Get a Man to Listen

An advanced skill my wife uses on me is simply to ask me to listen. She'll say, "Oh, I'm so glad you're home. I've had such a day. Would this be a good time to talk about it? (pause) You don't have to say anything. (little pause) I'm sure I'll feel so much better if I can just talk about it."

By inviting me to listen in this way, she gives me what I really want—a chance to make her happy—and she gets what she needs most—the opportunity to talk, share, and nurture her female side.

When women support their male partners in supporting them, everybody wins. With practice, sympathetic listening can eventually become easy for a man. Paradoxically, what women need most from men can be given with a minimum of effort.

What a woman needs most from a man is to be listened to, a hunter's skill which actually comes naturally to him.

Although listening in this special way is a new requirement for men in relationships, it is a talent we have spent thousands of years preparing for. Since the ancient hunter's major task was to silently watch and listen, men are good at it. Once he acquires the knack of applying this traditional talent to listening to his mate, a man can give a woman the special, focused attention she finds so wonderfully fulfilling.

The Art of Listening

The art of listening to a woman does not entail solving problems or offering advice. Conversely, a male listener's goal should be helping his partner regain her feminine/masculine balance.

This new job description clarifies his goal and thus guides him to silently watch and listen while giving her the sympathy she craves, not the solutions.

Men must remember, a woman talks about her problems not to solve them but to nurture the female side of her psyche.

To develop skill in listening, a man needs to recognize that when a woman is upset and seems to be demanding solutions to her problems, it is only because she is still operating primarily from her male side. By not responding with solutions he assists her in finding her female side; she will then eventually feel better. Men are easily tricked into thinking that if they can give solutions women will then feel better.

Remembering this is particularly helpful when a man feels the woman is upset with him. To explain why she shouldn't be so upset with him only makes matters worse. Although he may have disappointed her in some ways, he must remember that her real complaint is that she is not being heard or nurtured as a woman.

To successfully dodge her attack, a man needs to remind himself that, even when his partner is upset with him, she has only temporarily forgotten how wonderful he is. Before she can remember, she needs her femaleness nurtured. Then she will be capable of, and eager to bestow on him, the appreciation and acknowledgment that he has earned.

> When his partner is upset with him, a man
> needs to remember that she has temporarily
> forgotten how wonderful he is. To remember,
> she needs to feel heard.

What Men Really Want

In the past, what a man achieved in the outside world largely satisfied his wife. Work done, he returned home to reap the fruits of his toil by seeing the smile on her face and feeling the love in her heart. These days, when a man gets home, his wife is not only overwhelmed but is generally needy. She may have love in her heart, but he doesn't see it.

A man knows he works as hard as his forefathers did, and deep in his soul, he expects his woman to acknowledge and appreciate his efforts and in some measure be fulfilled by them. When she does not seem happy to see him, something very significant begins to happen. His tender but passionate desire to please her, protect her, and provide for her is dampened and is eventually snuffed out.

Men don't generally pinpoint what is happening inside themselves because they are more concerned with trying to make women happy. Yet the more a woman acts and reacts from feelings of unhappiness, something inside a man switches off. When his hard work seems to count for nothing, his life and relationship lose all magic and meaning for him.

Remember, what a man really wants is to make his partner happy; if he loves a woman, his primary goal is her fulfillment. Her happiness signals to him that he is loved. Her warm responses are like a mirror reflecting back to him a shining image. When she is not happy, he feels like a failure and eventually gives up trying to fulfill her.

When a woman is unhappy, a man may feel like a failure and may eventually give up trying to fulfill her.

Understanding Our Differences

This understanding of what men really want does not imply that a woman doesn't care about her partner's happiness as well. Certainly, when a woman loves a man, she wants him to also be happy, but note this crucial difference between men and women:

A man can be stressed out from a day at work, but if his partner is happy with him, he feels fulfilled. When he senses her appreciation for his labor, his stress level dissipates; her happiness is like a shower that washes away the stressful grime of his day.

However, when an exhausted woman returns home to a happy man, he doesn't make her day. It's great that he appreciates her hard work to help support the family, but it doesn't in the least diminish her unease. As we have discussed, she needs to communicate and feel some nurturing support before she can begin to appreciate him.

A man thrives on appreciation because it directly nurtures his male side. A woman thrives on communication because it directly nurtures her female side.

By understanding and honoring that men thrive on appreciation and women on communication, we gain the knowledge and the power to create mutually fulfilling relationships.

Even if you only read this chapter and apply these insights, your relationships will change forever for the better. However, to most effectively utilize this advanced understanding, in the next chapter we will explore a new job description for both partners in a relationship. Just as in business we must update our skills, so also in our relationships we need job retraining.

CHAPTER 3

A New Job Description for Relationships

The reason there are so many problems in relationships today is that we just don't understand each other. Men, in particular, don't understand what women need to be happy, and women don't know how to communicate their needs in a language that men understand. Old relationship skills are no longer effective, and are many times counterproductive. With an updated understanding of modern pressures and needs we can begin to formulate a new job description for relationships which can nurture and support both men and women.

Old relationship skills required men to be effective providers and protectors while women learned to be pleasing and accommodating. If strictly observed today, these old skills would go from being the solution to being the problem. When modern men focus on being better providers and protectors, they only burn out, working more and spending less time sharing in their relationships.

Let's look at a playful example of how times have changed. When men were hunters, it was much easier to have relationships. It used to be fine if a man was late getting home. When eventually did return home, his wife was happy that he was still alive.

The harder and longer he worked, the more she felt taken care of. Now, when he is late it is taken as a sign that he doesn't care, and he is in the doghouse. Our fathers had a much easier time in their relationships; not only were they not rejected but they didn't even have to remember to call home.

On the other hand, women didn't mind being pleasing and accommodating to a man when he came home because he was generally very tired and went to sleep. But now, with men spending more time at home, women begin to feel like they give more than they are getting in return. From this playful perspective, our mothers seem to have had it much easier when men spent more time away from home.

When modern women, however, focus on being more pleasing and accommodating, they end up feeling like martyrs who sacrifice their own needs to ensure harmony in the relationship. For women, practicing old relationship skills today is like setting a time bomb. They gradually become so overworked that they explode, feeling resentful, overwhelmed, and unsupported. Although they love their partners, it is hard to *be* loving. Men, seeing that their mates are not happy, assume that they have failed as providers and, in time, withdraw completely.

The only antidote to despair and divorce is the application of new, advanced relationship skills based on new job descriptions for both men and women.

Practicing old relationship skills today is like a time bomb. The only antidote to divorce and despair is the application of new, advanced skills based on new job descriptions for both sexes.

Our Parents Never Told Us It Would Be Like This

If a woman is unwaveringly pleasing and accommodating according to the old ways—as my mother was with my father— her man will never get the message that she needs a different kind of support. My father didn't have a clue as to what my mother really needed on an emotional level. He was too busy feeling the pressure to be a better provider. My mother rarely complained, but when she did, he heard it simply as her wanting more, which implied that he wasn't giving enough. Not knowing what to do, he would just go to his room. That's classic male behavior. Feeling unappreciated, a man who uses old relationship skills commonly reacts by doing less. He figures that if this isn't enough, then why bother trying to do more.

No wonder so many contemporary women feel so hopeless about men. Without retraining in advanced relationship skills for communicating their needs to their partners, it is nearly impossible for men to satisfy them.

New relationship skills are imperative for women today to get what they need from men.

In previous generations, women could focus on being pleasing, accommodating, and nondemanding because men were well trained and knew their jobs. Women didn't need to ask for help or learn how to successfully communicate their wishes to men because men received a clear job description from their fathers and their culture. A woman did not need to instruct her partner, instead she could focus on appreciating his efforts and forgiving his mistakes.

Doing Less but Supporting More

What women need most today besides good communication is for their partners to do more in the home. For men, however, the thought of having to do more is many times a strong message that they are not doing enough. Feeling unappreciated, it is difficult for men to find the energy and motivation to do more.

When a man hears that he is not required to solve her problems or do more in the home, but is primarily needed to listen when she wants to talk and be supported emotionally, then when she talks he can relax and begin to really listen.

When a woman gives a man the message that he can do less and support more by listening, he will slowly but surely begin to have more energy and will automatically begin offering to help out. When a man truly understands a problem, an inner energy then emerges to assist him in solving it. But when he is told he is the problem and must do more, he feels little energy and is very resistant.

While women want men to do more, men want to feel that they are doing enough. The most successful approach in a relationship is to focus first on creating good communication, where a man can feel appreciated for being empathetic, sympathetic, and understanding. As he begins to listen more and is appreciated for supporting her in this way, he will almost magically begin to do more.

To get what they need from their men, women must learn how to communicate needs and desires without demanding or finger-pointing. In most cases, as we will discover, a woman can be made happier by a man who is actually doing less because he is supporting her differently, according to new rules which are infinitely more effective. When a man understands this truth, his motivation to do things differently greatly increases.

Part of a man's frustration is that when a woman wants more he mistakenly assumes that he has to do everything she needs. He does not know that as long as he is taking small steps toward helping her around the house, coupled with better communication, she will be immeasurably happier.

As both partners begin successfully to give and receive the support they really need, they will happily give more and more. He will give her more and more of what modern women most need and appreciate. She will give him more and more of what men really want.

Under the new job descriptions, men give women
what they most need and appreciate, and women give
men what they really want.

B.B.C.—Before Birth Control

To discover the behavior patterns that nourish femininity and masculinity, let's return for a moment to the world of the male provider and his nurturer mate. Religion and social convention encouraged differences between men and women, particularly through assigning specific roles. "Men's work," as we've seen, to a great extent was providing, protecting, and leading, while "women's work" was generally nurturing, homemaking, and supporting. This division of labor held steady for millennia, well into our parents' time.

The hunter's day was filled with risk and danger and was primarily focused on the single task of successfully protecting the home and bringing home the kill. The life of his family depended on his competence, assertiveness, aggressiveness, and skill. Men evolved in specific ways to cope successfully with the pressures of "men's work."

A nurturer's day was a flow of repetitive and detailed tasks that sustained her children, her family, and her community. The life of her family depended on her ability to communicate, negotiate, accommodate, and cooperate. Women also evolved in specific ways to cope successfully with the stresses of "women's work."

> **Traditionally, men's work was providing, protecting, and leading, while women's work was nurturing, homemaking, and supporting.**

Today, the lines dividing men's work and women's work are dramatically fading. As men take a more active role in parenting and enjoying their relationships in the home, women are developing the focus and competitiveness required for traditional "male work." This generational shift away from rigidly defined gender roles is a definite step toward wholeness and promises great eventual fulfillment, but it also presents new challenges. Through understanding and respecting how our ancestors coped with stress, we can be better equipped to support each other during this dramatic transformation.

Today, we can detect a definite generational shift
away from rigidly defined gender job roles and
toward wholeness.

How Our Ancestors Coped

On a very basic level, our brains and bodies have, over the millennia, developed specifically to deal with the unique stresses of traditional men's and women's work. Although modern lifestyles are rapidly dispensing with those roles, evolution has yet to catch up and produce new coping mechanisms.

Chief among the traditional female coping mechanisms is communication. For the nurturer women of long ago, talking in a non-goal-oriented way, while giving and receiving sympathy, was essential to peace of mind and generated feelings of security and belonging. Years ago, women with children were much more vulnerable and were dependent on the goodwill of others. Before government welfare programs and expanded legal rights and educational opportunities, women had to rely on others for security and safety. If her husband left her or died, a woman depended on her family and community to take care of her, so she had to maintain strong relationships with those around her. Talking connected her to her support network and made her feel secure. When a modern woman today is upset and begins talking, she is automatically connecting with that time-honored feeling of security.

Why Women Need to Talk About Problems

As a common practice, nurturer women shared their problems with each other not to directly ask for help but to share sympathy and community. Problem solving was secondary to the exercise of the cooperative spirit.

Women supported each other unconditionally, without being asked and expecting nothing in return. This cooperative sharing strengthened relationships within the community and ensured a woman's and her children's survival should she be widowed.

Talking about problems, sharing feelings, and articulating desires became a feminine ritual to create greater intimacy and express loyalty to the community. Today, when a woman goes to a counselor, she is seeking out that same support. Most counselors and therapists, it should be noted, are trained to listen attentively rather than focus on problem solving. Hence, the process offers tremendous support for women in coping with day-to-day stress.

Through talking and feeling heard in therapy, women come to feel nurtured, and the weight of their problems lifts. Once able to relax and proceed at a more easygoing pace, they can begin to deal with their problems.

When Men Offer Advice

Men instinctively don't understand this and, unlike therapists, are not trained in how to support feelings effectively. When a woman talks about her feelings, he assumes she is seeking his help to solve her problems and instinctively responds to her feelings by offering help or advice.

Take a fireman, for example. When he receives a call, he must get the size and location of the fire as quickly as possible and then do something to put out the fire. Asking a lot of extra questions and offering empathy is not part of his job description.

Imagine this scene. A fireman receives a call and responds by saying, "You have a fire. How awful. How does it feel? Really. Have you ever been in a fire before? It *is* hot. I've been to a lot. I'm sorry it's so hot. Are you all alone?. . . " Obviously, this kind of empathetic response would be out of place.

This simple but dramatic example helps women to understand why listening without offering solutions can be so difficult for men. It is truly a new job description for a man to learn to listen without trying to immediately put out the fire.

When a man becomes restless while listening to a woman it is not because he doesn't care about her. It's because every cell in his body is saying: If there is a fire, let's get out of here and put it out. If there is a problem, he wants to do something about it and not just talk about it.

Modern men need to understand that modern women need, more than anything else, the opportunity to talk about their feelings without focusing on solving the problems that cause them. By responding with empathy, sympathy, and understanding, he makes sure that her female side is nurtured so that she can throw off her feelings of being overwhelmed. Gradually, as she shifts back to her female side, her heart will be full of appreciation and love for him. In a practical sense, by just listening he frees her to forget the urgency of her problems and remember what a great guy he is.

In a practical sense, by just listening a man frees a woman to forget the urgency of her problems and remember what a great guy he is.

When a woman is unhappy and talks about problems, a man must remind himself that it is not him but modern culture that demands that she must bear the stress of having two full-time careers—homemaker and wage earner—at once. Remembering that he is not the prime source of her frustration helps him to not feel blamed when she is unhappy. This awareness frees him to better sympathize with her rather than defend himself.

How Men Cope

Men commonly cope with stress differently. For instance, by working at achieving a simple goal like driving the car, or hitting a tennis ball around, teeing off, or shooting hoops, a man sorts out his thoughts and concerns, clarifies his values and priorities, and develops a plan of action. It gives him a sense of security.

Remember, a hunter's survival is ensured by moving quietly and then striking. Through his hunting—or problem-solving—skills, his family's security is ensured. It is the subconscious hunter, buried deep inside the contemporary man, who feels secure when he lobs a paper ball into the wastebasket across the room.

If a man can put his feelings into action, he begins to feel more in control. By simply pacing back and forth when he is frustrated, he can find the same relief a woman might feel through talking. Through understanding this vital difference, men and women can more effectively support each other.

If a man can put his feelings into action, he feels the same relief a woman does by talking.

Why Men Don't Understand Women

When a man solves a problem, he feels relieved and happy. So when a woman talks about problems, he mistakenly assumes that to feel better she needs to solve them rather than to talk about them and be heard.

Without being taught that she needs to be heard, he will interrupt by offering solutions. When she doesn't feel appreciative of his solutions, he then also feels upset. Instead of getting the nurturing she needs in order to cope, a woman feels even more stressed. Instead of successfully solving her problems, he feels like a failure.

After a few arguments like this, she will close up to avoid making things worse. In the long run, this will only increase her level of stress. She will become increasingly overwhelmed, and communication will become more and more difficult.

Silently Sitting on a Rock

It's crucial to remember that one of the most significant differences between men and women is that while women cope with stress through sharing in nurturing relationships, men cope through solving problems. Traditionally, men have dealt with their problems by silently and patiently thinking up solutions. Ancient

hunters would sit on a rock and silently search the horizon, looking and listening for their prey, or looking across the plains at their
target, studying its movements and planning the attack.

This process of sitting, waiting, scheming, and planning
allowed him to relax and conserve energy for the inevitable
chase. Focusing kept his mind off the fear of being attacked or
of missing his target, and when he achieved his goal he returned
home a happy, stress-free man.

> **Women cope with stress through sharing in nurturing
> relationships, men by solving problems.**

Why Men Watch TV

When a modern man comes home, quite commonly he sits in
his favorite chair and either reads the newspaper or watches TV.
Like the ancient hunter who needed to recover from the stress
of his day, he instinctively finds his rock to sit on and begins
gazing off into the horizon.

Through reading or listening to the news he is, in effect,
looking out over the world or scanning the horizon. As he picks
up the remote control and begins searching through the sta-
tions, or turns the pages of his paper, he is once more in control: he silently and swiftly continues his hunt.

As he assumes this ancient posture, deep and reassuring feelings of security begin to emerge. Feeling in control, he is able to
most effectively cope with the stress of not having immediate
solutions to the problems of his life.

Through this instinctive ritual he is able to temporarily forget his problems at work and is eventually ready for the relationship.

When Women Don't Understand Men

When men today attempt to fulfill their need to be solitary, the
modern woman commonly misunderstands. She mistakenly

assumes that he wants her to initiate a conversation. She thinks he is waiting for her to notice that he is distressed, and that he wants her to ask him what is bothering him. She does not realize that he really wants to be left alone.

When she persists in asking, he becomes increasingly annoyed and sends her what he thinks are clear messages to leave him alone, but she misinterprets his cues. Here is a common pattern.

She Says:	He Says:
1. *She says:* "How was your day?"	1. *He says:* "Fine."
She means: "Let's talk, I'm interested in your day, and I hope you are interested in mine."	He means: "I am giving you a short answer because I need some time alone."
2. *She says:* "How did your meeting go with your new client?"	2. *He says:* "It was OK."
She means: "I will keep asking you questions so you know that I really care and I am interested in your day. I hope you will be interested in my day. I have a lot to say."	He means: "I am trying to be polite and not reject you, but would you stop bothering me with more questions?"
3. *She says:* "Did they like your proposal?"	3. *He says:* "Yes."
She means: "I suppose it must be hard to talk about it, so I'll ask a more neutral question to get us started. It's OK if you don't open up right away. I am here for you, and I am interested. I	He means: "Look, I don't want to talk right now. Would you just leave me alone? You're bugging me. Can't you tell I want to be alone? If I wanted to talk I would talk."

She Says:	He Says:
know you will really appreciate it, and then you will want to hear what I have to say."	
4. *She says:* "What's wrong?" She means: "I can see that something happened that is upsetting you. You can talk to me. I will listen, I care. I'm sure that by talking about it you will feel better."	4. *He says:* "Nothing's wrong." He means: "Nothing's wrong that I can't deal with alone. After a while I will forget my problems and then be available for the relationship. So would you just ignore me for a little while and then I will be much more open and interested in you. I just need to shift gears to get back home."
5. *She says:* "I can tell something is wrong. What is it?" She means: "I know something is wrong, and if you don't talk, it will get worse. You need to talk!"	5. *He says nothing and walks away.* He means: "I don't want to get mad at you, so I am just walking away. After a while I will be back, and I will not be mad at you for annoying me."

How Women React When Men Don't Want to Talk

Inevitably, when a man resists conversation and a woman doesn't understand his need to be alone to recuperate from the day, she will have a variety of misinterpretations and begin to panic. These are some of the ways in which she may then react:

She Thinks:	She Reacts:
1. She thinks there is some big problem in the relationship and he doesn't want to be with her.	1. She reacts by feeling rejected, and to clear things up insists on discussing their relationship.
2. She thinks he doesn't trust her to care about his feelings.	2. She reacts sympathetically by asking lots of questions and trying to show that she cares. Eventually, she feels frustrated when he resists her loving attempts to help.
3. She thinks he must be angry with her.	3. She reacts by feeling inadequate and confused.
4. She thinks he doesn't want to talk because he is hiding something that might upset her.	4. As a result, she does get upset worrying about what it might be.
5. She thinks he is selfish and only cares about himself and not about her.	5. In reaction, she doubts his love for her.
6. She thinks he is trying to punish her by withholding his love and attention.	6. She reacts by getting angry back and withholding her attention and love.

She Thinks:	**She Reacts:**
7. She thinks he is dissatisfied with her.	7. She reacts by feeling unappreciated for all she does for him.
8. She thinks he is just lazy.	8. In reaction, she feels resentful because she is giving so much more than he is.
9. She thinks he has lost interest in her.	9. She reacts by feeling ignored, isolated, and powerless to get what she needs. She may also begin to feel unattractive, boring, and unworthy of love.
10. She thinks he has a deep fear of intimacy brought about by his dysfunctional past and that he needs therapy.	10. She reacts by feeling powerless to ever get what she needs until he is healed.
11. She thinks he is hiding something from her.	11. She reacts by feeling afraid that she has done something bad or that he has done something bad.
12. She thinks she got involved with the wrong man.	12. She reacts by thinking other men are not this way and longs for a more sensitive and talkative man.

In each of these examples, the woman's reaction is based on a misunderstanding. If a woman is to support a man in coming back to the relationship, her new job description requires her to understand this difference and accept his need for space. As we will continue to see, this doesn't mean that she must sacrifice her need for conversation. What is required, however, is a new sense of timing.

> For a woman to get a man back into a relationship, her new job description requires her to accept his need for space.

Why Men Pull Away

When a woman learns the skill of temporarily postponing her needs and allows a man the time he needs to shift gears from his work life to his home life, she creates a fertile ground for him to find his love for her and then act on it. As he grows accustomed to this support, he begins to anticipate it. At this point, just the thought of returning home begins releasing his stress. The more he gets this kind of support, the less he needs to pull away from his mate.

Without this advanced relationship skill a woman unknowingly prevents her male partner from successfully making the transition from work to home. Through her demanding more of him or reacting negatively to his need for private time, he may never relax enough to come back into the relationship. If the downward spiral continues, it can actually hinder a man from contacting his loving feelings. He may even believe that he doesn't love his partner anymore.

> When a man arrives home to a needy woman, he continues to pull away.

When a man arrives home to a needy woman, he continues to pull away and never learns how to open up. The more he feels pressured to talk or be "in relationship," the more he needs to back off to relax. He can most effectively forget the demands of his job when he feels no pressure or demands from his mate.

When a man returns home to a nondemanding woman, he feels free to take the time he needs to relax. He can then automatically shift gears and give his partner the love she deserves. When a man is not expected to give more, he automatically wants to. Literally thousands of women who have studied advanced relationship skills report that this single insight has magically transformed their relationships.

When a man is not expected to give more, he automatically wants to. ·

When Men Don't Understand Women

When a woman is emotionally distressed, a man mistakenly assumes that if she is to feel better, she needs some solitary time just like he does. He will tend to ignore her and give her lots of space because that is precisely the kind of support he would want. To ignore her, however, is the worst thing he can do.

Even if he asks her what is bothering her, he may misread what she really needs. Again, let's look at a common pattern.

Tom says to Mary, "What's wrong? You seem upset."

Mary says, "Oh, it's nothing." Mary is silently saying, "Nothing is bothering me, unless of course you really care. Then you will show me by standing here and asking me more questions."

Tom says, "OK," and walks away. He is silently saying, "It's OK if you don't want to talk about it. I understand if you want some space. I'll support you by acting like everything is OK. I trust that you can handle it."

Tom actually thinks he is being supportive and has no idea that he has just failed the test. Most men think like Tom, but almost any woman would instinctively understand that when

Mary said, "Nothing's wrong," she really wanted him to ask more questions and draw her out. When a woman says "Nothing's wrong," something usually is, and she needs to talk about it to a listener who is interested and cares. She wants to be asked questions that will eventually help her to open up.

> **When a woman says "Nothing's wrong," something usually is, and she wants to talk about it with a sympathetic listener.**

Let's look at some other common ways in which men misunderstand women.

1. He asks: "Do you want to talk about something?"	1. She says "No" but really means "Yes, and if you really care, you will ask more questions."
2. He asks: "Do you want any help?"	2. She says "No, I can do it " but really means "Yes, and if you really want to help, then watch what I am doing and join in."
3. He asks: "Did I do something wrong?"	3. She says "No" but really means "Yes, and if you care to make things better you will figure out what by asking more questions."
4. He asks: "Is everything OK?"	4. She says "Yes" but really means "No, and if you want to work it out, then you will ask more questions about what might be upsetting me."

In each of these examples, the woman is, in a sense, testing to see if it is safe to talk about her feelings. If he understands her hidden meaning, then she is assured that she can share her feelings and that her needs will be supported.

Without a clear job description of what he is supposed to do at such times, few men have a clue and just walk away thinking they are being helpful.

When Women Talk About Feelings

After feeling neglected for some time, when a woman does eventually talk about her feelings a man will again misunderstand. Commonly, he misinterprets her complaints and assumes that he is required to be a better provider instead of hearing that she really needs more attention and nurturing at home. Let's look at some common examples.

She Complains:	He Misunderstands:
1. When she complains about the house, she is really only wanting to share her frustrations and be heard.	1. He thinks that he has to earn more money for a bigger house before she will be happy.
2. When she complains about her job, she is really only wanting to share her day and reconnect with her partner.	2. He thinks that he has to make more money so that she doesn't have to work, and only then will she be happy.
3. When she complains about having to do housework, she is generally sharing her feelings of being overwhelmed and is asking for help if he has the energy.	3. He thinks that he has to either provide a maid or become one for her, and only then will she be happy.
4. When she complains about the weather or other problems with no solution, she is generally seeking a little	4. Emotionally, he begins to feel as if he has to earn more money so that they can move to a better

She Complains:	He Misunderstands:
sympathy for what she has been through.	climate before she will be happy.
5. When she complains that he works too hard, she is wanting him to know that she misses him and would love to spend more time together.	5. He thinks that he now has to make more money so that he doesn't have to work so hard, and then she will be happy.

In every case, when the woman is distressed the man feels on a deep instinctual level that he has to work harder to be a better provider. This instinct to succeed more at work causes him to be less present in the relationship. When he does become more successful, or when he does exert himself to solve her problems and she is still unhappy or unfulfilled, he feels ever more intensely the frustration of not being able to make her happy. To cope with this frustration he begins to turn off his romantic feelings of caring about her fulfillment.

Why Men Don't Commit

This same principle applies to many single men. When they don't attract the woman of their dreams, they begin to feel as if they have to make more money. Instead of recognizing that they need to work on relationship skills, they may focus too much on their careers.

Some men give up on the thought of marriage because their particular talents make it seem unlikely that they will earn big money, or they feel that they'll have to sacrifice themselves too much to make a large salary. Some men may have the woman of their dreams but are afraid to commit because they don't make enough money.

Jackie and Dan are a very dramatic example of this. They had been living together for nine years. She wanted to get married, but he didn't. He assured her that he loved her, but something inside was stopping him from getting married. He claimed that he just wasn't sure. Then, one evening while talking about a movie they had seen, she happened to say, "I'd love you even if we were always poor."

The very next day, he went out and bought the ring.

All Dan needed was a clear message from Jackie that he didn't have to make a lot of money to successfully provide for her happiness. Then he could make the commitment. Like most men, Dan was able to commit to the relationship when he felt his ability to provide for a woman was enough to make her happy.

While all men are not as obsessed with making money, they do need to feel confident that they can provide for a woman's happiness before making a commitment to marriage. Advanced relationship skills help a man realize that, regardless of how much money he makes, he can provide emotional support and a woman will be much happier.

Why Men Become Preoccupied with Work

When a man experiences the stress of thinking that his family is unhappy, he instinctively focuses more and more on succeeding at work. He focuses to such an extent that he doesn't realize how much time he is away. For him, time may pass very quickly, but while she is waiting for him to come home it passes much more slowly. He doesn't realize that in modern times, his presence at home is at least as important to her as his success at work.

Tunnel Vision

The more work stress a man experiences, the more he focuses on solving problems. At such times it is extremely difficult for him to release his lock on the problem and bring his full attention back to relationships. He can become so focused that he forgets everything else and unknowingly neglects his wife and family.

It is as though he is looking through a tunnel and only takes in what is relevant or useful to achieving his goal. He doesn't realize that he is not listening or responding to the people he loves because he is so utterly focused on solving his problem. At such times, he has temporarily forgotten what is really important to him. He does not recognize that he is pushing away the people he loves the most.

> **Men are often so totally focused on problem solving, that they do not realize they are not listening or responding to loved ones.**

When a Man Ignores His Family

When a man withdraws from intimacy to focus on his work problems, it is hard for a woman to recognize it as an automatic reaction. She views it as a deliberate act of coldness and indifference because for a woman to focus on work issues and ignore her family would require a deliberate decision on her part and, in most cases, would also signal that she just doesn't care.

When a man is focused on his work, he doesn't just decide to ignore his family. He truly forgets. He doesn't decide to forget picking up his daughter at school, it is an automatic byproduct of increasing his focus on solving his problems at work. It is not a sign that he has stopped caring. If anything, it is a sign that he does care but is just not adept at coping with his stress.

This same tendency to focus on one thing and forget everything else causes a man to procrastinate about doing things he really is willing to do. Many times a woman will ask a man to do something he really intends to do, but then he forgets. Because it is actually hard for her to forget, she mistakenly assumes that he is deliberately trying to get out of it by putting it off.

Men and the Stresses of Work

A man today cannot simply make a kill like his ancestors did and then come home to celebrate. His life is much more complex. It may take months to finish a deal and hopefully make a killing. During that time his mind is consumed with planning and thinking and rethinking how to solve his problems. He thinks at work, at home, and in his sleep. He can remember every detail required to achieve his work goals, but he then forgets to bring home the milk no matter how many times his wife reminds him.

Shifting Gears from Work to the Relationship

A man's tendency to be absorbed in his work is not only counterproductive for a woman, but it is also counterproductive for him. Until a man can apply advanced relationship skills and directly nurture a woman's feelings, his instincts will urge him back to his work when she is upset or unfulfilled.

There are basically three ways in which a man is able to shift gears between work and the relationship. To various degrees, all three are simultaneously required.

1. Success
The first is success. The more successful a man feels when he leaves work, the easier it is for him to forget his problems and enjoy his relationships. A successful day at work makes him feel that the hunt is over and he can now return home and more easily relax. When a man is not succeeding as much as he would like, or as much as he thinks he should, then the next two ways become more important.

2. Distraction
The second is distraction. To forget the problems of his day, he distracts his focus from work to sitting on his favorite rock and watching TV, reading the paper, listening to music, going to the movies, or any other easy and nondemanding activities requiring focus.

Another practical way for him to shift gears through distraction is to physically work out, focusing his mind on exercising his body. This can be vigorous activity or even something as easy as going for a walk. To free his mind from solving problems at work, he just needs a new challenge that requires focus.

A man forgets his real problems by focusing on other problems he can easily solve or problems he is not responsible for solving. Playing games, fiddling or tinkering with things, cheering on teams, playing sports, and watching the news are the most common stress reducers. When he mentally solves the world's problems or figures out how to get his team to win, he feels competent again and confident about facing his real-life problems.

Indulging in a hobby also allows him to forget the really pressing and important problems. Hobbies are very important even if they seem trivial, because without them a man may not be able to disengage from work and can become overstressed.

Without a hobby, a man may not be able to disengage himself from work and can become overstressed.

Through these kinds of distractions, a man actively engages himself in some easy activity and succeeds in disengaging from his work projects. This stress reduction technique is perfect for men and has taken century upon century to develop. To encourage or expect a man to be in his female side and talk about his problems in many cases goes against his nature. In some cases, talking about his day before he is relaxed may increase his stress by bringing his awareness back to work, with all its frustrations, disappointments, and worries.

Once the stress is reduced, then a man can begin to open up and share in a relationship from his female side. This order is very important. First he needs to forget his problems and then he feels like he has something positive to offer. He will then automatically remember what is most important to him—his wife and family or the desire to have one. This shift in awareness to what is really important to him is also essential for him to recharge.

> Once his daytime stress is reduced, a man can begin
> to open up and share in a relationship from his
> female side.

3. Appreciation

The third means to shift gears from work to the relationship is to return home anticipating the support of his partner. A woman's accepting and appreciating love is something he begins to look forward to. To anticipate this support makes him feel that he is a success even if he didn't achieve his goals at work.

The very thought of returning home to a loving partner can wash away much of a man's stress. Then, if he still needs to take some alone time, he won't need to retreat nearly as much.

On the other hand, when a man anticipates arriving home to an unhappy partner, he becomes even more consumed with his work. It is then harder for him to release the pressures of his job.

In my relationship with Bonnie, there are a variety of little things that I can do when I get home to ensure that I get this appreciation. Without much effort at all when I get home, I can find her, give her a hug, ask her about her day, and listen for a few minutes, and I am certain of being appreciated. The more I feel her appreciation and love welcoming me home, the less I need to distract myself from work when I get home. In addition, I tend to acknowledge and recognize my success each day so that I can more easily leave the problems at the office.

A New Job Description

> With a new job description, both men and women
> can learn to effectively support each other through
> thick and thin.

With a new job description, both men and women can learn to effectively support each other. When a man comes home, he can easily learn to be more responsive to his partner—but it takes time and retraining in advanced relationship skills. This process can be achieved much more quickly with his partner's support. To assist a man in this process requires new training for women as well.

It becomes easier for women to understand this extra time a man needs to be open to the relationship if we compare it to a different arena in which she requires more time to open up. For example, to enjoy sex after a stressful day, most women will strongly relate to feeling the need for more time, attention, conversation, and romance first.

In a similar way, it is as difficult for a man to open up to a relationship when he gets home as it is for a woman to open up to sex after a long, stressful day. A man needs more time and space and lots of appreciation to make the shift from office to home.

In some ways, it is as difficult for a man to open up to a relationship when he gets home as it is for a woman to open up to sex after a stressful day.

By correctly understanding a man's tendency to focus and forget, a woman can be more forgiving, accepting, and appreciative. She does not take it so personally when he is withdrawn. This accepting awareness, combined with advanced relationship skills for communicating, gives her new power not only to get what she wants but also to support a man in letting go of his stress and opening his heart.

Advanced relationship skills give women new power to not only get what they want but also to support a man in letting go of stress and opening his heart.

Likewise, as men begin to understand women, they can apply the new skill of providing emotional support and not focusing primarily on physically solving women's problems. A man can learn to listen when his partner speaks without it causing him to feel that he is being required to do more. By learning these new advanced relationship skills, men happily discover that without having to change who they are, or do a lot more, they can support their mates much more.

Emotional Role Reversal

When a woman is more on her masculine side, and her female side is neglected, an emotional role reversal occurs. She begins to function from the needs of her male side, not her female side. While most modern women can easily recite a litany of valid work- and relationship-related problems and injustices, often the real culprit responsible for their general dissatisfaction is this emotional role reversal.

For women to feel happy in relationships, they need to regain the balance of their male and female sides. Both men and women need to work together to assist the woman in coming back to her female side. A man's new job description requires him to assist a woman in nurturing her feminine self after a long day's work.

> A man's new job description requires him to assist a woman in finding her feminine self again after a long day's work.

The Problems of Emotional Role Reversal

The stress of switching back and forth from the masculine to the feminine side every day has an invisible but devastating effect on lasting romance, passion, and intimacy. Just as a ball rolling downhill gathers speed, so a woman continues to spiral farther into frustration if there is no conscious intervention to relieve this stress. Without an understanding of this underlying dynamic, a man's logical attempts to solve partnership problems can be disastrously counterproductive.

When emotional role reversal occurs and a woman is more on her male side, then she automatically feels a greater need to solve problems. It is not enough for her to do what she can do and then relax through talking about everything that is not done. Instead, she feels a strong pull to solve all the unsolved problems before she can relax.

At those times when she feels a need to solve problems, a man can best support her by listening. I remember when I first recognized the symptoms of emotional role reversal in my own marriage but didn't have a clue about correctly supporting my wife.

Bonnie and I had just returned home after playing a really enjoyable tennis game.

"I can't wait to take a nap," I told her.

"That sounds so good," she agreed. "I'd love to take a nap."

As I was walking up the stairs to our bedroom, I noticed that she wasn't behind me and called, "Aren't you coming?"

"I'd love to," she called back, "but I can't. I have to wash the car."

How could she make washing her car more important than taking a nap on a day off? I thought to myself. At this point, I realized we definitely were from different planets.

I did not suspect that she was stuck on her male side and locked into solving her problems. I did not know that through nurturing her female side with some conversation that it would assist her in releasing her burdens and responsibilities. Without an understanding of how I could support her in relaxing, I continued upstairs and instantly dozed.

I woke refreshed and was looking forward to a romantic evening—until I went downstairs and discovered Bonnie in a bad mood.

I casually said, "You should have taken a nap. I feel great." This comment did not go over big.

She responded icily, "I have no time for naps. I still have to do laundry, help with the kids' homework, clean up the house. And I still have to make dinner."

Not realizing that she needed to talk, I continued trying to solve her problems by suggesting we go out for dinner.

"You don't understand," Bonnie insisted, "I have food in the refrigerator that needs to be cooked. And Lauren still hasn't finished her school project."

I said, "This is the weekend. You should be relaxing."

"I can't relax," she said. "You just don't understand!"

At this point I was also in a bad mood. Whatever romance I had inside me quickly dissipated. Bonnie was even more upset because I didn't listen sympathetically, and I was ticked off because she had rejected my solutions.

Now, when Bonnie is feeling overwhelmed, our conversations sound quite different. Instead of feeling rejected or defensive, I know just what to do. She needs to talk to come back to her feminine side, and she needs my help to do it. This is an example of a conversation we might have when Bonnie is overwhelmed and having difficulty switching to her feminine side:

John: "What's wrong?"
Bonnie: "I don't know, there's just too much to do."
John: "Oh."
Bonnie: "I don't have enough time."
John: "Tell me about it."
Bonnie: "I still have to do laundry, and dinner isn't even started."
John: "Hmmm."
Bonnie: "I was supposed to take Pearl to the dentist today and I completely forgot."
John: "What did you do?"
Bonnie: "Oh, I don't even want to think about it."
John: "Hmmm."
Bonnie: "Pearl was so worried, she thought something terrible had happened. (pause) I never forget things like that."
I said nothing, just took a deep breath and shook my head back and forth.
Bonnie: "It worked out OK, though. We just rescheduled another time."
John: "That's good."

Bonnie: "I don't know what to do about dinner. I haven't planned anything."

John: "Hmmm, I don't know either."

Bonnie: "Do you mind eating leftovers tonight?"

John: "Sounds good to me. What do we have?"

Bonnie: "Oh, I don't know. I really don't feel like making anything."

John: "Let's just go out to eat, and then we'll have some time left for us."

Bonnie: "Great!"

What a difference a few years of practice makes! Without my knowing how to support Bonnie with the advanced relationship skill of nurturing conversation, we would probably just argue, eat leftovers, and go to sleep frustrated and turned off.

When Women Don't Feel Free to Talk

When, over the course of a relationship, woman don't feel free to talk, they disconnect from the natural happiness that comes when their female side is nurtured. Even more distressing is the fact that, as they lose touch with their female side, they may also lose the awareness of what they need. All they know is that "something is missing," and generally, the man in their lives gets blamed.

The more a woman disconnects from her female side, the less receptive she is to a man's support. Meanwhile, her partner feels frustrated because he can't fulfill her and feels powerless to change things.

Why Women Need More Talk

To cope with the added stress of leaving the home to work, today's woman has a much greater need for partnership support. When she gets home, she needs to talk more. She needs the security of being able to open up and share feelings that may not always make sense or be related to the bottom line. She needs to feel that someone understands what she's going through and cares about her.

Men must understand that when women talk to relieve their daily burdens, they are looking *not* for solutions but for a sympathetic ear. This is what happens when a man tries to "solve" a woman's problems:

Anatomy of a Misunderstanding

1. She claims "You are not listening" or "You don't understand."

2. He explains that he was too listening or he couldn't have offered such a great suggestion.

3. She continues to insist that he's not really listening to her and that he doesn't understand her problem.

4. He begins to feel frustrated and tries to prove that he does understand and that his solution is the right one.

5. They begin arguing.

He thinks she is saying that he doesn't understand the problem or that his solution is the wrong one. What she is really saying, though, is that she's not getting the empathy or sympathy she craves. When she says "You don't understand," she really means "You don't understand what I need from you. I just need you to listen and empathize."

Men don't readily know how to respond to work-stressed women because they never saw their fathers do it. In most cases, our mothers spent their days nurturing their feminine natures through communicating with other women. I don't remember ever hearing my mother complain to my dad that "We never talk." By the time Dad came home, she had already talked enough. However, women of our generation don't have this luxury. They are required to be mindful of the time and always to get to the point when talking. They are pushed toward maleness.

One comedian put it this way: God gave women an average of six thousand words a day and men two thousand. Quite commonly, by the end of a workday they have both used two thousand words. When she comes home she still has four thousand left. No wonder she feels neglected. She wants to talk, but he has already spent his allotted two thousand words.

While this is a fun way of understanding the problem, the problem is very real.

> **The lack of communication in relationships
> is the number one reason contemporary women
> are dissatisfied.**

Literally thousands of relationships dramatically improved in an instant as men began to understand the female need to be listened to.

> **Thousands of relationships have dramatically
> improved in an instant when men began to
> appreciate and act on the female need
> to be listened to.**

Remember, when men talk about problems, they are generally looking for solutions. Most of the time, however, a man looking to recover from the day doesn't want to talk. The calm he achieves through not talking, women achieve through talking.

> **The calm men achieve through not talking, women
> achieve through talking.**

In simple terms, a man needs to remember that even when an overwhelmed woman shares a list of problems that demand solutions, the only one that has to be solved immediately is her need to be heard by someone who is not trying to talk her out of her feelings or solve all her problems. Women must remember that when men don't listen it is mainly because they don't understand why "feeling heard" is so important to women.

> Women must remember that when men don't listen it
> is mainly because they don't understand why "feeling
> heard" is so important to women.

By recognizing that the working world prevents women from nurturing their female sides and finding happiness, men can at last begin to make sense of the feminine need to be heard. Men really do want to make their partners happy, it's just that until now they haven't understood how.

A man can more easily endure the lack of feminine values in the workplace because he has from time immemorial come home from work to a female in order to find balance. But since women rarely work outside the home in a nurturing feminine environment, and they do not have a female to come home to, it is much harder for them to find balance.

Not only do men not know how to support women, but women don't know how to successfully communicate their need for support. Women either expect men to be mind readers and know their needs, or they let their needs build up until they are resentful and then demand more. Neither approach works.

Why Women Don't Like to Ask

As we have explored, times have changed, and all the relationship rules have changed. Although women are wanting more, even they don't know exactly what they need. In our parents' day, if a man loved a woman he would do what she wanted without being asked.

That is because what she wanted was also what his father taught him to do and her mother told her to expect. He learned from his father how to be a good provider. She didn't have to teach him. Each day he focused on being a better provider. He was not expected to be a domestic helper, and she was not expected to be stressed out and overwhelmed.

When Men Are Self-Motivated

When a man loved a woman according to the old ways, he would go to work to provide for her and would willingly give up his life to protect her. That was his most precious gift to her. He did not rely on her to tell him what to do. If he loved her, he motivated himself to provide for her. That self-motivation expressed the extent of his love.

Because men knew what was expected of them and had been trained by their fathers and other mentors, women were not required to tell a man their needs or ask for support. When a man loved a woman he *offered* his support as a provider. If he offered his support, then a woman knew he loved her.

Now women want things our fathers were not required to do. If a woman is to receive a new kind of support, she is required to educate her partner about her needs and to ask in pleasing ways for more.

> If a woman is to receive support, she is required to educate her partner about her needs and to ask in pleasing ways for more.

Having to ask is not easy for women. If she has to ask, then it doesn't feel like she is being loved. In addition, she really has had very little exposure to a woman asking for what she wants in a way that works. For this reason, I recommend first improving communication, and then beginning to practice the art of asking for more. Once there is good communication and a man begins to understand her feelings more deeply, he will automatically understand her problems better and will slowly but surely do more.

For centuries, the sign that a woman was loved was her not having to ask. Now, when a man appears to a woman as if he is not motivated to support her needs, it weakens her self-esteem and humiliates her. She feels that she is not worthy of his love.

In a similar way, when a man feels that he is unfairly being asked for more, he may not feel that his self-esteem is weakened, but he certainly doesn't feel like giving more. When he returns home from work, he will feel increasingly lifeless and lethargic.

To Ask or Not to Ask

It used to be that the squeaky wheel got oiled. Today, however, the squeaky wheel gets replaced. Asking for more can easily begin to sound like nagging. Men hate to hear it, and women hate to do it. Without understanding how to assist a man in taking the time to listen to her feelings, a woman is left with only two alternatives. She can become a martyr and settle for whatever she gets, or she can try demanding and nagging for more.

Neither alternative will work. To get the love and support she needs, it is crucial for a woman to focus on what is most essential. Ask him to listen, and gradually, over time, as he understands her feelings better, she can begin to ask for more physical support.

To sustain love and good feelings in a relationship, it is essential that a woman learn to express her feelings and needs in a way that can work for both the man and herself.

> To sustain love and good feelings in a relationship, it
> is vital that a woman learn to express her feelings
> and needs in a way that can work for both her man
> and herself.

I am in no way suggesting that women not express themselves, but I am saying that if they want to be heard and respected, advanced relationship skills and new job descriptions are definitely required.

Just as women underestimate the power of appreciation and positive reinforcement of a man's behavior, men underestimate the power of listening with empathy to a woman's feelings and then offering a little help and attention here and there. Most men have no idea of what women really need today. A little focused attention on her and her needs can go a long way.

What to Expect

When approached in the right way and at the right time, men are happy to do more. With a few months of good communication without demanding anything more, and several doses of appreciation, any man will be willing to do more. A man's idea of "more" and a woman's may be dramatically different. Men can give more only in small degrees.

Men can give more only in small degrees.

It is unrealistic to expect a man to suddenly be motivated to do 50 percent of the housework if he has been used to doing much less. Likewise, if he is the quiet type, it is not probable that he will immediately open up and share his feelings.

It is equally unrealistic for a man to expect his female partner to greet him at home with great appreciation and feel fulfilled when she has also spent all day working. These unrealistic expectations create unnecessary resentment and alienation in both men and women.

Remember that for century after century, men were not expected to be nurturers in the home. Domestic inclinations were not required of them because women didn't need men to listen to feelings and help with the chores.

Both women and men can get the support they need, but it doesn't happen overnight. Just as a business takes hard work, dedication, and the application of new strategies to succeed, so also do relationships require patience, persistence, and rewritten job descriptions rooted in advanced relationship skills.

As women begin to accept the fact that they can ask for and get more without having to nag or complain, they give up their resistance to giving a man the daily appreciation he requires. They assume full responsibility for communicating needs, confident that they can get them fulfilled. They don't expect men to know what they need instinctually, but patiently and persistently appreciate what they do give and gradually ask for more.

**Just as a business takes hard work, dedication,
and the application of new strategies to succeed,
so also do relationships require patience, persistence,
and rewritten job descriptions rooted in advanced
relationship skills.**

Adjusting Our Expectations

Just as a woman needs to adjust the expectation that a man will automatically listen to her feelings and will equally share all domestic duties, so also a man must adjust his expectation that a woman will speak in a loving, pleasing manner, make no demands of him, and be fulfilled when he gets home. In essence, women need to release the expectation that men will do everything they want, and men need to release the expectation that women will always be loving and happy.

Through practicing his advanced relationship skills, instead of feeling annoyed by her feelings of discontent he can begin to see them as opportunities to make her happier. When a woman is not getting the support she wants, she can see it as an opportunity to take the responsibility for getting what she needs. She can view it as an opportunity to practice expressing greater power, but in a feminine way. This is generally something her mother could not tell her.

When a woman is unhappy and talks about problems, a man doesn't have to feel blamed. He can reverse this pattern through understanding her real need to share. When she claims to feel a lack in the relationship, he realizes that it is not because of his deficiency (although it may always sound that way) but is because our modern culture doesn't sufficiently support her feminine side. This frees him to truly consider and feel her feelings rather than defend himself. It also greatly clarifies what he is required to do.

When a woman is disappointed by her partner, instead of taking it personally she can reverse the pattern and recognize his loving intent and willingness to support her more, but in small steps. Through adjusting her expectations she can eventually connect with the grace of her feminine spirit, which does not demand perfection but seeks to love and embrace life just the way it is. She realizes that it is not personal but that he was not trained by his father's example in how to fulfill a modern woman's new needs.

In the next chapter, we explore how to more effectively apply these skills through understanding how men and women are different.

How Men and Women Are Different

With an awareness of how men and women are different, we are freed from the tendency to try and change our partners at those times when we are not getting what we want. With a greater level of acceptance and understanding, not only does love flourish, but we can also much more wisely and effectively apply new skills for getting what we want.

Through understanding our historical and evolutionary development, we can take what is useful from our past and update it in ways that do not reject our genetic makeup, and can expand or stretch ourselves to be more of who we can be.

Trying to ignore differences, however, only creates more confusion and frustration between the sexes. The generalizations I make about men and women are certainly not true for everyone at all times, but they are true for a lot of people. When they do not apply to your situation or experience, just set them aside like an outfit that others may buy but that you don't. What is most important is that when the differences do show up, you will have positive and useful relationship skills for coping with them.

Understanding these broad categories of differences helps

you to accept them in a noncritical way, and then assists you in working *with* them instead of against them. I have found that these differences begin to show up even more when couples begin to have intimate relationships; in some cases, they begin to show up even more when the couple has children.

Brain Differences

In recent years, a multitude of scientific studies clearly indicate many differences between men's and women's brains as well as in the way they use them. While these studies do concretely show differences, it is still too soon for scientists to know exactly what these differences mean.

In general, however, it can be said that women tend to use both sides of their brains simultaneously, while men use one side or the other. This means that a man tends to use either his left brain language skills or his right brain spatial problem-solving skills, while a woman uses both at the same time.

Studies have revealed that some women have much more corpus callosum, or connective tissue, between the two hemispheres of the brain, which would account for a woman's tendency to use both sides of the brain simultaneously. Even though some women do not have more connective tissue, MRI brain scans reveal that these women still have a tendency to use both sides of the brain simultaneously. While some men may have more corpus callosum than some women, these men still use only one side of the brain at a time, while the women use both. The impact of this difference is staggering.

While we eagerly wait for more studies that will reveal how men and women use their brains differently, what has already been discovered can dramatically assist us in understanding some of the great mysteries between the sexes.

Bodies, Brains, and Hormones

Over the course of evolution, men's and women's bodies, brains, and hormones have become specialized to best support their different roles and activities. A man, for example, is most efficiently wired to cope with strong emotions by silently problem solving. As a hunter and protector in the jungle, he adapted to his role and coped with strong feelings of fear, anger, and loss through silently problem solving. By planning his strategies to protect himself and his family, he was able to most effectively cope with his feelings.

Women, on the other hand, have adapted to their role of nurturer and have learned to cope with feelings and problem solving primarily through talking and sharing with others in the family and community. Not only does this reflect a woman's tendency to use both sides of her brain at the same time, but repeatedly in scientific testing women show an advantage when it comes to left brain language skills, while men have an advantage when tests require right brain spatial skills.

How Our Brains Are Organized Differently

That talking is an integral part of femininity makes perfect sense when we learn that the female brain is organized in a way that allows her to communicate feelings more efficiently. Females' extra connective tissue, which is comprised of billions more neuroconnectors between the feelings and the language center of the brain, allows little girls to develop language skills before little boys do. Most commonly, at an earlier stage of development girls will use many more words than boys. This difference is repeatedly validated in the testing of children.

While a girl's brain is developing to express her communication abilities, a boy tends to develop his spatial skills. Spatial skills, for example, help us to determine how far to throw a ball, or where to run to get help and how to get there. The development of spatial skills allows a boy to "do something about it" when he is emotionally distressed. Spatial skills for him are an integral part of problem solving.

As any parent knows, at an early age a girl's impulse is to

talk, sometimes without thinking, while a boy's impulse is to act, sometimes, as well, without thinking. When a girl feels supported in talking without the fear of rejection or loss of love, then she is eventually able to grow the neuroconnectors that allow her to feel, speak, and think at the same time.

As an adult, when she is upset and is not thinking clearly, she will instinctively want to talk to someone who will just listen. This support helps her to reconnect her thinking to her feelings and make sense of the situation to determine what to do. When a woman is distressed, she seeks out help in the form of someone to listen to her articulate her feelings.

On the other hand, when a boy feels safe to act without fear of abusive punishment or the loss of love, he has the freedom to act, make mistakes, and then think about what he did and correct his behavior. This self-corrective mechanism allows him to learn from his mistakes. Eventually, he can grow the neuroconnectors needed to feel and then think before acting.

When a man is upset and not thinking clearly, he will instinctively want to move around. He may simply pace back and forth just to satisfy his urge to do *something* before he has figured out the right thing to do. Any simple, mindless activity will help him to express his feelings of wanting to do something while he is trying to use the right side of his brain to figure out what to do.

Just as spatial skills are required for playing games like basketball, soccer, and football, they are also required for the hunter to stalk his prey, accurately throw a spear, and then find his way back home. When we consider how long men have specialized in being the hunters and protectors, it is no wonder that our brains are organized so differently.

While a woman may be quicker to speak out about her feelings, a man will tend to more quickly act to solve a problem. While she will want to explore a problem more fully through talking, a man will be restless to do something about it. While neither approach is necessarily better, the best approach is when we work together.

From the dawn of time, a man's ability to throw spears was

essential for his survival, just as a woman's ability to talk and form relationships was responsible for her survival. It is no wonder that our brains develop so differently, with a woman able to more efficiently communicate her feelings, while a man can more efficiently detach from his feelings to consider a problem and its solution.

A man generally has to think about a feeling before he can talk about it. A woman can feel, talk, and think all at the same time. She most efficiently sorts out her thoughts and feelings by talking. He, however, silently mulls things over.

A man must think about feelings before he talks about them, while a woman can feel, talk, and think all at the same time.

Different Brain Maps

We can visually imagine that as a girl's brain develops, billions of neuroconnectors are mapped out from her emotional centers to the talking center in the brain. In a boy's brain, other priorities are operating. The right side of the brain, required to shoot arrows, hit a target, and then find the way back home, develops first. Eventually, a boy does develop his language center and a girl develops her action center, but the way we use these centers as adults ends up being very different. As a result of this different order of development, a man's emotions are more tied into action problem solving and not talking, while a woman's emotions are more tied to communication and then problem solving.

A man's brain first develops billions of neuroconnectors between his emotions and his action center. When he is emotionally charged or upset, he generally wants to do something about it. Finding a solution is his priority. Certainly, a woman will also act to solve problems, but because of the way her brain develops, her initial tendency is to first talk about it.

A woman has billions of neuroconnectors between her feelings and the talking center. In a sense, she has superhighways connecting her feelings to speech. When a man attempts to put his feelings into words, he needs to first think about what he wants to say. For him to express his feelings in words, there are no freeways and he has to take winding back roads.

First he has the feeling, then he wants to do something, then, in analyzing the feeling and what he can do about it, he decides if it is useful to talk about it. He then has to move over to the left side of the brain and begin formulating the words for these feelings. After he talks and new feelings come up, the whole process then has to start over. This is hard for a woman to instinctively understand because, as mentioned before, she tends to feel, talk, and think all at the same time.

Boys Will Be Boys and Girls Will Be Girls

This difference in brain development is most commonly seen in various childhood behaviors. One study revealed this difference in a very dramatic way. In the experiment, a mother was asked to enter a room where her toddler was already sitting. In the room, the mother was separated by a glass wall from her child. She was instructed to stand in front of the glass wall with a neutral expression. The results of this experiment showed a very clear difference in the way boys and girls responded.

If the toddler was a boy, he would see his mother, become distressed that she was not holding him, and begin crawling to her. When he arrived at the glass wall, he would attempt to push it over or try to climb over it. Eventually, his mother would reach over the wall and pick him up.

When the toddler was a girl, she would see her mother and, like the little boy, she would become distressed that she was not being held. But then instead of crawling to her and trying to overcome the glass wall like the little boy toddler, the little girl would make eye contact and then cry out. The boys consistently expressed their feelings through action, while the girls expressed their feelings verbally.

Male and Female Cognitive Development

At a later stage in the brain's development for both boys and girls, the logical or cognitive centers begin to develop. At this stage of development, billions of neuroconnectors are made to the cognitive or thinking parts of the brain. Again we see this development reflected in common male and female tendencies.

When a woman is upset, her first tendency is to talk about it, then as she continues to talk, her cognitive abilities set in and she can think about what she is saying and feeling and thus *sort it out*. She starts out in the feeling part of the brain, then she travels to the communication part, and from there she goes to the thinking portion. This is her most natural route because this is the order in which her skills developed. Gradually, over time, she develops the ability to feel, talk, and think at the same time.

For a man, his process of dealing with feelings is different because his skills developed in another order. First his feeling center develops, next his action center, and then his thinking. When he is upset, his first tendency is to do something about it. Action leads him to clearer thinking. Gradually, over time, he develops the ability to feel, act, and think at the same time.

Because of these very significant differences in the way our brains develop, men and women behave and communicate very differently. Men use communication primarily as another tool to express their thinking in order to achieve some goal or solve a problem. Women use communication for this reason as well, but they also depend on communication as a way to connect with their feelings and as a way to clarify their thinking. Communication has a much greater significance for a woman.

In a similar way, action is more significant to men. Action is like a pump that activates the thinking part of a man's brain. Like men, women use action as a way to solve problems, but for men it is much more. Action is the most significant way for a man to find mental clarity and to express his feelings for someone.

How Our Differences Affect Our Relationships

Women do not instinctively understand a man's need to silently reflect on his feelings and thoughts at the times when she would want to talk and share. Conversely, men don't instinctively understand a woman's need to talk about problems. As a result, we experience endless frustration in our relationships with the other sex. Quite commonly I hear women express the following complaints:

1. When he is upset, he will not talk.
2. After we get close, he pulls away and doesn't want to talk.
3. When I talk about my feelings, he can't just listen and feel what I am feeling, instead he starts problem solving.
4. He feels very uncomfortable when I cry.
5. He rarely, if ever, says he loves me.
6. He doesn't open up and share his feelings.
7. He just doesn't understand what I need when I am upset.
8. When he argues, he always has to be right.

Understanding our brain differences can help us to understand why these complaints are so commonly expressed by women about men. For example, when women are upset, they commonly tend to resolve their feelings by talking. Through talking, they are able to think about their feelings, sort through or "process" conflicting feelings, and find resolution.

Men "process" feelings differently. They silently feel their feelings and think about what is bothering them, and then begin problem solving. Simply by using his right brain to problem-solve, he temporarily disengages from his feelings and automatically cools off. This is what happens when, as I put it in *Men*

Are from Mars, Women Are from Venus, a man retreats "into his cave" to cool off.

Understanding Men

With this extra insight from understanding how our brains are different, women can begin to understand the answers to their biggest questions about men. Let's look again at the eight complaints listed above and explore briefly how both men and women can solve these problems. In later chapters, we explore the specific skills needed to apply this new understanding.

1. When he is upset, he will not talk.

It is not necessarily a fear of intimacy that causes a man to withdraw emotionally and not talk about his feelings, but it is commonly his most efficient way to cope with strong feelings, negative or positive. His brain is organized to problem-solve as a way to minimize feelings and regain control of himself.

While many men will always do this, they can, however, eventually learn to open up later, after they have sorted things out, and then share what was bothering them.

2. After we get close, he pulls away and doesn't want to talk.

When a man gets close, many times strong feelings come up. To a certain extent, when these feelings come up, his mind goes blank and he loses a sense of control. As we have discussed, it is not easy for him to feel and think at the same time. He feels awkward and really doesn't know what to do or say. To regain his grip, he feels a pull to engage himself in some easy problem-solving activity before he can return again to intimacy.

While men, to various degrees, will always pull away after a period of closeness and intimacy, the amount of time a man needs for himself eventually becomes less and less as he feels that his partner accepts this tendency. On the other hand, if she is always wanting to be close to him, he will feel a greater need to pull away.

3. When I talk about my feelings, he can't just listen and feel what I am feeling, instead he starts problem solving.

While it is easy for women to feel, talk, and think at the same time, it is much more difficult for many men. A man will tend to listen and talk (left brain activity) or he will feel, think, and problem-solve (right brain activity). When a man listens and connects with a woman (left brain activity), he suddenly wants to minimize the uncomfortable feelings he begins to feel through problem solving (right brain activity).

To shift to problem solving, he has to use his right brain and hence stops listening, or using his left brain. Remember, men use either one side of the brain or the other, not both at the same time like women. While this may work for him, it actually interferes with her way of processing feelings.

To a great extent, for a man to listen (left brain activity), after a while he will always feel a need to begin problem solving (right brain activity). This does not mean, though, that he can't be a great listener.

Once a man really understands that when a woman is upset the problem she needs solved is her unfulfilled need to feel heard, then he can stay focused on her feelings without problem solving because he doesn't feel immediately responsible for solving her problems. He can listen better because he is motivated to stay on the left side of his brain. He knows he can support her best by listening to what she is saying and trying to understand why she must be feeling the way she feels.

When he recognizes that no matter what she is upset about, he is solving her problem by understanding the validity of what she is saying, then his left brain mental activity of listening is not disturbed by his usual tendency to shift to the right brain to solve problems.

4. He feels very uncomfortable when I cry.

After listening and connecting to what she is feeling (left brain activity) while she is crying, he then moves back to his right brain to feel his feelings in reaction. As his right brain feelings emerge, he then automatically begins to problem-solve.

After offering his solutions, he doesn't know what to do because she is not in a place where she is open to solutions. Feeling powerless, he becomes increasingly frustrated, which makes him feel the need to find a solution even more, which then increases his frustration.

This pattern is easily transformed when a man understands that by listening and understanding her feelings without offering solutions he *is* solving her problem. With this awareness he can relax and not get frustrated because he knows that he is doing exactly what is needed.

5. He rarely, if ever, says he loves me.

Quite commonly, when a man feels emotionally connected or attracted to a woman, he will suddenly become inarticulate when asking her out on a date. It is hard for him to think straight and communicate when he is feeling strong feelings. Remember, he has less connective tissue between his feelings (right brain activity) and the communication center of his brain (left brain activity).

The stronger his feelings, the less he is able to put them into words. When he feels strong feelings of love, he is commonly speechless. This is hard for women to understand because they are not.

Certainly, men do say "I love you," but when they do, it is not just a spontaneous expression of a feeling easily translated into speech, instead it is expressed to solve a problem. It is his way of letting her know his intentions. In essence, when he says "I love you," there is a "point to saying it." And once he has said it, he doesn't instinctively have a reason to say it again and again.

Once a man learns that women thrive on being told they are loved, then a man has a reason for saying it more often. If saying it will solve a problem, then the feeling of love is more easily translated into speech. With a little practice, it can almost become spontaneous. Not only will she benefit, but he, too, will experience the pleasure of feeling his love for her each time he says it.

6. He doesn't open up and share his feelings.

This is hard for women to understand because when they have a problem they generally feel a need to talk. Repeatedly, this difference in brain wiring is revealed through MRI brain scans. When women use the language centers of their left brains, they also use the problem-solving skills of their right brains.

When a man is bothered by something, he first needs to calm down by trying to solve his problems by himself. By using the right brain to silently solve it, he can get a grip on the problem and begin to relax. If, however, he immediately talks about it, using his left brain, he loses his right brain grip and can easily be swept away by emotions of fear, frustration, et cetera.

Most of the time, he withdraws to mull things over and eventually he minimizes the problem and his negative feelings go away. He may say to himself, "It is no big deal, I will just forgive and forget." Then, when he is back and available for a relationship, because his feelings are released he has nothing to say. This creates a lot of confusion. She commonly misunderstands and thinks he is withholding his feelings when, from his side, there really is nothing to talk about.

If a man and a woman have a tense interaction or unpleasant argument, it is very healthy to take a time-out. With this understanding of men, it helps a woman give the man the time he needs to cool off and mull over what happened.

To reconnect, however, it is very helpful if the man initiates a conversation about what happened. This is a new skill for men to learn. Instinctively he feels there is no point to talking because he has already resolved his feelings and has nothing to say. However, taking into consideration a woman's need to talk, he now has a reason to initiate conversation even when he has little to say. Advanced relationship skills require a man to initiate conversation not because he wants to talk but because he knows she needs to talk to feel connected.

To initiate a conversation after he has cooled off is important because a woman generally panics when he doesn't want to talk about what happened. A woman fears that he is suppressing his feelings and that they will eventually turn to resentment. She is afraid because if *she* doesn't talk, she instinctively knows she will begin to feel resentful.

Through understanding this potential problem, a man can learn to solve it by initiating a conversation even when he has little need to talk. When he is back and feeling better, then he can easily initiate a conversation in order to assist her in talking and feeling that she is heard. Men don't generally do this because the last thing they would do is start a conversation when they have little to say. The situation changes when he understands the value in supporting her in talking more.

7. He just doesn't understand what I need when I am upset.

When a man is upset, he moves to his right brain to problem-solve, cool off, and feel better. He does this through analyzing what is bothering him, thinking of solutions, and minimizing the problem. When a woman is upset, rather than encourage her to talk more, which is what she needs to do, he attempts to prevent her from talking by offering solutions. He doesn't realize how he is making it worse for her.

When she says "You don't understand," he becomes even more involved in explaining his solutions to prove that he understands. With this new perspective, a man can eventually learn to support her by focusing on understanding why she is upset rather than offering to solve her problem. When a man experiences how helpful it is for her if he just says nothing and tries to empathize with her feelings, then it becomes much easier for him to be a better listener.

By learning to stay calm and centered while listening to a woman, a man is actually developing more connection between his left and right brain. This will eventually give him the ability to share his own feelings in a calm and centered way.

8. When he argues, he always has to be right.

When a man experiences strong emotions, it is imperative that he use his right brain to problem-solve and find control, otherwise he has the tendency to do something without thinking. There is a reason why 90 percent of the people who go to jail are men. These men had strong feelings and acted on them without thinking. It is not that they were necessarily bad people, but instead they hadn't developed the billions of neuroconnectors in their brains to restrain themselves from acting on strong feelings. As a result of their crimes, they then go to jail where, hopefully, they can learn to think before they act.

When a man is upset, it is imperative for him to calm his feelings through clear thinking. Then, based on clear thinking, he can act successfully. This is why men instinctively feel a need to be right when they are upset. If they get upset and they are wrong, they not only cause a lot of trouble but also get into trouble.

Women do not feel such a strong need to be right when they are upset because they are not about to do something. When women are upset, they are more apt to talk first rather than suddenly doing something without thinking. This difference shows up statistically in the number of women who go to therapists to talk about their feelings. Ninety percent of the people who see therapists are women. This, however, is not so surprising when we understand how women use their brains differently.

When women are upset, they are not emotionally attached to finding the "right thinking to solve the problem"; instead, they are emotionally attached to being heard so that they can sort through their feelings, and then if there is a problem that needs to be solved, they can focus on the solution.

Unfortunately, a man's tendency to be right has the effect of making a woman feel that her feelings are wrong. When she is upset with him, he instinctively explains why he was right in what he did or said. As a direct result, she feels he is saying that she does not have the right to be upset.

Once a man understands this problem, he can solve it.

Instead of being right, he can focus on solving the problem by "doing the right thing." As he learns that listening and validating her feelings is the best solution, he can let go of his defensive tendency to explain away her feelings and be right.

Understanding this difference is also very important for women. If a man is upset and wants to be right about a certain point, the only way to be heard is to postpone the conversation and give him time to cool off. As a general rule, the more upset he gets, the more he will want to be right and the less able he will be to empathize or sympathize with her point of view.

Take a Deep Breath and Count to Ten

We have all heard the old adage that tells us to take a deep breath and count to ten when we get angry. This particularly applies to men. When a man counts or does math problems in his head, he begins moving to the problem-solving part of his brain and his turbulent emotions gradually subside. This shifting to the right side of his brain gives him more objectivity to understand what is bothering him and what he must do about it. It protects him from acting on his feelings without first thinking.

This shifting is particularly helpful when he is using his left brain and is about to say something to communicate his angry feelings. The best thing he can do is to not talk but to shift gears by moving to his right brain through counting to ten or doing math problems.

This technique is not designed for women, and it doesn't work as well for them. Instead of counting to use her right brain, it is much more helpful for a woman to use her left brain. When a woman moves to the left side of her brain to formulate her thoughts to talk, it actually helps her to gain the objectivity she needs to better understand herself and the situation.

How Men Deal with Feelings Differently

When a man puts his feelings into action, he is able to more effectively sort them out. Simple, goal-oriented activities like sports allow him to more fully activate the thinking part of his brain and more effectively deal with emotions.

A close male friend of mine was given the very terrible news that his daughter had cancer—which I knew about from my wife before he called to tell me. After a normal exchange of greetings, he announced that he had bad news, then paused.

"I already heard from Bonnie," I said to spare him having to go through the bad news again.

After another pause, he asked me if I was free to play some tennis. I said I was, and we arranged to meet at the neighborhood courts in a few minutes.

When I told Bonnie where I was going, she understood perfectly and told me to give my friend a hug for her.

During the game, when my friend and I changed sides or went to the net to retrieve balls, we'd exchange a few words. Then we'd play some more, then talk some more. For him, playing tennis—something he did well and enjoyed—allowed him an opportunity to express his feelings about what had happened. Talking was how he could sum up his ideas and then receive my feedback and support. But the way he connected with his feelings in the first place was by playing tennis.

In focusing his attention and energy on keeping the ball in the court, he was able to contact and express his frustration at not being able to remove the cancer: when he hit it long or wide, he was connecting with the pain of not being the perfect father and reflecting on possible mistakes he had made; when the ball stayed in, he connected with his desire to do the right thing and be the best father he could. By connecting with his desire to beat me and win, he fueled his desire to beat this cancer and save his daughter.

After the game, sitting on a bench by the court, we explored different ways of effectively supporting his little girl through the coming ordeal. Throughout our conversation, he automatically connected with and occasionally expressed his fears of losing his daughter, along with his deep feelings of love for her. At this point, I gave him a hug from me, followed by the one Bonnie had asked me to send him.

This story has a happy ending. My friend's child was successfully treated, and today is fine.

In pointing out how men need to do things to help process their feelings, I don't mean to imply that it is not helpful for a man to talk about his feelings. Every man has a female side, and talking is the means by which it can most effectively be nurtured. However, he must first take care to think and cool off before talking.

> Every man has a female side, and talking is the means by which it can most effectively be nurtured. However, he must first take care to think and cool off before talking.

How Men Receive Love Differently

It is through his actions that a man can most directly connect to his feelings, and it is through acknowledging and appreciating his actions that he feels most loved. Appreciation of a man's decisions, efforts, and actions is the most direct route to his heart. Likewise, it is forgiveness of his mistakes or actions that also nurtures his masculine side. This acceptance frees him to most effectively experience the fullness of feeling loved, and in return become more loving. Women do not instinctively understand this because their feelings are directly connected to the brain's talking—not acting—centers.

> Direct appreciation of a man's decisions and actions and forgiveness of his mistakes nurtures his masculine side.

Women mistakenly give the kind of loving support they themselves want without intuiting a man's needs. When a man is distressed, women think they are being very loving by trying to get him to talk. They do not instinctively realize that the best thing they can do is to lovingly accept him by giving him lots of space and then, when he is directly supportive, to respond warmly in a way that says she is glad to have him in her life. With this new awareness of how men feel loved, women can begin to focus their support in ways that matter most to their mates.

Nurturing the Female Side

A woman lets love in primarily through talking and feeling heard and understood. Men don't readily understand this because talking is *not* their direct link to feeling loved.

When a woman talks about her feelings, she naturally connects with her more positive and graceful aspects. At such times she does not need an immediate solution to feel better. This feminine process of non-goal-oriented problem sharing is an alien concept to modern men and women alike.

After working all day in a traditionally male, goal-oriented job, women have a hard time coming back to a more relaxed style of communicating. They become like men, focused and bottom-line-oriented. Without a conscious and concerted effort on her part to shift this tendency, a woman's female side suffers. For a woman to be happy, her female side needs to be nurtured. A man's assistance in this process is greatly needed.

Similarly, when a woman uses her thinking abilities to most efficiently achieve business goals, but is deprived of the opportunity to talk and share cooperatively with others, she may temporarily lose touch with her warm and tender female nature. Men do not instinctively understand how to support a woman through communicating because they cope with stress differently.

How Men Cope with Stress

In prehistoric times, there were those occasions when a hunter did not return home with the kill. To cope with the strain of not having adequately provided, he developed strategies for shifting his focus from critical problems to less important ones that he could handle successfully.

Men became experts in temporarily forgetting their real

problems by focusing on lesser ones. They came to depend on hobbies, sports, or any other activity that would distract them from thoughts of providing. Today's men, following in ancestral footsteps, likewise rely on distractions to relieve the pressure generated by a bad day at the office.

The Importance of Hobbies

A hobby is a freely chosen activity that a man performs in his spare time. While making very few personal demands, it's challenging because it requires skill. Although a hobby has little real-world importance, it matters to a man's peace of mind and ultimately supports his competence and skill in solving problems of significance.

Competition and Sports

Competitive sports allow a man to redirect and channel his aggression. They enable him to express his frustration at not being able to solve real-world problems. Instead of killing his prey or potential enemies, he focuses on beating the other team or player. The male instincts that are required to kill, hunt, and protect find free expression in sports.

The male instincts that are required to hunt, kill, and protect find free expression in sports.

In order to function fully as a stress reliever, a hobby or activity must be one at which the man excels. Even if he feels down because he didn't accomplish what he wanted to at work, beginning to do something he is good at makes him feel more in control. This transition prepares him for reconnecting with his partner.

By releasing his focus from work through some seemingly unimportant activity, he gradually remembers what is most important to him—his love for his wife and family, and the desire to be there for them and with them.

> By releasing his focus from work through a
> seemingly unimportant activity, a man gradually
> remembers what is most important to him—his love
> for his wife and family, and the desire to be there for
> them and with them.

Hunting, Fishing, Tennis, and Golf

If a man can't solve the problems of work, he can still stalk game or bring home some fish. This is why hunting and fishing are such important leisure activities. After a successful outing, somewhere deep in his male spirit he feels he has solved his problem and can now relax and receive his partner's love and support. For other men, watching a favorite sports team on TV or attending a game brings this same relief.

Tennis and golf are also perfect distractions to relax through doing. The focused activity of these sports allows men to use their right brain enough to connect with their feelings and then they can talk for a while with their left brain. In this way, back and forth they connect.

Two men feel much more at ease being together and occasionally talking if they are also doing something. Instead of saying "Let's go for a walk and take in this beautiful day, looking at scenery," they say "Let's play some golf or go fishing."

Movies

Many men enjoy going to the movies because the images are bigger than life and allow them to shift focus by absorbing their attention. Through identifying with the characters on the screen, they are temporarily released from their personal problems. Action movies are particularly helpful if a man has a sit-down job. Suspenseful thrillers are helpful if he has a routine kind of job. Violent movies are helpful if he has to be loving all the time. At the movies, men connect with feelings that their "day jobs" don't allow them to feel or process.

Reading or Watching the News

Watching or reading the news can help a man shift his focus back to his family because when he concentrates on world problems, his own suddenly seem smaller. He is able to relax because he does not feel any immediate responsibility for solving these problems. They are out of his control.

TV and Fire Gazing

Contemporary man's most common leisure-time activity is watching TV. Most women don't understand this at all. Some women hate a man's watching TV because it gets all his attention. Others actually think men watch TV to get even. But while TV is a recent invention, watching it is the contemporary form of an ancient ritual which men have been enacting since history began.

Although TV is a recent invention, watching it is actually an ancient ritual which men have been enacting in some form since history began.

While visiting communities so primitive that they didn't have TV, I noticed that at dusk, while the women were occupied in talking and performing tasks, the men were sitting silently in a circle gazing into a fire.

Fire gazing is the most ancient and potent of male stress reducers. When men today stare into the TV, they are, in effect, mindlessly looking into the fire. It allows men to redirect their focus, stop thinking, and just relax. This relaxation rejuvenates the body, releasing the stress and tensions of the day.

Fire gazing is the most ancient and potent of male stress relievers; when men today stare into the TV, they are, in effect, mindlessly looking into the fire.

How Men Can Accomplish More by Doing Less

When a man who copes with stress by forgetting problems gets home to a partner who wants to talk about problems, there is generally much frustration. This problem can be solved when a man learns how to listen without feeling responsible for solving a woman's problems. As a man gets good at this, he can actually learn to de-stress from the day by listening to his partner.

One of my most relaxing activities is watching the news. It is relaxing because these are not problems I feel I have to solve. Once I really realized that I didn't have to solve my wife's problems for her to feel better, then listening to her became as relaxing as listening to the news. And even better, she appreciates me for it and the TV doesn't.

Most men do not realize that by actually doing less in a relationship, they can support themselves and their partners much more. By learning to listen to a woman's feelings in a sympathetic way and focusing less on solving her problems, not only can he make her much happier, but he can also relax. Although the end result is enhanced mutual ease and support, it will take some extra start-up effort to excel at this advanced relationship skill.

It is common for a man to hear a woman's feelings of unhappiness after a hard day's work and conclude that he must do more to make her happy. When he does more and she is still overwhelmed, he naturally feels frustrated and unappreciated and eventually stops giving. Pleasing an overwhelmed woman becomes an impossible task.

When a woman is overwhelmed, she needs *emotional* support. In most cases, she first needs to talk about her feelings with a partner who understands and sympathizes with her. Then and only then can she appreciate his physical efforts to solve her problems.

Doing More Is Not the Answer

The way to support a woman best is to nurture her female side so that she doesn't feel an urgency to do everything now. Men do not instinctively realize that her overwhelming feelings are not "fixed" or illuminated through helping her solve her problems. To support her, a man needs to remember that her overwhelming feelings are released only through nurturing conversation. Doing more so that a woman will have less to do is not the answer to making her happy.

Doing more so that a woman will have less to do is not the answer to making her happy.

As we discussed in chapter 3, a woman's work *is* never done. There will always be more to do. However, by learning to initiate conversation and listen respectfully, a man can free her from the urgency to do it all now. From this centered and loving perspective, she can then accomplish what is humanly possible in a more relaxed manner.

Men Who Do Too Much

When a man focuses on solving problems for his partner rather than providing initial emotional support—despite the fact that his efforts and actions are indeed motivated by love and caring—he will make matters worse by doing too much. Let's look at some common examples.

Like so many men, Tom was frustrated by hearing his wife, Sharon, complain about having too much to do. His way of dealing with the problem was to attempt to divide domestic responsibilities along guidelines that she agreed were fair. Though this scheme seemed like the answer, it brought them to the verge of divorce.

They came to me for counseling as a last chance to save their marriage. Tom began by complaining that even after he started doing half the work at home, Sharon still wasn't happy. "I can't stand it anymore," he told me. "I'm willing to do more chores if it makes her happy. But if she's still going to be unhappy, I'm through."

Tom made the classic mistake of expecting Sharon to be

happy by solving her problems. What he didn't know was that
Sharon would always need to talk about her feelings; no matter
how many problems he solved for her, there would still be
problems she felt compelled to talk about.

> **What Tom didn't know was that Sharon would
> always need to talk about her problems; no matter
> how many he solved for her, there would still be
> some she felt compelled to talk about.**

As it turned out, Sharon was every bit as dissatisfied as Tom.
When he began doing more chores, she felt as if she'd lost the
right to complain. At this point, he had become so supersensi-
tive that whenever she was overwhelmed or upset, he would
automatically shake his head and either sulk or criticize her for
being negative.

In their sincere attempts to solve the problem, they had
unknowingly made it worse. Look at how it went:

1. Because he was doing more at home, Tom expected
   Sharon to be happier.
2. When she occasionally felt overwhelmed, he felt even
   more frustrated and unappreciated.
3. Now she couldn't freely talk about her feelings because it
   upset Tom too much.
4. In time, Sharon began to feel more and more overwhelmed.
5. The more she had to control her feelings, the more urgent
   her need became to identify and solve problems.
6. It was now impossible for her to relax and enjoy her life
   and relationship.

Doing Less but Supporting More

Through acquiring advanced relationship skills, Tom and
Sharon were able to find a creative solution to their dilemma

and save their marriage. Tom's new job description would not include doing more at home and trying to solve problems, but listening and comforting Sharon. He would practice giving nurturing support.

Sharon agreed to practice appreciating Tom for what he did at work without demanding more at home. She would focus on asking him to listen to her feelings while making sure that he knew how much she appreciated his emotional support. As he got better and better at listening to her feelings, he would eventually be able to do more without expecting her to always be happy or appreciative. They solved this common problem in two stages.

Stage One: No Solutions

Initially, they both agreed that Tom wouldn't try to *do* more for her but would focus just on listening.

He practiced being sympathetic to her feelings while making sure that he did nothing to directly solve her problems. Sharon had already given him the clear message that he was already *doing* enough, and that the only request she was making was to share her feelings.

With this dynamic in place, Tom was able to listen to Sharon without becoming frustrated. He was amazed by how effective just listening was. Sometimes she would simply say, "Thanks for listening, I feel much better." At other times she would say, "I feel so much better now. I love being able to talk like this with you. I feel relieved to know I can." With this kind of feedback, it wasn't long before Tom was able to understand what was truly required of him by his wife. Not only was it sometimes pleasurable to do but it was actually easier than trying to solve her problems.

Sharon, on the other hand, was amazed by Tom's attentiveness when he knew nothing except empathy was required of him. Tom said he now felt as free as when they'd first met. He didn't feel responsible for Sharon's problems or take them personally. Since he didn't *have* to do more, he found himself naturally wanting to do more. After several weeks of successful practice, he suggested they start stage two.

Stage Two: He Offers Help

Tom was to continue listening as before but now was able to offer help in problem solving by doing more for her—in very small increments.

I recommended that Tom start by listening to Sharon's litany of problems and offer to help solve the easiest. He was surprised to learn that he was not expected to solve her toughest problems. What she needed from him was to feel that she was not alone in dealing with her problems. In fact, Tom discovered that by offering to do several small things, he gave Sharon more support than trying to tackle one big problem.

When a woman is convinced that she is not alone in coping with and solving life's problems, she feels deeply comforted.

Without feeling pressured to solve her problems, Tom not only became a better listener but—using his own feelings as a gauge—he learned to regulate how much he could give without expecting his mate to be happy all the time.

When he felt frustrated that his partner was not happy, he recognized it as a signal that he was giving too much, not that she was asking too much. Sharon loved this. No longer feeling responsible or protective of Tom's feelings, she could freely share her emotions and talk openly with him about her life. A deep, feminine part of her being was at last being nourished.

Over time, Tom began to give more and do more as he felt appreciated for his efforts—not because he was trying to get rid of her negative feelings but because he truly sympathized with her needs and wanted to help. He realized that most of the time, she really just needed to talk. Tom was able to rewrite his job description successfully because he was properly prepared.

Preparing a Man to Listen

Whenever a woman shares overwhelming feelings, a man tends mistakenly to feel frustrated or blamed. Amazingly, it only takes one simple statement to prepare him properly so that he can avoid feeling blamed and be an attentive listener. I myself went through the gradual process of learning that problem solving was not what my wife needed or wanted from me. I remember how Bonnie cleverly applied advanced relationship skills to help me support her better.

In the first years of our marriage, Bonnie would occasionally feel overwhelmed and complain about what had happened at work.

Each time I would listen for a few minutes and then offer her what I thought was sage advice: "If you don't like your job, why don't you just quit? You don't have to put up with that!" She would proceed to tell me what else had happened to bother or stress her. I would then tell her again that she should change jobs. I would point out why she should quit, and she would defend her job. After a while, I didn't even want to listen. I kept thinking, Don't keep complaining about something if you're not going to do something about it.

She felt as if I didn't care about her feelings and was too controlling. We argued frequently.

Then one day she tried something new, which changed everything. She told me, "I'd like to talk about my day, but first I want you to know that I love my job and I don't want to quit." Then she proceeded to complain. It was amazing. Every time she paused, I wanted to say, Why don't you just quit that job? but I couldn't because she had already answered it by saying that she loved her work. Having nothing to say, I listened without speaking or solving.

I had been prepared.

Then she proceeded. After a while I truly saw that without any solutions on my part Bonnie was indeed much happier. Preparing me for what she was about to say made it much easier for me to listen.

Properly preparing a man makes it easier for him to listen.

What Frustrates Men

A woman can prepare a man to listen by letting him know in advance what it is that she needs. This allows him to adjust his instinctive expectations to learned expectations. For example, when a man has worked hard or was particularly successful that day, his instinctive expectations are much higher. When she talks about her problems, he fully expects her to respond favorably to his solutions and doesn't relate to her need to communicate feelings and talk about problems as a way to feel better. He instinctively feels that as a result of his actions that day she should be happy. Without some preparation from her, it is easy for him to be frustrated.

Success and Relationships

When a man begins to realize that he has gone about as far up the ladder as he is going to go, and his partner is still complaining, he despairs of ever receiving the support he wants most. As he was moving up, there was always a little voice in the back of his head saying "When I get a little more successful, she'll appreciate me. When I make a little more money and take her on that vacation, she'll be happy." But when he finally levels out at a fixed income, it becomes very hard for him to handle her unhappiness. This stress is relieved when he understands what she really needs and that it is not about how much money he makes or whether he can solve her problems.

Women and Wealth

Women also have new hurdles to overcome when their partners become better providers so that they no longer have to work. A woman who doesn't have to work is expected to be categorically happier not only by her husband but by everyone she knows. However, it is the lack of nurturing relationships that creates unhappiness in women, not the lack of wealth. A woman who doesn't have to work each day also needs to be emotionally nurtured.

As any well-off person can tell you, money does not eliminate problems. If anything, it makes life more complex. The greater the wealth, the more momentous the decisions about spending it, using it, and protecting it. Money definitely doesn't prevent women from feeling overwhelmed.

Money doesn't prevent women from feeling overwhelmed.

If a man can use his money to create more time away from work to spend with his wife, and also be understanding of her daily frustrations and problems, then money can help a relationship. Generally, however, making a lot of money without ruining a relationship takes a disciplined and conscious effort on both the man's and woman's part. He must strive to listen and she to appreciate him.

To create wealth without damaging a relationship, a man must strive to listen and a woman to appreciate him.

Why Women Feel Overwhelmed

Women feel overwhelmed when their daily relationships are not nurturing to the feminine spirit; it has nothing to do with money. Greater wealth may either assist her in, or prevent her from, finding more nurturing. Since women with money tend to get less sympathy, they are frequently overwhelmed.

Not only are less well-off women disinclined to respond sympathetically to her problems, but a wealthy woman's husband becomes increasingly intolerant because he instinctively believes that money should buy her happiness. When she is not happier, he feels he can never provide enough to satisfy her. He doesn't realize that what she needs is not more money but more of his attention and nurturing.

For all of the above reasons it is essential for a wealthy woman to learn how to support her male partner in giving her the support she deserves. Sometimes all it takes is just a few well-chosen phrases to prepare him to listen to her feelings. When he is able to listen and understand what she goes through, she can more easily give him the appreciation he needs.

The Contrary Role of Wealth

Jeff is a successful lawyer, and Teresa is a wife and mother who doesn't have to work. For the first ten years of their marriage, they were in love, and their relationship flowed. When Teresa expressed feelings of unhappiness, Jeff could be understanding because although he was working long hours, they didn't have a lot of money. When she complained, he could be sympathetic because he appreciated her sacrifices. He also felt that one day he would be a success and have lots of money, which would finally make her happy.

So he prospered, but as women have done for centuries, Teresa continued to talk occasionally about her problems. Now, however, he couldn't deal with it and took it personally. He felt he was still not doing enough, and that no amount of money would ever be enough to satisfy her. Whenever she complained about her day or wanted more from him, he felt that she wasn't appreciating his hard work.

In counseling, Teresa would insist that she didn't care about the money, the cars, or the house. She wanted Jeff's love.

I immediately asked her to take a brief break because I could feel Jeff react to those words with a desire to attack. "I know how you feel," I told her, "but I also know how that must sound to Jeff. Money is his most precious gift to you. He has worked hard for it. Let's find another way to share those feelings without rejecting him. While I understand that you want to feel loved, do you also appreciate the lifestyle he provides for you?"

"Well, of course," Teresa responded. "Jeff is a great provider. In that sense I feel very lucky."

"Good," I told her. "Now this time, before you share how you feel, first prepare him by letting him know how much you appreciate all he does give you."

Teresa needed only a slight shift in direction to make everything she said clear to Jeff. This is what she told him:

"I want you to know that I feel so lucky to be married to you. You work so hard, and you provide me with so many comforts that my friends don't have. Some of my friends don't even know if they can pay their rent this month. I also have a lot of other feelings. I miss you. I would like to spend more time with you. I feel like your clients get the best of you, and when you get home you are too tired for me. All these years I have looked forward to being able to spend more time with you. In the past, you had to be busy so we could survive, but now I would most love the luxury of spending more time with you."

Jeff was able to hear her this time without getting defensive and suddenly became much more cooperative. I explained how important it was for women to feel heard and have their feelings validated. Jeff learned that it was normal for his wife to have emotional needs, and that overwhelming feelings were perfectly appropriate for her to experience.

Jeff gradually learned to listen without feeling as if Teresa didn't appreciate what he was providing for her. This took a lot of practice and patience, but they both did successfully rewrite their job descriptions through the use of advanced relationship skills.

Teresa learned to be playful about their learning experience, and Jeff greatly appreciated it. Sometimes before sharing difficult feelings, she would prepare Jeff by saying things like, "I am really happy that we have so much money! I love it, and it really makes me happy. I also had an awful day, would you take a few minutes to just listen? You don't have to say anything, and I will feel better!"

Over time, Jeff became a much better listener, and without Teresa having to demand it, he started spending more time with her. As communication improved, she became much less overwhelmed and happier to see Jeff at the end of a day. Gradually, he began to do more to help, but most important, he focused on learning to listen without feeling responsible for solving Teresa's problems.

How Women Unknowingly Turn Men Off

Quite commonly, a man gets turned off to a woman because he doesn't understand a woman's need to talk about feelings and problems. While she thinks she's just making conversation and letting him know that she is open to him, he misreads the situation and feels that he could never make her happy and decides to not get involved.

A limousine driver I had occasion to speak with put it like this when I asked him about women and relationships. He was thirty-two, single, and experienced. He claimed he had had seven relationships that he considered "special." I was curious to discover what went wrong. After we talked for a while he said, "I think I'm jinxed. I'm only attracted to women with psychological problems."

I laughed and then said, "Let me see if I can guess what happened. In the beginning these women were very warm and pleased by you. You felt really good about yourself when you were with them. You cared for them and wanted to make them happy. Then, as each relationship progressed, they would begin to talk about problems. It seemed as if no matter what you said, they just came back with more problems."

"Yeah, that's right!" he exclaimed. "How did you know?" I assured him that these women did not have psychological problems. As I explained to him why women feel overwhelmed and what they really need, he—like most men—began to feel relieved and expressed a renewed interest in pursuing the relationship he was just ending.

While this is a nice story, there are still millions of men out there who don't understand how to react when a woman talks about her feelings. If women are to stay feminine and share their feelings, it is essential that they learn the advanced relationship skill of preparing a man to listen to them.

Many times it takes only one sentence to remind him in a playful way that she appreciates his listening, knows it must be hard to listen, and that she really doesn't need him to say anything or do more to make her feel better.

Once a woman masters the art of preparing a man to listen, she will begin to experience a new freedom of expression in her relationship, whether she is starting a partnership or is already involved in one. And, as with all advanced relationship skills, it only requires a small shift that doesn't involve changing who you are.

Successful Giving and Receiving

Without becoming overworked himself, a man *can* learn to be more effective in supporting his partner. At each step, her appreciation will motivate him to do more. It will not entail a major sacrifice nor will he feel controlled. With a deeper understanding of men, a woman can learn how to support a man in providing her with the support she needs.

> With a deeper understanding of men, a woman can learn how to support a man in providing her with the support she needs.

Men *want* to be the providers, they *want* to take credit for a woman's happiness, and they thrive on feeling successful in making a difference. They just need to feel appreciated for it. This is the kind of love and support that a man craves most from a woman.

Men and women complement each other in a very magical way. Men thrive on successfully caring for their partners, while women thrive when they feel cared for. Certainly, women also love to care for their male partners but primarily need to feel cared for themselves. I have never heard a woman say "My partner completely ignores me, but I still *love* giving to him." In a similar way, men need to feel cared for but primarily need to feel successful in fulfilling their partners.

> Women love to care for their men but primarily need to feel cared for themselves. Men need to feel cared for but primarily need to feel successful in fulfilling their partners.

Why Couples Break Up

In listening to hundreds of couples on the verge of partings, I hear the same message over and over. Women say they give and give and are tired of giving and not getting back. They want more.

A man's discontent is similar but different in a very significant way. Men say "I give and give, but no matter what I do, it is never enough to make her happy." This is because his condition for fulfillment is primarily based on fulfilling her needs. When she is happy, he is happy.

A woman's fulfillment in a relationship is largely dependent on the man's supportive behavior, while his happiness is much more linked to her response to his support. When she is fulfilled, he is more willing to do more. When she is not fulfilled, he believes his efforts are not valued and naturally resists doing more.

Men who don't want to give more simply are not feeling sufficiently appreciated. Before asking him for more, a woman must convince her partner that he is already doing enough. To read him a list of what he is doing wrong only creates more resistance. Appreciating what he does do, however, and making specific requests in small increments, is the key to getting more.

> When men feel they are doing enough, they eventually are willing to do a little more.

This simple approach of man as giver and woman as receiver does not mean that men don't need women or that women should not give. Women will always give, and men will always be happy to receive. That is not the problem. The problem is that women give too much and feel overworked, while men give only what their fathers gave and expect to receive the same measure of support.

Modern women give too much and feel overworked, while men give only what their fathers gave and expect the same measure of support.

Why Women Feel They Give More

Women today feel they give more, and in return expect men to give back more. They feel exhausted and overwhelmed because they are certainly getting less than they need, but that doesn't mean men are giving less.

Men today give by going to work (as their fathers did) and feel unappreciated if they are asked to do more. They expect to leave their work at the office and relax when they get home.

The secret of successful relationships is to clearly understand this basic difference. It is not that the man gives less. He is giving what men have always given. Through understanding the problem without blame, both men and women are motivated to solve their share of the problem.

To solve this basic problem we must first recognize that it is not really about how much more she does. Instead, it is about what she is not getting in order to be fulfilled. As we have explored, the real need that women have that is not being fulfilled is the need to be heard.

As men learn how to provide emotional support through using advanced relationship skills, then and only then will women begin to feel greater warmth and appreciation. Then, as a woman truly feels more centered and appreciative, a man is naturally motivated to gradually do more in the home.

Just as a weight lifter gradually builds muscle by slowly increasing his weights, a man can and will do more and give more at home to nurture his partner if it is a gradual process. Once he begins to experience his partner's appreciation, his resistance to doing more melts away. Instead of feeling like a child being controlled by his mother, he begins to welcome her requests for more and is happy to respond to her.

> Once a man experiences his woman's appreciation,
> his resistance to doing more melts away. Instead of
> feeling like a child controlled by his mother, he begins
> to welcome her requests for more.

In the next chapter, we will explore how men can use ancient warrior skills to duck and dodge when they feel verbally attacked in conversation. By putting a new spin on old skills, they can easily learn to listen to a woman without getting upset with her. After focusing on skills that men can use, we will then focus on advanced skills that women can use to communicate so that men will listen and truly understand.

CHAPTER 5

Masculine Skills for Listening Without Getting Upset

To give a woman the emotional support she requires, a man needs to listen in a new way, using advanced relationship skills. When she is upset, his most powerful means of assisting her in feeling better is to listen without getting upset that she is upset. To do this successfully, he does not have to make major changes in himself. Instead, he is required only to reconnect to his ancient warrior skills.

By learning to duck and dodge what he hears as blame, mistrust, and criticism, a man can gradually learn to listen patiently and not get shot to pieces. Through listening in a skillful manner so that he is not hurt by her words and feelings, he will begin to hear her calmly.

While he is perfectly capable of mastering this advanced relationship skill, it is not as easy for him as women assume. His every positive step needs to be acknowledged and appreciated. His mate's conscious assistance in this process can greatly speed up his progress.

> **Every positive communications step a man takes
> needs to be acknowledged and appreciated.**

We have already discussed that hearing a woman talk about problems is particularly hard on a man because he is inclined either to offer solutions that she doesn't appreciate or feels blamed for what is bothering her.

If a man simply practices listening passively for more than ten minutes without clear guidelines, and without doing something to make his mate feel better or at least defend himself, he will become increasingly frustrated and upset.

Even if she does not intend to attack or blame him when she talks about her feelings, he may feel that she does. Merely listening is too inactive for him. It is as if he is standing in front of a firing squad. When she begins to talk, he either wants to fight back or put on a blindfold.

Instead of allowing himself to be wounded by his partner's words, a man can practice the advanced relationship skill of ducking and dodging. When he feels under attack, he can actively support her by not taking it personally. He is superbly equipped to do this because protecting himself from harm is the most basic of warrior skills. If he has survived this long, with a few adjustments he can begin applying his skills in conversation.

> **Merely listening is too inactive for him. It is as if he is
> standing in front of a firing squad.**

Emotional Self-Defense

The instincts that sent warriors boldly into battle to defend themselves and protect their loved ones come into play when a modern man tries to listen to a modern woman. A modern man is still required to be a warrior, but with a new twist. He must now defend himself without attacking back. To prevail, he must learn to successfully duck and dodge.

A modern man is required to be a warrior but now must defend himself without retaliating.

Ducking and dodging require new mental strategies for correctly interpreting the situation. Instead of reacting to blame and criticism, a man learns to hear the correct loving message in her words and responds in ways that diminish friction and conflict. Ducking and dodging allow a man to keep his cool and respond respectfully to a woman's need to communicate.

When he listens to a woman *without* ducking and dodging, he will be repeatedly assaulted by her words and begin to feel blamed, criticized, unacknowledged, misunderstood, rejected, mistrusted, or unappreciated. No matter how much he loves her, after about three direct hits he will no longer be capable of listening to her in a supportive way. War breaks out.

When a man is struck by a woman's words, it is much harder to restrain his ancient warrior instincts to intimidate, threaten, or retaliate. Once these defensive responses are triggered, he will either attempt to change her mind through arguing or protect her from his own aggressive reactions by emotionally withdrawing. However, through advanced relationship skills of listening without getting struck, he can easily sidestep provocative reactions.

Women Still Want to Be Protected

Although modern women are independent and assertive, their female natures still seek out strong men who can provide protection. They still want to be protected, but in a different sense.

Women now look to men to provide the emotional climate in which they can safely explore and express their feelings. When a man can listen to a woman's feelings and allow her to articulate them without responding negatively, she is not only very appreciative but more attracted to him as a result.

Through ducking and dodging, a man will avoid getting upset along with his partner and will create a new dimension of protection for the woman he loves. This new ability and strength not only helps her but ensures that he too will get the love he deserves.

> **Through ducking and dodging, a man will avoid mutual upset, create a new dimension of protection for his partner, and ensure that they both get the love they deserve.**

Security is the most important gift a contemporary man can give a woman. In hunter/nurturer societies, that security was primarily physical. Today, it is emotional as well. When a woman feels secure enough to share her feelings with the man she loves, and he can listen without being wounded, the relationship will thrive. Let's explore an example.

> **When a woman feels secure enough to share her feelings with the man she loves and he can listen without being wounded, the relationship will thrive.**

Buying a Computer

I'll never forget the day I first discovered this truth in my own marriage. Before then, even knowing that women needed to be heard and feel understood, I didn't realize that safety was an even more important element to them.

> **Safety is even more important to women than being heard and feeling understood.**

On the last day of the year, I decided to buy a new computer. I had put off this decision for a long time but finally decided to do it on New Year's Eve so that I could take it off that year's taxes. When I mentioned this to Bonnie, the force of her reaction stunned me.

"*Why* do you need to buy a new computer?" she demanded. "You already have one."

Although I didn't like being "questioned," I paused to consider her request, then began to explain by simply saying, "Well, for a lot of reasons."

By saying as little as possible, I was again able to "duck" and avoid getting hit by her inevitable emotional reaction to my gut reactions. If I hadn't ducked, we would have clashed. By doing so, I prevented the situation from escalating into a full-blown fight.

"What's wrong with the computer you already have?" Bonnie persisted.

I again paused, then observed, "You seem upset. What's the matter?"

"Have you researched the market?" she persisted, not answering my question. "How much is this computer going to cost?"

Although she was again asking me demanding questions, I knew Bonnie was upset and needed to talk. If I started giving complicated explanations of why I needed a new computer, not only would she continue to be upset but I would become upset because it would feel like she didn't appreciate my explanations. Instead of directly answering her questions, which would amount to being provoked, I chose to answer briefly, turn the conversation back to her, and draw out her feelings.

Men should duck answering a woman's direct questions if they are provocative, turn the conversation back to her, and keep their responses to a minimum to draw her out.

Drawing Out Her Feelings

Here's how it went:

John: "I think before we talk about the computer we should first talk about how you feel. I want to understand what you are feeling and why you are upset."

Bonnie: "Well, I am upset. Whenever you want something, you just go out and get it. I don't know why you have

to get another computer. Yours works fine. If we are
going to spend money, there are other things we could
spend it on."

John: "OK, what do you think we should buy?"

Bonnie: "It's not that I have this all thought out. It's just a feel-
ing. I feel like you get what you want and I get seconds.
Maybe I am mad that you want so much more than me.
When I want something, it doesn't seem so important."

John: "What do you want?"

Bonnie: "I don't know. But it feels like everything we do is
for you and not me. We always do what you want to
do, and you always get your way. I'm afraid I will not
get what I want."

John: "I can understand that feeling."

Bonnie: "We have been waiting six months to redo our floor.
Our couch needs to be recovered. I still need a kitchen
cupboard. There are so many things we need to spend
money on in the house and you are buying a computer.
It just feels like you don't care about me. You are going
to buy what you want, and that's it. What I have to say
doesn't matter at all."

As the conversation progressed in this way, I was vigorously
ducking and dodging. As I continued to hold back and not
retaliate, I realized that I could only take so much more.

John: "I really want to understand your feelings *and* it really
is hard for me. It's starting to sound like you're saying
I'm this selfish person. Don't I do anything nice?"

Bonnie (softening): "Of course you do. I don't mean to upset
you. I just have a lot of feelings coming up. I really
appreciate you trying to listen. Just the fact that I could
talk about my feelings without you getting upset with
me makes me feel so loved."

She then burst into tears, and I gave her a loving hug.

The Importance of Safety

At that moment I realized how important it was for Bonnie to feel safe enough to express her feelings. When I share this story in my couples' seminars, women repeatedly get misty-eyed relating to Bonnie's feelings. The freedom to express emotions safely with their mate's help is of paramount importance to them.

> The freedom to express emotions safely with their mate's help is vital to women. Men inevitably express surprise at how much women need to feel safe.

When a man seeks an intimate partner, he wants primarily to be needed and appreciated. When a woman seeks a mate, a man's ability to protect her is a key job requirement. This is a very primal feeling directly connected to her emotional well-being.

> When a man seeks an intimate partner, he wants primarily to be needed and appreciated. When a woman seeks a mate, a man's ability to protect her is a key job requirement.

Down through the centuries, women have looked to men for protection because it was crucial to their family's survival. This protector role carries over into our generation of relationships, but now, as we've said, it is more linked to emotional security.

Emotional security guarantees that a woman is safe to share her feelings without an invalidating argument and interruption from her man. It means that she can talk without worrying about hurting him and without reprisal. It means that she can be in a bad mood without her mate's holding it against her or ignoring her. Emotional security frees her to be herself.

> Emotional security guarantees that a woman is safe to share her feelings without invalidating argument and interruption from her man. It is the force that frees her to be herself.

The Emotional Freedom to Be Herself

Women are under such constant pressure to be loving and sweet that the freedom to be themselves is the greatest gift a man can give them. Even if he doesn't really understand her feelings, the attempt to do so calmly makes her feel powerfully supported.

Sometimes a woman doesn't understand her own feelings until she freely talks about them. If she doesn't have to worry about her man's losing control or withdrawing his love, she is doubly relieved and deeply grateful. Even if she remains upset *with him* after receiving this support, it becomes much easier for her to draw deep from her loving center the strength to forgive and forget.

> Sometimes a woman doesn't understand her own feelings until she freely talks about them. If she doesn't have to worry about her man's losing control or withdrawing his love, she is doubly relieved and deeply grateful.

Back to my computer story: By talking about her feelings, my wife was able to process emotions—not just about the computer—that had been building up steam over time. By verbally sorting them out, Bonnie was able to shed her emotional resistance and support me.

> Generally speaking, when anyone, male or female, has a strong emotional reaction, it is to a combination of many elements, not just the subject at hand.

The Right Time for Problem Solving

After taking Bonnie in my arms, I began to address her questions. Now that she felt heard, it was time to put aside emotions and concentrate on problem solving.

"I've been researching this computer for six months," I began. "It's a great deal. And if I buy it today, I can claim a tax write-off this year. But I've got to get to the store before they close.

"I understand you want things for the house," I assured her. "When I get back, why don't we sit down and plan what *you* want? Sound good?"

"Sounds good," she answered with a smile.

So I got my computer, and Bonnie got refinished floors. Most important, we both got the satisfaction of knowing we had somehow spoken each other's language, fully communicated, and grown together in love.

It's All in the Timing

Timing is essential when offering solutions. I personally discovered that I became most upset with Bonnie when she continued to be emotional or argumentative after I offered suggestions. As a man, I believed my most valued gift to her was to provide a solution. It was like offering my most precious jewel and having the woman I loved reject it.

Gradually I learned that when a woman is upset, she rarely has the ability to appreciate solutions. This is because what she needs then is to be heard, not fixed. In some cases a solution makes matters worse by minimizing or even invalidating her feelings.

When a woman is upset, she needs to be heard, not fixed. She rarely has the ability to appreciate solutions.

Blaming Bonnie for not appreciating my solutions when she is upset and needy would be like blaming a hungry lion for biting my hand after I put it in its mouth. Although I can understand intellectually that there are times when my wife can't fully appreciate my solutions, it still feels like rejection.

The art involved in offering solutions is first to make sure a woman is receptive to attempts to help. By offering a solution before she is ready to hear it, a man is setting himself up to feel rejected—significantly decreasing his ability to continue listening without getting more upset.

By offering a solution before a woman is ready to hear it, a man is setting himself up to feel rejected— significantly decreasing his ability to continue listening without getting more upset.

Once he is hit, he will almost inevitably be struck again, with each successive emotional blow growing more and more painful. After the third strike, it is advisable to take time out to cool off, think things over, and then resume the conversation when you feel more centered.

The Inner Mechanics of Ducking and Dodging

To some women, the above dialogue might sound like John Gray is this loving guy who can hear his beloved wife because he loves her so much. The truth is that I do love her with all my heart, but in the computer incident, we avoided getting into an ugly argument and a clash of wills because I have spent years practicing the skills of ducking and dodging, and Bonnie has supported me in that process.

In the beginning of our marriage, Bonnie and I would often fight and argue because in essence we weren't speaking the same language. Now, after rewriting our job descriptions and practicing advanced relationship skills, communication is much, much easier.

When conversations repeatedly turn into fights, one or both partners will eventually begin to close up, and passion will start to fade. When men begin to understand this, they are motivated to listen more. However, without becoming agile at ducking and dodging, it's a hard row to hoe. Men attending my seminars are uniformly grateful for advice on ducking and dodging and always ask for new tips.

Without the advanced relationship skills of ducking and dodging, conversations repeatedly turn into

fights, eventually one or both partners will close up,
and passion will start to fade.

Let's revisit "the computer incident," but this time noting
the inner reactions and reflexes exercised as ducking and dodging that allowed me to patiently listen and give my wife the consideration and support she deserved. This description of what it
takes to be a good listener may astound women and assist them
in being more appreciative of what a man goes through. An in-
depth understanding can help her to be more accepting and
patient when he needs to take a time-out and not talk for a
while.

Preparing to Dodge

Before even mentioning the computer, I have to prepare myself
for Bonnie's resistance, because every instinct in my body is
telling me she'll disapprove. For starters, she doesn't have the
same appreciation of electrical gadgets and gizmos that I do.

Her resistance is making the conversation much harder for me
to start. In some ways, I feel like a child or a subordinate asking
permission. I don't feel very manly, in fact I feel like a weakling.

I am able to overcome my resistance by reminding myself
that I don't need to get her approval, but that I am supporting
her by respecting her need to be included in the decision. To feel
respected, she needs me to seriously consider any opposition or
suggestions she might have.

Although the computer is a purchase exclusively for me to
use, Bonnie is my equal partner in life and deserves to be
included in any major financial decision. For her to feel equal,
she needs me to take her emotions into account.

I plan my words carefully with an eye to keeping them as
brief as possible to give her room for whatever reaction she
needs to have. After all, I've spent six months working through
my resistance, weighing the pros and cons of a new computer—
why shouldn't she have some resistance as well? With this
preparation, I begin the conversation.

The Importance of Containment

John (casually): "For several months I've been thinking about buying a new computer. I know just what I want, but I also want to include you in the process. How do you feel about it?"

Bonnie (shocked): "*Why* do you need to buy a new computer? You already have one."

I pause and consider her question. Before answering, I "contain" my gut reaction and practice the advanced relationship skill of ducking and dodging. While taking a calming breath, I remind myself, It is OK for her to be upset. It doesn't mean I can't get what I want. I don't need to get upset back. Let her talk. This was a quick duck.

Bonnie: "What's wrong with the computer you already have?"

John: "Hmmm."

At this point I quickly dodge and reassess the situation by thinking that although it sounds as if she is trying to control me, she is not. She is not saying I am wrong for wanting a computer nor is she acting like my mother and telling me I can't buy one. I don't need her permission, but she deserves my consideration.

However, she is upset and needs to talk before she can be more supportive. This may take twenty minutes. It is crucial that I relax, get comfortable, and let her explore her feelings out loud. Although it will sound like blame, it is not. I must not take it personally.

While I am doing my best to dodge, I still feel like shouting, "How dare you tell me what to do! Why do you have to get upset because I want to buy a computer?" Fortunately, I appreciate the wisdom of containment and duck by not indulging in expressing my gut reaction.

Women Don't Demand Agreement

Men don't realize that an emotionally upset woman is not demanding agreement or submission from him. She just wants to be considered. He mistakenly assumes that he has to fight to be himself when she only wants to feel heard, not stop him or control him.

Men don't realize an emotionally upset woman is not demanding agreement or submission but merely wants to feel heard.

A man does not instinctively understand this because he is so much more goal oriented. Generally speaking, when a man is upset and he talks, then his goal is to get his listener to agree with him so that some problem can be corrected.

When a man is upset and he talks, then his goal is to get his listener to agree with him so that some problem can be corrected.

When a woman is upset, she first wants to talk about it and decide later what she thinks should happen. A man mistakenly assumes that he has to give in to her feelings and sacrifice if he wants to please her. He mistakenly concludes that he has to agree with her point of view before she can feel OK again. If he doesn't agree and doesn't want to give in, he feels driven to point out the deficiencies in her argument to get her to agree with him.

Through understanding this difference, a man can contain his tendency to argue when a woman is emotional. When I use my brains instead of my guts, I can easily duck and dodge. This does not mean that I should disregard my gut reactions. They are inevitable. What is required in a relationship is that men control their instincts when they are feeling blamed or attacked and not retaliate.

What is required in a relationship is that men control their instincts when they are feeling blamed or attacked and not retaliate. A woman can handle his being upset if he can contain his gut reaction and respond respectfully.

Certainly there will be times when a man is struck by her words and gets upset. It's only to be expected. A woman can handle a man being upset if he can contain his negative reactions and respond respectfully. As long as he contains his feelings and doesn't lose control by dumping them on her, it counts as support. However, one loose derogatory zinger can undo twenty minutes of attentive support.

When emotions are involved, it is important for men to think before they act. Whenever I contain my reactions and use my brain to respond, both Bonnie and I win. Otherwise, we both lose. I may win the argument, but I will eventually lose her trust.

> When emotions are involved, it is important for men
> to think before they act. Otherwise, they may win the
> argument but will eventually lose a woman's trust.

What Women Admire in Men

A woman admires a man if he has the strength to control his emotions and the sensitivity to consider the merits and validity of what she is saying. He doesn't have to put his tail between his legs and do whatever she wants. He just needs to respectfully consider her point of view as a valid perspective.

> A woman admires a man if he has the strength
> to control his emotions and the sensitivity to
> respectfully consider her point of view
> as a valid perspective.

Women are turned off by passive and submissive men. They don't want to be the boss in an intimate relationship. They want to be equal partners. If a man respects a woman's primary need to be heard, she will respond by becoming equally respectful of his wishes.

> If a man respects a woman's primary need to be
> heard, she will respond by becoming equally respect-
> ful of his wishes.

Dodging the Challenge

Back to Bonnie and me and the computer. As the conversation
continues, she says in a mistrusting tone, "Well! Have you
researched the market? How much is this computer going to
cost!!?"

I am now livid and silently feel inside, Who is she to doubt
my competence? I don't need her telling me how much money
to spend on a computer. I don't need another mother!

Before these emotions become real, I make sure to nip them
in the bud by remembering my goal—to provide a safe place for
her to share whatever feelings she has.

I find it useful to always keep my objective in mind. I need
to remember that I am not trying to win a court case. Instead, I
am trying to give my wife nurturing support at a moment when
she has little to give me.

If I were a litigator, my objective might be to immediately
invalidate her credentials. Not only would I attempt to discredit
her competence, but I would establish my own competence in
the field of computers. After all, I used one and she didn't; in
addition, I used to be a computer programmer. How could she
dare challenge my authority?

This kind of approach in conversations creates immediate
conflict and friction. It may convince a judge, but if a man uses
such tactics in his intimate relationship, he'll end up using them
next in divorce court.

> The worst move a man can make in discussions with
> a woman is to invalidate her feelings.

Rather Than Be Right, Do the Right Thing

When a woman is emotional, any attempt on a man's part to explain the correctness of his point of view invalidates her feelings. Instead of trying to be right, I attempt to see what is right with her feelings. This way, she will in turn be able to be more supportive of me.

> When a woman is emotional, any attempt on a man's part to explain the correctness of his point of view is taken as invalidation.

To remain supportive in our conversation, I need to remember that Bonnie isn't intending to discredit me. Interrogation is an automatic reaction when women don't feel safe enough to share their feelings. So, instead of responding, I dodged the missiles of mistrust and remembered that she was caught in the middle of a process and was really not intending to be derogatory about my competence.

Rather than feeling challenged, I have learned to interpret my wife's questions as a plea for me to "hear" her. When women get emotional, they generally ask questions as a sign that they need to be questioned themselves so that they can explore their feelings.

> When women become emotional, they generally ask questions as a sign that they need to be questioned themselves so that they can explore their feelings.

Bonnie's doubt and fear were less about my competence than about whether or not I was interested in her feelings. This doubt was valid, because on a gut level, I didn't want her to interfere. But on a heart and head level, I do care about her and did want to give her the respect she deserves.

Now let's get back to our dialogue.

The Prime Objective

In response to Bonnie's questions, I reject arguing from my guts in favor of realigning myself with my prime objective, to support and be supported back.

John: "I think that before we talk about the computer we should first talk about how you feel. I want to understand what you are feeling and why you are upset."

This kind of steady focus is required if arguments are to be minimized. Even if a man is practicing advanced relationship skills and intentionally not solving a woman's problems, her questioning can catch him off guard. Suddenly he is giving answers instead of asking more questions.

The more a man says, the more there is for a woman to question, and the more upset he will become. The more words she speaks, the more heard she can feel and the more appreciated he will be. The advanced technique to remember here is to delay answering questions by asking more questions. Answer her question by asking her to talk more.

A man should delay answering an emotional
woman's questions by asking more questions.
He should answer her questions by asking her
to talk more.

A man will always be tempted to defend his point of view. He instinctively feels that if he could only share *his* understanding of the situation she would feel better. In truth, she will feel better only when he shares in her understanding of a situation. When a woman feels understood and validated, she can relax. Otherwise she feels she has to fight to be heard.

Delayed Solutions

At this point in the computer conversation, I am restraining myself from offering Bonnie solutions. I do not explain that as a writer, I am as dependent on my computer as a cowboy is on his horse. That I love computers and can certainly afford one. That my extensive research has made me certain this model and price is the best deal around. Or that because it's a business write-off that I could use this year, I'm actually saving money by buying it today. But all of these arguments are futile until I first find out what is really upsetting her.

If she wasn't upset and needing to talk when I told her about the computer, she would simply have said, "Really. You want another computer. What kind of features does it have?" As she listened for a while, quite naturally she might say, "What is it going to cost, what do your magazines say about it," et cetera, and I would discuss it with her.

On this day, however, she isn't responding in such a cheerful way. To avoid making things worse at such times, I have learned never to get logical and try to have a solution-oriented technical conversation. When a woman is upset, it is extremely difficult for her to appreciate a man's explanations, or indeed his entire attempt to exercise a rational approach. When Bonnie presents negative emotions, I take it upon myself to understand her feelings before offering any solutions or answering any questions.

When a woman is upset, it is extremely difficult for her to appreciate a man's explanations, or indeed his entire rational approach.

Ducking the Generalizations

To my question about her feelings, Bonnie replies, "Well, I am upset. Whenever you want something, you just go out and get it. I don't know why you have to get another computer. Yours works fine. If we are going to spend money, there are other things we could spend it on."

When she acknowledges that she is upset, my inner voice goes: Yes! Now I can get her to talk about it, and soon she will feel better. Be careful, John, don't correct anything she says, silently listen. Remember, feelings are not to be taken literally. They are poetic expressions to indicate one's passing emotions. They are not intended to be taken as factual statements. Nor are they about me.

Whenever Bonnie begins to use incorrect statements or make sweeping generalizations, I relax because it is a clear reminder to me that we are not having an intellectual or factual conversation. She is expressing the need to feel heard. When she eventually feels heard, the resistant feelings pass away.

Most men fear that if they don't correct a woman's statements, she will continue holding on to them as fact. This is true in court but not in a relationship. In a courtroom, if she said, "Whenever you want something, you just go out and get it," I would be required to point out the incorrectness of her statement. I would defend myself by reminding her of all the things that I want that I don't get. I would point out to her all the times I had sacrificed my wishes for her. While this may be the way the wheels of justice turn, it will not work in an intimate relationship.

Explaining that I also make sacrifices—such as waiting six months to buy the computer—would only confirm that I didn't understand her general feelings. It would also stimulate her need to talk about her sacrifices. Before we knew it, we would be arguing about which of us sacrifices the most.

Ask Friendly Questions

As the computer conversation continues, Bonnie completes her comments by saying, "There are other things we could spend our money on." She pauses. This is my opportunity to be civil and ask what she thinks we should buy.

When she pauses, I have a choice. I can ask a question in a friendly or at least neutral tone to draw her out more. Or I can undo everything I have accomplished by asking something condemning like "How can you say that?"

What most men don't understand is that the more a woman feels the right to be upset, the less upset she will be. If a man doesn't criticize her for being critical, or blame her for blaming him, he gives her an opportunity to release any criticism or blame she may be harboring.

> The more a woman feels the right to be upset,
> the less upset she will be. If she isn't criticized or
> blamed, she is given the opportunity to release
> any negative feelings she may be harboring.

Why Men Argue with Feelings

Men assume that an emotional woman is inflexible in her thinking. They don't realize that at such a time, when a woman talks about her feelings she is not making conclusions or expressing fixed opinions. When a woman shares negative emotions, she is generally in the middle of the process of discovering what she believes to be true.

> When a woman shares negative emotions, she is
> generally in the middle of the process of discovering
> what she feels to be true. She is not stating an
> objective fact.

She talks to "discover" the range of feelings within herself—not to give an accurate description of objective reality. That's what men do. Instead, she is more concerned with discovering and describing what is going on in her subjective, inner world.

Meanwhile, I'm waiting for Bonnie to answer my question about what *she* feels we should buy instead of the computer, but she's still in the midst of discovering what her feelings are. Finally, she tells me, "It's not that I have this all thought out. It's just a feeling. I feel like you get exactly what you want and I get seconds. Maybe I'm mad that you want so much more than I do. When I want something, it doesn't seem so earthshaking."

I realize that "It's not that I have this all thought out" means she's still talking feelings, not facts. But even with her help, I'm still struggling to dodge and duck from feeling criticized and unappreciated. Inwardly, I'm fuming.

How can you say you get seconds? I silently demand. I do so many things for you. I work hard so that you can have practically anything you want. How do you have the nerve to even suggest you're not important to me! Although these are my true gut reactions, I thoroughly appreciate how counterproductive it would be to express them.

If I were to "tell her what I think of her," it would only be to try and convince her that she is wrong or is being very unfair. I would succeed only in invalidating her feelings and confirming her doubts and mistrust. But by listening without attacking her, I am giving her the time and opportunity to talk more, remember the good things about me, and let go of the negative comments *on her own*. Despite my resentment, I'm convinced that she soon will.

When a woman has a chance to share her feelings freely, she begins to feel more loving. Sometimes she may realize how wrong, incorrect, or unfair her statements sounded, but in most cases she just forgets them as she begins to see things from a more loving perspective.

When a woman has a chance to share her feelings freely, she begins to feel more loving despite what she may have said.

It's hard for men to relate readily to this mood change because it's foreign to their natures and they just can't fathom it. When a man is upset and talks with the person who is upsetting him, he tends to remain upset unless that person agrees with him in some significant way or until he can find a solution. Simply listening to him and nodding your head in sympathy is not enough if he is really upset.

After a woman shares a negative feeling, a man mistakenly takes it as her "final" conclusion and thinks she is blaming him. He doesn't know that her feelings will change if he just lets her talk them out.

After a woman shares a negative feeling, a man mistakenly takes it as her "final" conclusion, not realizing that her mood will change if she can just talk through her emotions.

Why Men Feel Blamed

Quite commonly in counseling, a woman will share her feelings and a man will feel attacked and blamed. This is how it goes:

He says: "You're blaming me."
She says: "No I'm not. I'm only sharing my feelings."
He then says: "But your feelings tell me you *are* blaming me. When you say you feel ignored, you're saying I'm not attentive. When you say you don't feel loved, you're accusing me."
She then says: "No I'm not. I'm just talking about how *I* feel. I am not saying something about *you*."
He says: "Yes you are! I'm the only one you are married to."
She says: "I can't talk to you."
He says: "There you go again blaming me for how you feel."

Without some intervention, they will go on arguing until they give up in frustration.

Men must understand what is really going on inside a woman when she sounds blaming. On the flip side, a woman can make communication much easier by appreciating why her partner imagines that she is blaming him.

As men begin to comprehend the female thinking and feeling process, they will see that from the woman's viewpoint, she really isn't blaming them.

For years I couldn't comprehend this when I was listening to my wife. It was really hard to dodge when I felt repeatedly blamed. While she shared her feelings, I would feel an urgent need to argue with her. Then one day all that changed. It was a realization that occurred while I accompanied her on a little shopping excursion.

A Shopping Trip

As I observed my wife shopping, I noticed a striking difference between us. When I shopped, I found what I wanted, bought it, and got out as quickly as possible, like a hunter making a kill and hurrying home with it. Bonnie, however, was very happy trying on many outfits.

When she finally settled on a shop that interested her, I was relieved and parked myself in a chair by the dressing room. She was very excited about several outfits. I was very excited because not only would she be happy but we could finally leave. How wrong I was!

Instead of simply buying an outfit or two quickly, she took what seemed like years trying on each one to get a feel for it. As she preened in the mirror, she made comments like, "This one's sort of cute, isn't it? I'm not sure though. Is it really me? The colors are good. I really love the length."

Finally she announced, "No, it's not me." This scene was repeated with outfit after outfit. Sometimes before changing out of one, she would say firmly, "I like this one."

After forty-five minutes of this, we left without her buying anything. To my surprise, she wasn't the least bit frustrated. I could not ever imagine putting that much time and energy into the hunt, coming home empty-handed, and still being happy.

How to Dodge Blame

As I reflected on that incident, I realized that this was the key to understanding why a woman sounds blaming when she claims she is not.

You see, an overwhelmed woman talks about her feelings the way she shops. She is not expecting you to buy a particular feeling any more than she is necessarily going to buy it herself. She is basically trying on emotional outfits to see if they fit. Just because she takes a lot of time trying on an outfit or testing an emotion doesn't mean it's "her."

In a similar manner, when women share their feelings, they are not committed to those feelings but are in the process of discovering what really fits their most loving selves. Just because a woman says something, it doesn't mean that she is going to take it home and wear it forever.

> **Women who share their feelings are not committed
> to those feelings but are in the process of discovering
> what really fits. Just because a woman says
> something, it doesn't mean she's going to take it
> home and wear it forever.**

Now, in the spirit of fairness, when my wife seems to blame me I pretend that we're shopping and she is just beginning to try things on. It may be an hour before we actually "leave the store," but only then can I know what she finally believes.

Negative Feelings Are Not Permanent

It is easier to dodge a woman's resistant feelings and not feel blamed if a man remembers that her feelings are not permanent and that she is just trying them on for size. If he argues with her, she will become defensive. Having to protect herself prevents her from getting immediately to the place where she can return her negative feelings to the rack and "buy" more positive ones.

Women speak negatives out loud to discover the positive, loving, and more accurate picture of what happened. Even if some mistake was made by the man, as she lets go of negative feelings, she is able to see the bigger picture and remember all the good he does as well.

> **Women speak negatives out loud to discover the
> positive, loving, and more accurate picture of what
> happened.**

Articulating negatives helps women accept men and love them just the way they are without expecting or even depending on them to be perfect. To find real love that does not demand perfection, a woman needs a man's support so that she can express her feelings without being held accountable for every word she utters. Her feelings need to be expressed in a free and fluid way if she is to connect with the love in her heart.

**Feelings need to be expressed in a free and fluid way
if a woman is to find the love in her heart.**

Feelings Are Not Facts

When a man expresses a feeling, it is more like a fact—something he believes to be true but doesn't have a lot of objective evidence to back up. This is not what a woman means when she shares her feelings. For women, feelings are much less about the outer world and more about their *experience* of the outer world. For women, feelings and facts are very different animals.

Bonnie's comment that "It feels like everything we do is for you and not me. We always do what you want to do and you always get your way" sounded like a critical comment about me. I heard her saying "You are selfish and you only care about yourself. You don't care about me. We only do what you want to do." I dodged by remembering that her feelings were not facts about me. When I can remember this, it helps her to remember it. I also felt assured because I knew that when a woman can expand, dramatize, or intensify her feelings about a situation and feel heard, she eventually can and will begin to see the positive facts more clearly on her own.

**When a woman can expand, dramatize, or intensify
her feelings about a situation and feel heard, she
eventually can and will begin to see the positive facts
more clearly on her own.**

How to Duck Criticism

To duck Bonnie's criticism I needed to remember that she really didn't intend her words to be a statement of fact. Her feelings were not a final critical statement about me and my actions. Translated into a language I could understand, she said:

"Sometimes when I am emotional and not thinking clearly, like right now, I forget what a wonderful guy you are and all the times you are there for me and begin to feel *as if* everything we do is for you and not me. It is *as if* we always do what you want to do. I feel *as if* I can't ask for what I want because you don't care. I know you really do care, but this is how I react *sometimes,* particularly when, like today, you really want something. When you really want something, you are so clear about it that it feels *as if* we are not partners anymore, and no matter what I would say, it wouldn't count. I really know I do matter to you, but these feelings do come up. Your consideration of my feelings would make me feel really good right now. Would you reassure me that I do count and that you do care about me by listening to my feelings?"

To expect her actually to say all that is unrealistic. It would go against her feminine nature to be extremely rational, logical, and objectively accurate when she is in the process of exploring, sharing, and releasing negative emotions. A man who doesn't demand this masculine, pinpoint accuracy at such times provides loving support that allows her to eventually reach objectivity with greater love, trust, acceptance, and appreciation.

A man who doesn't demand masculine pinpoint accuracy from an emotional woman allows her to reach objectivity with greater love, trust, acceptance, and appreciation.

To dodge criticism successfully, a man needs to remember that all feelings are temporary. By listening to a woman's negative emotions, he allows her the opportunity to discover her positive feelings as well. In return, a woman can help *him* duck and dodge by making supportive comments. These comments we will explore more thoroughly in the next chapter.

Feelings Change

Another tip for successful dodging is to remember that negative feelings can shift 180 degrees in just a few minutes without a man's saying anything. If a man reacts in a negative way to a woman's negative feelings, she doesn't feel understood and must continue explaining those feelings before she can move on. Reacting in a negative way only prolongs the process.

It is not a contradiction—in fact, it's perfectly normal—for a woman to say in a single conversation "I feel like you only care about yourself" *and* "You really are a very caring person, you give me so much support."

Once aware of a woman's inherent flexibility, a man can relax and listen instead of focusing on how to change her mind. When a man doesn't know how to dodge, he resists by "spilling his guts," which in turn forces a woman to lose her flexibility and become closed, rigid, and righteous.

By listening to a woman, a man focuses on how he can change her mind. When he resists, he forces a woman to lose her natural flexibility and become closed, rigid, and righteous.

Disarming by Asking More Questions

Whenever a man asks a woman questions, he sends her the *disarming* and soothing message that he cares and that he is there for her. By asking questions or making statements like "How can I help you?" or "Tell me more," he releases her from feeling she's fighting an uphill battle. You'll find a list of "disarming" questions in chapter 7.

You win by asking more, you lose by talking about your gut reactions.

The secret of supporting a woman who feels upset or overwhelmed is to help her work through her feelings by getting her to speak more words—negative or positive, accurate or inaccurate, defensive or vulnerable. The more words he can hear and dodge, the more she will feel heard and seen, which will shift her attitude back toward love.

The secret of supporting an emotional woman is to help her work through her feelings by getting her to speak more words.

Bottom Line Advice for Men to Support a Woman

Remember, if a woman doesn't have to focus on getting a man to listen to her, she can do what is most natural for her—talking and shifting her *own* attitude. To support her in feeling more loving and accepting, here is some bottom-line advice for men:

1. When you suspect she is upset, don't wait for her to initiate the conversation (when you initiate, it takes away 50 percent of her emotional charge).
2. As you let her talk, keep reminding yourself that it doesn't help to get upset with her for being upset.
3. Whenever you feel an urgent need to interrupt or correct, don't.
4. When you don't know what to say, say nothing. If you can't say something positive or respectful, keep quiet.
5. If she won't talk, ask more questions until she does.
6. Whatever you do, don't correct or judge her feelings.
7. Remain as calm and centered as possible, and keep a lock on your strong reactions. (If you lose control and "spill your guts" even for a moment, you lose and have to start all over at a disadvantage.)

Delivering Support

Just as ducking, dodging, and disarming are all fighting skills, so also is delivering. In a real fight, a man needs to wait and watch for the right moment to deliver his punch and make contact. In a loving conversation, a man needs to apply this same skill. He needs to watch and wait for the right moment to deliver a word or phrase of support that will end the battle.

In a loving conversation, a man needs to apply the warrior skill of delivering.

During the computer conversation, after hearing many of Bonnie's feelings I waited for her natural pause to ask her what she wanted. By supporting her in expressing desire—even if she doesn't know yet what she wants—I open her to feeling my desire to support her.

Asking her what she wants doesn't mean I have to give up what I want. It does mean that I will have to expand my awareness to see how I can support her wishes as well as mine. It shows her that I consider her needs as seriously as my own. This kind of equal respect is a soothing ointment that nurtures her wounded female soul.

Equal respect is a soothing ointment that nurtures the wounded female soul.

What It Means to Understand Feelings

To illustrate my next point, let's again return to the computer conversation. As Bonnie expresses her feelings, I am waiting to deliver another supportive statement to assure her that I'm on her side. After she says she's afraid she can't get what she wants, it's easy to support her.

I say, "I can understand that feeling."

By saying I understood, I didn't mean that I agreed with her fear. I was not saying "Yeah, you should be afraid of never getting what you want. You are married to a real selfish guy!"

By saying "I understand that feeling," I was really saying "I understand what it is like to feel afraid of not getting what you want. I have certainly felt that way at times in my life. It is painful and uncomfortable."

During an emotional conversation, a man needs to be alert and ready to offer simple gestures of his support. The most common and most powerful are eye contact, occasional nods of the head, and physical contact like reaching out and taking her hand, touching her shoulder, giving her a hug, or making sympathetic sounds.

During an emotional conversation, a man needs to be alert and ready to offer simple gestures of his support like nodding his head in agreement, giving her a hug, or making sympathetic sounds.

The Importance of Eye Contact

When women are upset, they want to be seen. Unlike men, they don't want to be ignored or left alone. The most important thing a man can do is to notice when his partner is upset. When she feels seen, she can more directly see herself and more efficiently explore her feelings.

When a man listens, his basic tendency is to look away in order to think about what is being said. It is hard for women to understand this difference because when they talk about their feelings with each other, they instinctively deliver their support by lots of eye contact.

If a man simply stares into a woman's eyes when she talks about feelings, his mind will start to go blank and he will space out. Without understanding that a woman needs more eye contact than he does, a man tends to look away to figure out what his partner means or how he is going to respond.

Learning to maintain eye contact not only delivers a very important kind of support but also helps a man to check his reaction to immediately attempt to offer a solution to her problems. The trick for a man is not only to remember to do it, but to do it without going blank.

This can be accomplished if he looks in a special way. Instead of staring, he should first look in her eyes for two to three seconds. Then, when he would naturally turn his head and look away, he should instead look to the tip of her nose. After that, he should look at her lips, then her chin, and then her whole face. Then he should start over.

This procedure keeps him looking in her direction and yet frees him from spacing out or going blank. It can also be relaxing because it is something else he can do instead of passively doing nothing.

Cold Fronts

When I notice a cold front coming from my wife's direction, my old approach to making her feel better was to assume that she needed space to be alone. After a while I would notice that it was getting colder and colder, and the chill was definitely directed toward me. I would grumble to myself that I didn't deserve Bonnie's cold shoulder and inwardly begin getting furious at her. Eventually we would negatively interact and sparks would fly.

Once I understood more about women, I no longer sat around ignoring my wife when she was cold and getting angrier and angrier as she grew more distant.

It eventually occurred to me that by giving her more space, I was only making things worse. I finally realized that Bonnie didn't want more space but wanted more contact and attention. Most of the time when I was feeling the cold front, it was not even about me, she just needed to talk in order to warm up. But when I didn't notice and come over to touch her and ask questions in a caring manner, it just made her more cold and distant. So, even though her feelings weren't initially about me, they soon became so.

Now I cope with cold fronts by preparing myself to put on a warm jacket and fly straight into the storm. By touching her and initiating a conversation, I know she will eventually warm up to me without my having to do anything else but dodge, duck, disarm, and deliver.

How to Warm Up a Cold Woman

Now when I sense a coldness coming from Bonnie, I immediately go up and touch her.

If she doesn't pull back when I make physical contact, I know that her distress is not about me. If she does pull back, I realize that I'm going to need to duck and dodge a lot more, but I also know she'll get back to loving me even more.

Not only do I touch to defuse her anger, but also to check the temperature. If she is really angry with me, I find out and ask the appropriate questions. If she isn't, I simply relax from needing to duck and dodge. To initiate conversation, I ask her how her day was or if she's upset with me. A complete list of questions to ask are detailed in chapter 7.

In most cases, a woman will respond to these questions with "Oh, it's not you. There is just so much going on," and will then continue to talk. Even if she *was* a little upset with her mate, she will quickly tend to dismiss those feelings because he's initiated the conversation. When she feels supported, she can be very generous with her love.

If she says "It's not you" before she begins telling a man what's bothering her, he of course finds it much easier to listen. She begins to warm up. He cools off, knowing he is not the cause of her upset.

If an overwhelmed woman says "It's not you" before
she begins talking about what's bothering her, it's
much easier for a man to listen.

What to Do When She Is Angry with Him

When a woman is angry with a man, the most powerful message he can send her is that she has a right to be angry, that it is safe for her to be angry, and that he wants to understand what he did to upset her so that he can stop doing it.

**When a woman is angry with a man, the most
powerful message he can send her is that she has a
right to be angry.**

When I touch Bonnie and she remains cold or pulls away, the most important thing for me to remember is not to be hurt or offended by her rejection. Since I'm testing the temperature, I am prepared for a possible rejection. If I were not prepared, I would instinctually react with anger.

Let's look at another example. One day I was feeling a cold front that had been building for several hours. I truly had no idea what it was about. The old me would have reacted by feeling unappreciated and unfairly denied. Instead, I knew how to quickly nip it in the bud by giving her a chance to talk about it.

When I touched her, she immediately pulled away. But instead of stalking off, I summoned up my advanced relationship skills and didn't take her action personally. I continued to stand there, and look in her direction, wondering what was bothering her. As it worked out, it took at least fifteen to thirty seconds for her to even realize that she had rejected me. Since I didn't react negatively, it was easy to rebuild trust.

I now knew for certain that she was angry with me. To protect myself from feeling hurt by her anger and blame, I was careful not to ask a question like "Are you upset with me?" or "Did I do something wrong?" To protect myself from getting hurt, it was best to at least start out with a question that didn't directly link me to her anger.

The Power of Gentle Persistence

The most effective neutral question to ask at times like this is: "Do you want to talk about something?" If the answer is no, it is easy to dodge because deep inside I can easily understand her not wanting to talk.

I say, "I really want to understand what happened." Again I am careful not to open myself up to much of her anger.

She pauses and says, "There's not much to say." That tells me that there is a lot to say. I begin preparing myself to duck and dodge.

My objective is to gently persist in my goal of being there for her. By holding my ground without demanding more, I earn her respect, and she gets the message that I really care.

When women don't want to talk, it is generally because they don't feel safe, don't feel that you care, or feel that you won't understand. This resistance can only be overcome with gentle persistence.

When women don't want to talk, it is generally because they don't feel safe, don't feel you care, or feel that you won't understand. This resistance can only be overcome with gentle persistence.

Bearing that in mind, I say, "Is it something I said or did?"

Her response is a deep inhalation and a long sigh, indicating that she really doesn't want to talk about it.

I say, "If it is, I really want to know," then, after pausing, "If I hurt you, I want to know what I did so that I won't do it again."

At this point she opens up and gently replies, "The other day when we were talking, you answered the phone right in the middle of what I was saying. Afterward, you didn't even ask me to finish the thought. I felt really hurt."

I say, "I'm sorry, that was insensitive of me." Although a surge of explanations come up, I quickly push them away and reach out to touch her shoulder. This time she receives it.

Bonnie proceeds to talk about her feelings, and after a while we feel very close again. I would never have known how to do this years ago. How could I? Nobody ever taught me. But now that I am "working" according to a new job description based on advanced relationship skills, I know better.

What It Takes to Duck and Dodge

Once you've mastered the elements of advanced relationship skills, it only takes a few moments to discern how to use them. It's similar to hitting a tennis ball or golf ball—a lot of practice goes into developing the swing, but once learned, it's practically automatic.

Learning to listen is similar to learning any new skill. When you first drive a stick shift, the mechanism seems very complex. You have to remember which gears are up and down, you have to let off on the gas, push in the clutch, shift the gear and slowly let out the clutch, and increase the gas. You have to notice when it is time to shift again and repeat the process again and again. To slow down, you have to do the whole process in reverse. If this is a chore to read, it's twenty-five times more a chore to learn. Especially because all this has to be done while keeping your car pointed in the direction you want to go.

After practice, though, the tedium quickly becomes effortless. A seasoned driver doesn't even think about shifting because the process becomes a series of reflex actions.

For a man, learning to listen attentively without getting upset or frustrated when a woman is upset is definitely a new and difficult skill. However, with a lot of practice it can easily become second nature.

For a man, listening attentively without getting upset or frustrated when a woman is upset takes a lot of practice but eventually becomes second nature.

If Only Our Fathers Had Known

If a man could have repeatedly observed his father listen to his mother hundreds of times while growing up, he wouldn't need intimate job retraining. But because our fathers and mothers did not know about advanced relationship skills, they are techniques all of us have to learn.

In future generations, when our children have a chance to

grow up watching their parents model these communication skills, they won't have to work on them so hard in their relationships.

Until that time, if men are to learn this important skill, the assistance of women is invaluable. In my own experience, the element that has helped me to learn most quickly is my wife's cooperation and support. By not expecting me to be perfect and by letting me know when I was helpful, she made my way easier.

In the next chapter, we will explore advanced relationship skills that women can use to assist men in being successful listeners. By drawing on ancient nurturing skills, they can learn how to love and nurture a man without mothering him. Women will learn to apply the skills of unconditional love that are so natural to women, while at the same time making sure that they get the love and support they themselves need.

Feminine Skills for Talking So a Man Will Listen

When women address men as they have always talked to other women, men either don't get it or just stop listening. It is as if women were speaking a different language that men tend to misunderstand. A woman can greatly assist a man in learning her language by making a few small but significant changes in her communication style.

By learning to pause and prepare a man before sharing her feelings, a woman immediately begins getting the kind of support she most needs. By making clear up front how she wants him to support her, she can relax and share her feelings without having to worry about upsetting him or losing his attention.

By making clear up front how she wants him to support her, she can relax and share her feelings without having to worry about upsetting him or losing his attention.

This formula for talking so that a man will listen can be as simple as saying the following phrase: "You don't have to say anything or do anything, I just need to talk about my feelings in order to feel better."

Through first pausing and then preparing him in this way, he doesn't feel an obligation to offer suggestions or think up solutions to make her feel better. Instead of focusing on attempting to solve her problems while she is talking, he can relax and really listen. By doing less, he can actually give her the emotional support she is really looking for.

Talking "Male" Versus Talking "Female"

Talking in a logical and focused manner is primarily how men communicate and business is done. For eight hours each day to varying degrees, a working woman is required to express herself in this way. If she limits herself to talking "Male," a man may listen more, but it pulls her away from her femininity.

When a woman gets home, her first priority is finding the balance to be feminine again. However, if she abruptly begins talking "Female" and tries to share her feelings without clear guidelines, it will inevitably ruin her intimate relationships. Eventually, she will either give up on men or close down the feminine part of her that needs to talk. Both such courses are disastrous to her happiness and fulfillment.

To relax and connect back to her warm, loving, feminine feelings after being combative, competitive, efficient, and goal oriented during the day, a woman needs the freedom, permission, and support in her relationships to communicate her feelings in a nongoal-oriented, nonlogical, nonaccurate, and nonrational way.

To recuperate from her day, she needs to freely expand through expressing her feelings. If she is always editing them to make sure they are correct, accurate, and presented in a logical manner, she stays in her male side. Without understanding what a woman requires to nurture her female side, men become overly frustrated with a woman's need to talk in a feminine way.

A man does not instinctively know this because his male side is nurtured when he talks in a focused, direct, clear, logical, and goal-oriented manner after a lot of silent thought, consideration, and deliberation. He doesn't realize that to demand this focused approach from his partner is counterproductive and will inevitably prevent her from being feminine.

A New Dilemma

The contemporary woman is faced with a new dilemma. Either she trains herself to talk like a man and loses a part of herself as well as an essential source of happiness, or she disregards a man's resistance and lets it loose. In response to her free expression of feelings, he stops listening, and she eventually loses his love and support. Since neither approach works, it's fortunate that there is another way.

Traditionally, women didn't depend on men for nurturing conversations, nor were they required to talk like men throughout the day. If a woman had to be more linear when she occasionally talked with a man, it was OK because she had the whole day to talk in an expanded female style. Women today have a much greater need to talk in a "Female" way with their male partners because they are deprived of it at work.

Women today have a much greater need to talk in a "Female" way with their male partners because they are deprived of it at work.

The need to communicate with men is a new challenge for both women and men. By applying new feminine skills, a woman can greatly assist a man in listening to her feelings. Once a man is prepared, a woman can relax and let go. This is the secret. By her saying a few words, a man can be conditioned to effectively deal with her different style of communicating. Even if her words would normally sound critical and blaming to a man in "Male" language, even if he is not yet good at ducking and dodging, if he is prepared correctly he can even handle a direct hit.

The Great Houdini

A man's ability to listen is dramatically increased if he is first properly prepared. My favorite example of a man's need to be prepared comes from the life of the great Houdini.

The magician Harry Houdini offered the challenge that he could get out of anything. He was an escape artist. He became famous for getting out of chained boxes, straitjackets, bank safes, and jails. The second challenge he made is less well known.

He made the challenge that anyone, no matter how big they were, could punch him in the stomach and he wouldn't be hurt by it. He could take any punch.

One Halloween night during the intermission of his magic show, a young college student came backstage and asked, "Is it true that you can take any punch?"

Houdini said, "Yes."

Before Houdini had a chance to prepare himself, the student gave him a quick jab. It was that quick punch that killed the great Houdini. He was rushed to the hospital but died the next day.

Like Houdini, a man can handle a woman's verbal punches if he is prepared and can, in a sense, tighten his stomach muscles so that he doesn't get hurt. If he is not prepared, then he is overly vulnerable and can easily be hurt.

There are a variety of ways in which a woman can prepare a man so that he can hear what she is saying without getting bruised. In this chapter I will suggest some that may be appropriate for you and some that may not be. As time passes, other ways of preparing may feel more appropriate as you and your mate grow into them.

Trying on Different Outfits

Treat these suggestions as if they were different outfits that you might like to wear. Try them, see if they fit, and if you like them, then check them out with your partner to see if your partner likes them as well. Take your pick.

I suggest the following examples as a springboard for developing other expressions as well. Once you get the hang of it, it will become a natural way of supporting the person you love most in your life. Eventually you will find yourself integrating these advanced relationship skills into all your relationships.

Giving a Man His Job Description

When a woman talks, a man commonly does not know what is required of him. Listening is difficult for him because he misunderstands what is expected or what she is really saying in her language. If he is not skilled in ducking and dodging, the more he *cares*, the more he will feel hit by what sounds like criticism in "male talk."

It is much easier for a man to duck and dodge in the business arena because he does not interact with such an open caring of others. In his romantic relationships, he is much more open and vulnerable, so when he gets hit he is much more hurt.

It is much easier for a man to duck and dodge in the business arena because he does not interact with such an open caring of others. In his romantic relationships, he is much more open and vulnerable, so when he gets hit he is much more hurt.

A woman's new task is to casually let him know what she needs before she begins to talk. By clearly giving him a job description in a language that he can understand, he can relax and not exert himself in trying to figure out what she wants. This is a new twist for a woman, but once learned it frees her to express her power as a woman in a new way.

Using Old Skills in a New Way

Although it has a new twist, "preparing" is really an ancient feminine skill at which women are very adept. Their instinctive nature demands that they prepare. While cavemen focused on the day's hunt, cavewomen prepared for the future.

There is an intuitive knowing in women that acknowledges that everything grows naturally in small steps when the right conditions are created and patiently nurtured. Her instinctive motto is: An ounce of prevention is worth a pound of cure.

Until now, a woman's traditional daily responsibilities reflected this tendency to prepare. Each day she would think ahead to plan and prepare meals for her family. To create a nurturing setting for herself and the family, she would prepare the home to make it as beautiful and uplifting as possible. To grow a garden, she would first prepare the ground before planting the seeds.

As mothers, women have always taken the time to prepare their children for the world, step by step. In guiding a child to play independently, a mother will first set up the appropriate toys or set the conditions. To prepare the child to read, *she* will read to the child. Through "preparing" a nurturing setting she knows that the child will automatically grow and flourish.

Traditionally, women put much more attention in how they dress and appear. When a women gets dressed, she instinctively takes more time to prepare so that her personal expression is appropriate to the event or setting. Preparing her face with the right makeup, preparing her skin because it is more sensitive, and wearing ornaments on her body to attract the appropriate attention are all expressions of this tendency to prepare.

Even biologically women require more preparation. To birth a baby, she prepares for nine months. To fully enjoy sex, her body requires much more time, stimulation, and preparation. Particularly before the convenient availability of sanitary napkins, a woman had to prepare in advance for her menstrual cycle.

Traditionally, a woman prepared herself for marriage by remaining a virgin. Before having sex and thus having a baby, she prepared herself by making sure that her partner was com-

mitted to her and could provide for her. Even life insurance is
an ancient female ritual of preparation. In ancient days, she prepared herself for the possibility of her husband's death by maintaining a positive image in the community.

Women are always preparing. It is their nature, and they are
good at it. One of their great hidden frustrations is that they do
not know how to prepare a man to listen. Without a clear
understanding of how men speak "Male" and not "Female," a
woman cannot intuit the necessity of preparing to have a conversation. She naively assumes that if he loves her, he will
instinctively understand her language.

Even so, women do prepare a man to listen but generally in
instinctive ways that would work with other women but not
with men. She mistakenly assumes that if she asks him lots of
questions about his day, he will be prepared to listen to her.
This kind of preparing doesn't work.

Preparing a man to listen is a new skill for women. Just as
men can extend their ancient warrior skills to duck and dodge, a
woman can transform an ancient feminine art into an advanced
relationship skill by learning to prepare a man to listen.

> Just as men can extend their ancient warrior skills to
> duck and dodge, a woman can transform an ancient
> feminine art into an advanced relationship skill by
> learning to prepare a man to listen.

Well-Meaning Men

Times have changed so that even a well-meaning, intelligent
man doesn't know what a woman really needs. While she talks,
he will consistently offer a string of comments, corrections, and
solutions. In response, she will say "You don't understand."

Misunderstanding is one of the most common complaints
women have about men. It is so worn that when a man hears it,
he immediately gets defensive, because in "Male," she is saying
that he is stupid and thus incapable of helping her.

This phrase "You don't understand" is so automatic to a woman that she has no idea that she is preventing a man from giving her the support she needs. Not only does this phrase sound like criticism, but it doesn't make any sense to him.

He feels that what he is doing demonstrates that he does understand what she is saying, and to maintain his pride he is willing to fight to prove it. Although he started out to help, he ends up wanting to argue.

How to Get a Man to Listen

When a woman needs to talk about feelings, she generally needs a man to listen with empathy. At those times, she wants him to understand that she is not looking for his help in solving her problems but just wants to feel his emotional support. When he gives his solutions, she instinctively says "You don't understand."

This recurring comment is an insult to him because he thinks that she is saying his solution is not smart, helpful, or good enough. This, however, is not what she means. When she says "You don't understand," she really means "You don't understand that right now I *don't* need a solution."

He, however, hears that she doesn't appreciate his solution and then gets hooked into arguing about the validity of his approach and explaining himself at a time when she only needs to talk. If a woman wants to get a man to understand what she really needs, she should avoid ever saying "You don't understand," even when she means it, because the phrase is so accusatory that it is hard for a man to hear her.

If a woman wants to get a man to understand what she really needs, she should avoid ever saying "You don't understand," even when she means it, because the phrase is so accusatory that it is hard for a man to hear her.

However, here's an alternative. First, pause and consider that he is doing his best to understand and then say "Let me try saying that in a different way."

When a man hears this phrase, it also conveys the message that the man has not fully understood her, but in a noncritical way. He is much more willing to listen and reconsider what she is saying. He does not feel criticized or blamed, and as a result is more eager to support her. Without understanding what makes men tick, it would be nearly impossible for a woman to figure out that a man would greatly prefer to hear "Let me try saying this in a different way" to "You don't understand." To a man, however, the difference is so obvious that he would never think to suggest it.

The Wisdom of Pausing and Preparing

When a man is offering solutions and a woman wants just to be heard, advanced relationship skills are available that do not offend him, through which she can assist him in giving her the support she wants. By learning how to "pause" and then "prepare" him to listen she can continue without getting interrupted by his solutions.

The sooner a woman makes it clear that she doesn't need a solution, the easier it will be for her mate to shift gears from the "fixing" mode to the "hearing mode." For example, if a man has been listening and offering solutions for twenty minutes and the woman then pauses to let him know that she doesn't need his solutions, he will feel foolish, unappreciated, and defensive.

Sometimes, when my wife, Bonnie, is talking about her problems, I begin offering little solutions. Even though I teach advanced relationship skills, I sometimes forget to duck and dodge.

Instead of expressing an immediate reaction like "You don't understand" or "You're not listening," she pauses and prepares me to support her. Instead of focusing on what I am doing wrong, she just reminds me of what I am supposed to be doing. This strategy is definitely an advanced relationship skill.

She says in a very casual matter-of-fact way, "Oh, you don't have to solve this, I just need to talk about it. I'm already starting to feel better. I think I just need to feel heard."

She does this in the same tone of voice as one might use with a dinner guest who after dinner starts washing the dishes. In that situation a gracious host would automatically say, "Oh, you don't have to bother cleaning up, I'll get to it later. It's no big deal. Let's just go in the living room."

When she gently reminds me in this way of my new job requirements, I am very happy to make the shift to support her more. When a woman uses this kind of casual tone when she reminds a man, she thereby minimizes his mistake and allows him to easily continue listening.

Helping a Man to Listen

Once, after listening to Bonnie for about ten minutes, I began to look pretty beat-up. When I first came home I felt wonderful, but after hearing her complain about her life for ten minutes, I felt like a complete failure. I also felt "bummed out" because I thought she was really unhappy and that there was little I could do to change it.

She eventually noticed how down I appeared and told me, "You look the way I felt."

This was a revelation for me, because I had no idea that she was feeling better.

"You mean you felt this way but you don't anymore?" I asked.

She said, "Yes, I feel much better now. I'm sorry you had to get bummed out, but I do feel much better."

I too suddenly felt much better. I told her, "Well, if you feel better, then I guess I do too. I thought we were destined to have a really awful evening."

I think that on an emotional level I was feeling we were destined to have an awful life. Bonnie's giving me a little positive feedback about how helpful my listening had been completely changed my mood.

Consequently, the next time we talked it was dramatically easier for me to listen without feeling defeated. Each time we talked *and* I experienced that she was happier as a result, it became easier the next time.

Helping Her to Pause with Reality Checks

I remember another time when Bonnie seemed really upset with me and said things like "I feel like you never spend time with me anymore. Your work is more important than me. We used to be so much happier. I feel like things are just getting worse." These were hard words to hear, but I just kept ducking and dodging. I remembered that she was not talking about me but was just exploring what was really upsetting her.

At a certain point, in order to avoid feeling hit and getting even more upset, I helped her to pause by making a reality check. I said, "It's starting to sound like I do nothing right. Is there anything that has gotten better? Do I do anything right?"

In that moment she said, "Oh, yes, in the past I would never have been able to talk like this. I feel so much safer with you. I just need to get this out, and then I will feel so much better. I know this is hard for you, and I really appreciate it."

I said, "OK, tell me more." All I needed was to be reminded that her feelings were not directed at me as criticism.

Being Fair

One time she paused in the middle of a feeling conversation and said, "I know these feelings sound really unfair, I just need to express them and then I can easily let go of them. OK?"

Instantly I was able to relax and listen without feeling defensive. I said, "Thanks. Sounds good to me." It made a world of difference because she took a moment to pause and prepare me to listen. Women in general are very unaware of how a few simple words can make a huge difference for men.

> Women in general are very unaware of how a few
> simple words can make a huge difference for men.

It Sounds Worse Than It Is

Another time in the middle of a difficult conversation she said, "I know this must be hard for you. I just need to talk about it. It sounds a lot worse than it is. It really isn't a big deal to me. I just want you to know what goes on inside me."

Those words, "It sounds a lot worse than it is" or "It really isn't a big deal," were like honey to a bee. Although a man should never say to a woman "It's not such a big deal," if a woman feels safe to share her feelings, and if she feels that he makes her feelings a big deal, then she can comfortably say "It's not such a big deal."

For many women, this saying of "It's not such a big deal" would be counterproductive, particularly if while growing up they repeatedly got the message that their feelings were not a big deal. However, as an adult, when she experiences her feelings being respected and considered, then it becomes easier to make the kind of comments that assist a man in listening.

> Although a man should never say to a woman "It's
> not such a big deal," if a woman feels safe in sharing
> her feelings, and if she feels he makes her feelings a
> big deal, then she can comfortably say "It's not such
> a big deal."

As a woman begins to understand men she realizes that a man will make her feelings much more important if she doesn't demand it. By preparing a man by saying "It's not really a big deal. I just want you to consider how I feel," he will listen much more attentively than before.

At other times when a woman wants to initiate conversation, a good technique to use to prepare the man to listen is to say "I have a lot of feelings coming up, and I would like to talk about them. I just want you to know in advance that it sounds worse than it is. I just need to talk for a while and feel that you care. You don't have to say anything or do anything differently." This kind of approach will actually motivate him to think about how he might make changes to support you more.

What to Say When He Resists Listening

When a woman senses in advance that a man is going to resist what she is about to say, there are new ways to prepare him so that he can more easily duck and dodge. One woman told me that she just says to her husband, "Thanks for helping me here, I really appreciate your trying to duck and dodge what I'm saying. I know it must be hard to hear."

This is a great advanced relationship skills technique because many times, once a man is acknowledged for doing something difficult, he is happy to accept the job. A woman commonly takes for granted that a man should listen if he loves her. She doesn't instinctively understand how difficult it is for him to hear negative feedback from the person he cares most about. The expectation that he should easily hear and understand her because he loves her actually makes it harder for him to listen. When, however, she begins to acknowledge the difficulty, he is much more willing to do what it takes to listen.

At work, a man is happy to do a difficult job if he is paid accordingly. If, however, he is asked to take on a more difficult task and is not acknowledged or compensated for it, he begins to feel taken for granted, and as a result resists doing more. Likewise in a relationship, if a man is required to do something difficult, he wants his efforts to be appreciated; otherwise he may feel, "Why bother?" Let's look at a common example.

Pearl and Marty

Frustrated that her husband, Marty, "commonly missed exits," Pearl felt justified in giving him unsolicited advice on how to drive. She had little idea of why this so totally turned him off. She could see his resistance, but she thought it was stupid and childish. So she continued giving driving instructions, and he continued hating it.

After taking one of my seminars, Pearl realized her mistakes. "I understand now that I should just let him drive and learn from his own mistakes," she shared. "I didn't realize before that this is a way I could give him the love he needs. But what about me? What if we are going to my daughter's wedding and we are late because he takes the wrong turns. Can't I ever tell him how to drive?"

The answer to her question is yes. Pearl can give him advice, but extremely sparingly and only in situations that measure a ten on a scale of one to ten in importance. If she has not been doing it all the time, Marty should be able to take it without getting annoyed.

One way to prepare a man to hear advice at those really important times when you have to give it is to react in a very accepting way at those times when he makes little mistakes.

One way to prepare a man to hear advice at those really important times when you have to give it is to react in a very accepting way at those times when he makes little mistakes.

For example, if your partner misses exits, don't give him driving instructions. Use the incident as an opportunity to prepare him for more important feedback at another time. Try saying nothing, and act as if it is perfectly normal for an extremely brilliant and competent man to be so focused on thinking about something that he forgets the exit. He will not only be very grateful but he will be more open to your suggestions in the future.

In any situation, if a woman can be accepting of a man's little mistakes, when the big ones come along he will be much more willing to hear what she has to say.

Getting to the Church on Time

In response to Pearl's question, I explained that if she was worried on the way to the wedding, the best thing was to warn him in advance in a way that respects his sensitivities. She could say "I know you hate it when I give you directions in the car so I try not to do it, but today, would you mind if I helped navigate? I am so nervous about everything. It would make me feel much better."

When he says yes, she should thank him as if he is doing her a favor. Not only has he been willing to listen, but this kind of support prepares him to more easily hear her comments or advice in the future.

It is as though she is saying "I respect your need to do things on your own, and I don't have the right to invade your sensitivities. I do not expect more from you than you can offer. I appreciate your flexibility in supporting me today."

This kind of consideration gradually opens a man up to hearing a woman's concerns and advice in the future about other things as well. The bottom line is that the more a man feels appreciated and trusted as competent and capable, the more he can openly hear her requests for more.

The more a man feels appreciated and trusted as competent and capable, the more he can openly hear her requests for more.

In my relationship, when we are late or if I am not clear about the directions, I will take it upon myself to set up the situation. I know it will be hard for Bonnie to refrain from giving directions, and the truth is that I could use her help. At those particular times I will say, "It's OK today if you want to help navigate, I would appreciate the help."

What to Say When You Don't Know How to Say It

Many times a woman senses that a man doesn't want to hear her but because she can't come up with a better way to say it, she mis-says it. To overcome his wall of resistance, she applies more force, and generally builds up her own sense of entitlement by remembering all the other times that he didn't listen. She forges ahead regardless of his resistance.

It is as if she has to say to herself, "I don't care if he doesn't want to listen. I have to tell him." This kind of aggressive assertiveness does not build bridges but usually turns him off and ensures his greater resistance in the future.

When a woman doesn't know how to say what she wants to say in a way that would be easy for a man to hear, the most effective technique is to let him know just that. He will appreciate her concern and try to help her. By having his support enlisted in this way, he will be much more accepting of any mistakes she makes and much more understanding of what she is really trying to say.

The most difficult female attitude for a man to cope with is the expectation that he should listen without getting bent out of shape by what he hears. If she senses that it will be hard for him to hear, she can start by immediately letting him know it. She could say, "There is something I'd like to talk about but I'm not sure I know how to say it. I am still in the process of working it out. I certainly don't want it to sound like criticism or blame, but I would also feel really supported if you knew what I was feeling. Would you take a few minutes to listen?"

By letting him know what he's in for, in advance, she says, in effect, that she knows it will be hard to hear and she doesn't mean it to be that way. Just this consideration makes it so much easier for him to hear her and try to explore what she is saying in "Female" rather than reacting to how it sounds in "Male."

You Don't Have to Change Your Mind

I remember once my stepdaughter Julie skillfully using an advanced communication technique when she was sixteen years old. I was very impressed. Bonnie and I had decided to take a three-day vacation while some work was being done on our house. For various reasons, Julie didn't want to go, but she also didn't want to stay in the middle of remodeling.

She said to me, "I have a lot of stay-home feelings about this and would like you just to listen. You don't have to change your mind, I just want you to consider my point of view." She then proceeded to tell me that she didn't like remodeling and wished we would do it in the future at a time when she could also be away from the house. As she shared her feelings, she became more emotional about it and then felt much better. I remember how much easier it was to hear her feelings because she had simply prepared me with the statement "You don't have to change your mind."

That one phrase set me free to listen. The result of that conversation was that in the future I was much more sensitive to her requests and made sure that we never left her at home with the remodeling again. It also made me more considerate in general.

This is the amazing thing about men. If they are approached in the wrong way, they get defensive and push away a woman's feelings and needs. Yet, in a positive sense, when a man is approached or prepared in a way that helps him to be support- ive, he is then much more considerate in general about every- thing.

It's Not Your Fault

The more a woman practices preparing a man, the less she will need to prepare him in the future. Each successful interaction assists a man in ducking and dodging more effectively the next time. As with the acquisition of any new skill, it is wise to begin with easy problems and then, as the skill increases, graduate to difficult ones. A woman's start-up assistance makes it much easier for a man.

Just as men need assistance in learning to duck and dodge, so women sometimes forget to pause and prepare. At such times a woman must remember that it is never too late to correct things. If a woman notices that her man is having a hard time or is getting frustrated or angry, she can then and there apply some pausing and preparing techniques.

She could say "It makes sense to me that you feel. . . ." These words are very validating to him and will help him cool off. Another major reason men get upset when listening is that they feel blamed. To help him dodge, just a few words can make a world of difference. I remember many conversations with Bonnie when she just said a few words and it allowed me to relax and listen instead of defend and fight.

Right in the middle of a conversation, when she sensed that I was getting bruised by her words, she paused and said, "I know this is probably sounding like blame. I don't want to blame you. You don't deserve that. I just need to talk about these feelings. I know there is another side to this. Let me first work through my feelings and then I will be able to appreciate your side of it."

After a few minutes, she started saying things like "I can see that you really didn't mean. . . . I just misunderstood because I thought. . . . I really appreciate your not getting too upset about this."

When she finished, I really didn't need to say much in my own defense. I just said, "Well, I understand why you were upset, and I am glad we had this conversation." Even though at a gut level I hated having to listen to what sounded like blame, from a heart and head level of my being I knew that conversations like this were an important part of keeping the passion alive in a relationship.

You Don't Have to Say Anything

Probably the most potent and powerful phrase a woman can say to prepare a man to listen is: "You don't have to say anything." This message is important because it lets a man off the hook of needing to defend himself. In addition, it gently reminds him that he doesn't have to solve her problems.

A woman would generally not think of this because with other women it would be rude to say "You don't have to say anything." When one woman talks in "Female," tradition commands that it will next be the other person's turn to talk; the unspoken agreement is that if I listen to you talk for five minutes, you must listen to me for five minutes.

With a man it is different. If she says "You don't have to say anything," it is not rude—quite the contrary, he will be relieved. It is an easy job description.

"You're Not Listening"

Another common expression women use that is a complete turn-off for men is: "You're not listening." When a woman uses this phrase, it frustrates a man because he usually *is* listening in some way, or at least trying to. Even if he wasn't, it is hard for him to hear it because in childhood it was used repeatedly by his mother when she was upset with him.

Hearing it in adulthood, a man feels as if his mate is talking down to him and treating him like a child. He hears it as not only "degrading" but very "controlling." Just as a woman doesn't want to mother a man, a man does not want to be mothered. He feels she is blaming him when she is really just trying to be heard.

When a woman says "You're not listening," it is generally because a man is not giving her his full attention. He is hearing her with only part of his mind when she wants his full attention. To say "You're not listening" doesn't convey the correct message, which is "You are not giving me your full attention."

To say "You're not listening" doesn't convey the correct message, which is "You are not giving me your full attention."

To a man, there is a world of difference between these two statements. He can't argue with the second message, but the first only pushes him farther away.

When a man is half-listening, distracted, or looking away while she is talking, women quite commonly communicate the message that he is not listening by raising their voices. Getting louder for a woman is another way of saying "You're not listening." The result, however, is the same; in the end he will listen less. Yelling at children also programs them to not listen.

Getting louder for a woman is another way of saying "You're not listening."

Negative critical feedback just doesn't work. For most women, the only other option is to get upset and walk away. Although her options seem bleak, there is hope. By learning to pause and prepare a man, a woman can immediately begin getting the results she wants. Let's look at an example.

The Thirty-Second Attention Span

Many times, when a woman talks about her day, a man will focus on her for a moment, realize that she is going to talk for a while, and then pick up a magazine and begin reading it until she "gets to the point." If he is watching TV, he will listen for a few moments and then shift back to watching TV.

At the most, he will listen for about thirty seconds and then, when he experiences that she is not talking in a linear fashion, he automatically finds another focus for his masculine side. The news is great for focusing, since in the first paragraph of each article he gets the bottom line of who, what, where, when, how, and why.

In my seminars, I commonly ask how many women have experienced a man picking up a magazine to read soon after she begins to talk. Almost all the hands go up. I do this so that the women in the room can see that it is not just *their* husband who "doesn't listen."

Martha was one of those women. Her husband didn't take the course, but by learning at the seminar how to prepare a man to listen, she experienced an immediate and dramatic change. She was able to break through the thirty-second attention span and began getting his full attention.

Martha, Robert, and the TV

Martha and Robert had been married for nine years. Quite commonly, when she talked he would briefly focus on her and then continue watching TV. Her reaction was to keep talking and then after a while get furious with him and complain that he didn't listen to her. Although this approach is certainly instinctive on her part, it doesn't work.

For years this pattern repeated itself. Even though Martha complained, Robert would still watch TV while she talked. If the TV wasn't on, he would pick up a magazine and read it while she was talking. Like many thousands of women, Martha was definitely not getting the support she most needed.

Robert didn't give her his full attention because he didn't feel the same need to talk about his day with someone giving him their full attention. It is not that he wasn't interested in *her*, it was that he wasn't interested in the details of her day.

To him, the details were unimportant unless they were directly related to some point. Men are used to organizing details in a logical manner to make a point or to figure out a solution. When a woman talks just to relax and connect with her partner, she commonly uses details that are not necessarily related to any point or solution. She is talking to share an experience, not fix it. When he recognized that she wasn't going to get to a point, he would then look back to the TV or pick up a magazine to find a point to focus on.

A man needs to have a goal or a focal point. At those times when a woman is sharing feelings, a man's mind begins to tense up while trying to find the point. When he realizes that it's going to be a while before she gets to her point, he relaxes his mind by focusing on a newspaper, magazine, or TV. He is generally not trying to be rude. Many times, he doesn't even know that he is doing it.

A man needs to have a goal or a focal point. At those times when a woman is sharing feelings, a man's mind begins to tense up while trying to find the point.

He Thinks He Is Listening

When a woman talks and a man looks away, he still believes he is listening. There is still a part of his mind following her words for when she gets to the point and his response is called for. In a sense, he is waiting for his turn to "do something." A small part of him is paying attention, scanning what she is saying for any problems that may require his full attention to solve. When she says he is not listening, it doesn't make sense to him because he knows that it's not completely true.

As long as she complains that he is not listening, he will never hear her actual message. What she is really saying is, "When you watch TV, I don't feel that I have your full attention. If you give it to me and turn off the TV, it will help me get this out much faster and it will feel very good." This is a message that a man can hear and understand. It also gives him a focus or reason to listen. Men don't realize how important and soothing their attention is to a woman.

Men don't realize how important and soothing their attention is to a woman.

When a woman doesn't understand the way a man thinks and talks, she mistakenly assumes that he doesn't care about her. Martha was ready to end her marriage because she had become convinced that TV was more important to Robert than she was. When he picked up a magazine as she talked, she thought he hated her.

Quite commonly, they would argue about whether he was really listening or not.

She said, "You're not listening."

He said, "I am listening."

She said, "You can't listen and watch the TV at the same time."

He said, "How do you know what I can do?"

She said, "Well, I know I can't talk to you."

He said, "Look, I'm watching TV now, and I am hearing everything you are saying. I can repeat back everything you have said."

She said, "I knew it, I can't talk with you."

Various versions of this same argument went on for years until Martha tried a different approach.

A New Approach

The next time Robert picked up a magazine, instead of complaining or storming off in frustration Martha practiced a new skill. She paused from talking and looked *with* him at his magazine. After thirty seconds, he noticed that she had stopped talking. By pausing, she got his attention, and he remembered that she was talking.

Then she said, "Thanks, I really appreciate it when you give me your full attention. This will only take about three more minutes. Is that OK for you?"

After talking for about three minutes, she then thanked him for giving her his full attention. Instead of fighting about who was wrong, Martha got what she wanted. Robert started giving her his full attention when she spoke. Whenever he'd forget, she knew just what to do to get it back.

By gradually experiencing how much Martha appreciated and thrived on his full attention, Robert was instinctively motivated to give her his full attention when she talked.

When a woman wants a man to listen, it is important to make sure that he feels there will be closure. He needs to know what is required of him, how long it will take, and what he will get in return.

In this case, Martha let him know in positive and clear terms that she needed his full attention (not just for him to listen). She let him know it would only take three minutes, and when she was done, she let him know how much she appreciated it.

Three minutes is a good starting-out time for a man to practice building up his emotional support muscles. As he can do that, then she can begin to go on for longer and longer periods of time. Gradually, Martha would increase the time of her sharing.

When she noticed him starting to get frustrated, she would again pause and prepare him to listen by saying, "It will only be another three minutes and I'll be done." This kind of support for him ensured that he gradually learned how to support her. If she had more to say, then she used another advanced skill. She "postponed" sharing her feelings for another time.

A Woman's Lifeline

Good communication is a modern woman's lifeline. Without it, she loses touch with her ability to feel the love in her heart and receive the loving support of others; she loses her ability to feel warm, tender, and sweet feelings. By learning to support a man in a particular way, she can ensure getting back the support she needs to nurture her female side.

To achieve this end, it is important for her to realize that men have never been required to be good listeners of a woman's feelings and that they don't know how. By clearly understanding this fact, it gives her the patience and the awareness to appreciate each step he makes toward her fulfillment.

Women generally feel that if a man loves them, he will want to listen to their feelings. A man doesn't feel this way because sharing feelings is not as important to him and, traditionally, women didn't want to share their feelings with men. When a man loves a woman, it doesn't mean that he will be motivated to initiate conversations, nor will it be any easier for him to listen.

When a man loves a woman, it doesn't mean that he
will be motivated to initiate conversations, nor will it
be any easier for him to listen.

It actually works the other way around. The more a man cares, if he hasn't learned how to duck and dodge it hurts more when he gets hit. When she is unhappy, it is much harder for him to listen without feeling blamed. It is harder because the more he loves her, the more he feels like a failure when she is not feeling loved and supported.

By understanding that a man really needs her support to support her successfully, a woman can then be motivated to help him without feeling as if she is begging for love. This insight that a man could deeply care but also resist her when she starts sharing feelings helps her to take responsibility for communicating in ways that are supportive for her and also for him.

The Importance of Timing

I've already mentioned how vital timing is to good communication. When a man is recuperating from the demands of his workday, it is counterproductive to make more demands on him. Until he becomes proficient in the art of listening, trying to converse when he first comes home feels to him like more work, which he will tend to resist. Even if he is eager, his mind will wander to something less demanding like the TV or a magazine. To fight this innate tendency is useless, but by working with it a woman can get what she needs.

In my book, *Men Are from Mars, Women Are from Venus,* and in chapter 4, I explored in great detail this tendency men have to temporarily pull away from a relationship to recharge and described it as cave time. I first heard this concept from a Native American woman who said that in her tribe, when a woman was married the mother gave her this wise warning: "When a man loves you, at times he will pull away and go to his cave. A woman should never try to follow him or else she will be burned by the dragon. After some time, he will be back and everything will be fine."

Cave time for a man is solitary time when he can most effectively recuperate from the day, forget his problems by staring off into the fire, and gradually connect with his loving feelings and remember what is most important to him. Once he feels better, he automatically comes out of the cave and is available for a relationship.

Cave Busters

To ensure mutually supportive conversations, a woman needs to postpone her immediate needs to share her feelings until her male partner is out of the cave. It is disastrous to initiate a conversation before a man is actually capable of listening and sharing. Through "pausing" in this way and waiting for the right time to share her feelings, a woman can get the support she most needs.

One woman in my seminar shared that she was a cave buster. She would use dynamite to get in his cave, only to find that her husband would dig deeper and deeper tunnels. Without an understanding that her husband needed solitary time, trying to get closer only pushed him farther away.

When a man can't take the time he needs for himself, it is extremely difficult for him to find the loving feelings that originally attracted him to his partner. In a similar way, when a woman doesn't get the chance to share her feelings and connect with her female side, she, as well, loses touch with her deep, loving feelings.

Understanding the Cave

Most women do not understand the cave, nor do they recognize when a man is out. A woman is easily frustrated because she feels the need to talk but doesn't know how long it will take before he comes out. She wants him to come out, but she doesn't know what she can do to help. This uncertainty makes her need to talk even more urgent.

Men in relationships experience a similar frustration when women talk about problems. A man doesn't know how long she will talk before she feels better. He is afraid she will never be happy. It is hard for a man to figure out when she wants his advice or when she just wants to talk.

In a similar way, it is hard for a woman to understand if he is watching TV because there is nothing else to do or if he is in his cave and is not open to having a conversation. To solve these common problems, we not only need to understand our differences but must learn new skills for getting what we need.

> A man's frustration in trying to figure out when he is expected to solve her problems and when he is supposed to just listen is similar to a woman's frustration with figuring out when a man is in his cave and when he is not.

The Need for Clear Signals

A woman needs clear communication signals to know when a man is open and when he is closed in the same way that a man needs to know when she is open to solutions and when she just needs to be heard.

Just as it is hard for a man to trust that a woman will feel better again after sharing negative feelings, it is equally difficult for a woman to trust that a man loves her when he pulls away and ignores her.

To pause before talking or making requests of a man, a woman needs to first know if he is in the cave. If he is not available, she needs to postpone getting her needs met by him. If she can support him in this way, not only will he spend less time in the cave, he will be much more loving when he is out of the cave.

Through persisting in this process of not trying to change him but instead trying to assist him in being successful in supporting her, a woman can dramatically improve her relationship.

When a man is in his cave, it is the time for a woman to be less demanding of him. This nondemanding and trusting attitude is very attractive to a man, and will definitely shorten cave time.

When Is a Man Out of His Cave?

Even when a woman begins to understand a man's need to be in the cave, it is still difficult to tell when he is out. Women persistently ask me, "How do I know when it is a good time to talk? How do I know when he is in the cave?"

My favorite example to answer this question has to do with my daughter Lauren. One evening when she was seven years old she had attended one of my lectures on the differences between men and women. Although much of the time she was playing in the back, she had actually taken in a lot.

In that lecture I talked about not going into a man's cave. I hadn't thought Lauren was listening, but on the way home she said, "Daddy, you said if you go into a man's cave you get burned by the dragon. Is that why sometimes you get angry at me? Is that just your dragon? Do you still love me?"

I said, "That's right. Sometimes I am in my cave and just need to be alone for a while and then I come out again. Even if sometimes I feel frustrated or angry with you, I still love you very much."

She said, "Thank you, Daddy, I'm sure glad I know about the cave."

The next day she came up to me while I was reading the newspaper and said, "Daddy, are you in your cave? I don't want to bother you if you are 'cause I don't want to be burned by the dragon." I told her that I was in the cave, but soon I would be out.

She then said, "Would you let me know when you are out, because I want to tell you about my day."

When I finished reading the paper, I then easily remembered to find my daughter and ask her about her day.

Simple Answers but Difficult to Practice

Sometimes the answer to the most complex problems can be right before our eyes. Volumes of books have been written trying to answer the question of how to get a man to open up and yet, given the right understanding, a little child could find the answer.

The way to tell if a man is in his cave is simply to ask. Although it sounds simple, it does take a lot of practice not to feel rejected if he doesn't want to talk. It is hard for a woman to ask because instinctively it is a shock to her when a man doesn't want to talk.

**The way to tell if a man is in his cave is
simply to ask.**

This is because when she loves a man and feels safe to share her feelings, then after a long day she looks forward to sharing and talking with him. When she wants to talk and he doesn't, it is embarrassing. It feels as though she loves him more than he loves her.

Initiating Sex Versus Initiating Conversation

A way for a man to understand a woman's sensitivity to this issue is to compare it to a man's sensitivity on the issue of sex. If he is turned on to her and she is not even interested in having sex, it can be very embarrassing to him.

When a man deeply loves a woman, one of the most potent ways he can feel her love is during sex. During arousal he is most sensitive to receiving and giving love. To be rejected when he is aroused is generally the most difficult challenge for him to handle in a relationship.

Every man who has passionately loved a woman knows how

painful it is to love her and want to make love to her and then feel rejected sexually. If he then continues to initiate sex and his partner is repeatedly not in the mood, he then automatically stops feeling his desire for sex with her.

Why Men Lose Interest in Sex

He may not even know why he is not so interested in sex anymore. The thought of sex may just make him tired. This fatigue sets in because he is suppressing his sexual drive. It takes up a lot of energy to suppress one's sexual feelings. When a man is repeatedly rejected, it happens automatically.

In a similar way, when a woman feels rejected because a man doesn't want to talk, she loses touch with the tender part of her femininity that wants to talk and share. The opportunity to talk may sometimes just make her feel more exhausted or more overwhelmed. The energy it takes to suppress her female side wears her out.

With this understanding, a man is much more motivated to make it safe for her to talk. Without this awareness, a man can't be sensitive to the ways in which he may be hurting her.

Although a woman needs to understand and accept a man's need for the cave, he can, however, be sensitive to her feelings about it. By making it clear to her when he is in and when he is out, it makes it much easier for her to handle.

In a similar way, to keep the passion alive in her man, a woman needs to give him clear signals about when she is in the mood for sex and when she is not. This information is extremely helpful to a man.

Signals That He Is Out of the Cave

The way a man can help a woman know when he is out of the cave is to give her clear signals in a language that she will understand. Touching a woman in a nonsexual but affectionate way is probably the most effective and simple way to signal that he is out of the cave.

When I am out of the cave and available for conversation, I search out my wife and touch her in some affectionate way or offer to give her a hug. This clear signal tells her for sure that I am approachable.

This certainty regarding when I am available and when I am not makes a world of difference for her. She does not have to worry or try to figure out my moods. She does not have to try to get me out of the cave or watch for when I am.

When a man is out of the cave, it is even more helpful for her to recognize it if he initiates a conversation. This does not mean that he has to talk much. It means that he briefly communicates the message that he is out and is open to hearing her. This is best done by simply asking her a question about her day.

Initiating a conversation is particularly helpful because women today are many times so much in their male sides that they don't even know they need to talk until they are asked. Particularly if she has been burned in the past while sharing her feelings she will not consciously feel the need to talk. With a clear signal from her mate initiating the conversation, she does not have to fear his lack of interest in what she has to share.

> With a clear signal from her mate initiating the conversation, she does not have to fear his lack of interest in what she has to share.

Pausing to Postpone Sharing Feelings

A woman has to work hard at not reacting in a way that says to a man that he is a bad boy and that he is not making "Mommy" happy. These kinds of messages can be very destructive to him. To succeed in supporting him, she is required to nurture him with an accepting love and not be a mother trying to teach him how to be "good."

Even if these messages are her true feelings, when he is on his way to the cave it is not the time to share those feelings. To accomplish this feat she needs to practice "postponing" her feelings until she has a more receptive listener.

These kinds of feelings are a negative influence on him and are best shared with a woman friend. Through putting off giving a negative message she ensures that he will come back sooner. It is much easier for her to give him this support when she clearly knows when he is in the cave and that he will come out of his own accord.

If I am in a bad mood and needing cave time, quite commonly I will generally go for a drive. All I need to say is, "I need to go for a drive," and my wife understands that I am in my cave. My car is actually black with a black interior. To me, it feels like a moving cave.

If I am watching TV and I am in my cave, then I will scan the channels with my remote control at the commercial breaks. If I am open and receptive to her, then at the commercials I put the TV on mute and talk with her.

Generally speaking, when a man does something that a woman thinks is a waste of time or is unproductive, he is in his cave. It could be fiddling with his computer or fiddling with an old car in the garage. For some men, their cave is the workshop in the garage, a walk over the hill, a jog around the neighborhood, a workout at the gym, or going to a movie.

Generally speaking, when a man does something that a woman thinks is a waste of time or is unproductive, he is in his cave.

How to Ask a Man to Talk

Unless a man understands the importance of making clear signals that he is in the cave, a woman must depend on herself to figure it out. Even if a man knows the importance of giving signals, he will inevitably forget at times to use them. This being the case, it is essential for women to be skilled in checking out when he is in the cave and when he is not.

Just as a man can test to see how upset a woman is by gently touching her and asking her if she needs to talk, a woman can test a man by asking him a few simple questions.

Just as a man can test to see how upset a woman is by gently touching her and asking her if she needs to talk, a woman can test a man by asking him a few simple questions.

When a woman wants to talk, instead of assuming that a man is immediately available she needs to first "pause" and then approach him to see if it is the right time for him. She can "check it out" in a variety of ways.

She can do what she normally does but with a new twist. When a woman wants to talk, she generally asks the other person questions. By asking a man questions about his day she can quickly tell if he is in the mood to talk.

If she says "How was your day?," when he gives a short answer like OK or fine, it's a clear signal that he is in his cave or that he is open to having a conversation but would prefer that she talk more.

She can then say "Is this a good time to talk, or would you like to do it later?"

If he is not deep in his cave, he will generally say "This is a good time." Although he may still feel some resistance, it is not because he is in his cave or because he doesn't care, but because he doesn't have much to say. Don't be disappointed if he doesn't say "Oh, thanks for asking, I would love to talk."

If he is hesitant but clearly says "Not right now," then she can say "OK, I'll check back later. How about twenty minutes?"

Generally speaking, that should be enough time. If, however, he needs more time, then it is important to be prepared to accept what he needs. The more gracious and nondemanding she is, the more he will think about taking the time to talk.

Healthy Expectations

This situation is similar to when a man reaches out and gently touches his wife; he cannot expect that she should always receive his touch with a warm, loving response. If she pulls back and he doesn't react with anger but dodges and remains open to her, then she is much more willing to open up to him.

In a like manner, the more space or acceptance a woman can give a man while letting him know that she is looking forward to talking, the more open and willing he will be to make the time to talk.

The Unspoken Rules for Communicating

If a woman wants to talk with someone, she generally waits for her turn. It is her way of being polite. She either listens for a while and then begins to talk, or waits until the other person asks her about her day.

These unspoken rules are foreign to most men. If a woman waits for her mate to talk first, she may never get the chance to talk because he doesn't automatically have a lot to say.

A man's unspoken rules are that if you have something to say, say it. He doesn't feel the need to wait to be asked. If he wants to talk, he talks. When he asks questions, he rarely has the expectation that she is supposed to ask questions back about him.

When a woman asks him questions and he does talk, he thinks he is pleasing her by answering her questions and doesn't even have a clue that after talking for a while he is supposed to take turns and ask her questions.

> **Men don't have a clue that after talking for a while they are supposed to take turns and ask women questions.**

Even if a man has learned that a woman wants him to ask her questions about her day, he will tend to forget. When she is asking him questions, he is so busy thinking of what to say that it is hard for him to remember to ask her about her day.

If a man gives short answers, a woman does not need to wait until he has had his turn. He doesn't mind if she begins talking about her day. It would not be rude to him if she began talking about her own day without first listening to him.

Men Who Talk Too Much

A single woman at one of my relationship seminars asked this question. She said, "You say men don't want to talk. My experience is with men who talk too much and don't listen to what I have to say. How do I get them to listen?"

I asked her if she herself was a good listener. She very proudly said yes. I then asked if *she* asked lots of questions. She again proudly said yes.

She then said, "I do all the right things, but they still don't listen to me."

I said, "You are doing all the right things to get a woman to listen, but not a man. If you want a man to stop talking and listen more, then you have to stop asking him questions."

The more a man has to think about answering questions, the less he will think about her or pause to let her talk.

To get a man's full attention, this woman first needed to stop asking more questions. Then, when he paused, she should say something like this: "That makes sense to me because . . ."

With this kind of lead-in phrase, a woman can get any man's attention. Men love to be acknowledged for making sense. These three simple words, "That makes sense," are so soothing to a man that he will immediately stop talking and listen to what she has to say.

Letting Him Off the Hook

The most effective way to get a man's full attention is to "prepare" him for the conversation by letting him off the hook of needing to talk more. By letting him know in advance that he doesn't have to talk, he can relax and listen instead of figuring out what to say. After all, she is the one who wants to talk.

This is a very important awareness. A man can be out of the cave and be open to conversation but not have anything to say. Instinctively, he doesn't feel the need to initiate conversation. When a woman senses that he doesn't have anything to say, she feels awkward talking more or asking him to listen as I have suggested.

It feels rude to her to say something like "Well, even if you don't feel like talking, I have a lot to say. Would you listen to me? You don't have to say anything." She doesn't know that to him this is not rudeness. It is directness, and it is not demanding. Men love this kind of support.

By being prepared in this way, a man doesn't need to resist the listening process because it is clearly stated that he doesn't have to say anything.

Why Women Don't Initiate Conversations

There are actually many times when a man is out of the cave and available to have a conversation but is waiting for a woman to initiate the conversation. She may not know this because at other times when he was in the cave, she tried conversations only to find that getting him to talk was like pulling teeth.

After a few futile stabs at conversations, many women give up without even knowing it. They actually believe that they have nothing to say and don't want to talk. When they get home, they go to their caves as well.

These women do not realize that they are missing out on the thing that can bring them the greatest happiness. Life has taught them that it is foolish to try and share feelings with a man. But with advanced relationship skills and a new job description, they can get the support and respect that they require in order to risk sharing their feminine feelings.

Still other women know that they are missing out, but blame the men for not wanting to talk. Their mothers did not teach them about the cave. The worst thing a woman can do is to blame a man for not wanting to talk. It would be like a man blaming a woman for talking too much. Neither approach is valid or productive.

To ensure good communication, a woman needs to understand her needs and persist in creating opportunities to get the attention and understanding that she needs from her partner. Using advanced relationship skills makes this a possibility even if her partner doesn't read this book.

> **A woman needs to understand her needs and persist in creating opportunities to get the attention and understanding she needs from her partner.**

Advanced Communication Skills

To ensure the best communication in a relationship, both men and women can begin applying new skills. An easy way for women to remember what is required of them is to remember the four P's: pausing, preparing, postponing, and persisting. In a similar way, men can remember the four D's: ducking, dodging, disarming, and delivering. A relationship will be easiest when both are doing their best. Without these insights, relationships are much more difficult than they need to be.

Even when a woman's husband or boyfriend has not read this book, by applying these skills she will begin to get so much more. Through applying these four skills over time, she will learn to talk in ways that are natural for her but that will also motivate him to listen and support more. This summary of the four P's can be helpful for a woman to remember what the basics are for getting the support she needs.

1. Pause
   A. Check it out. Ask him if this is a good time.
   B. Don't interrupt him if you know he is in the cave.

2. Prepare
    A. Set a time limit. Tell him how long it will take. When a man doesn't know where the conversation is going, he begins to panic. When he knows there is a time limit, then he can relax.
    B. Give him a clear job description. Tell him that he doesn't have to say anything or make other supportive comments.
    C. Encourage him. Occasionally remind him that he is not being blamed or that you understand it is hard to listen.
    D. Appreciate him. Each time when you are finished talking, let him know that you really appreciate his listening and that you feel much better because of his support.

3. Postpone
    A. When he is in his cave, postpone sharing your needs for another time when he is more available and able to give.
    B. Put off expecting him to do more until he has become proficient in listening more to feelings, then begin to ask for more physical help in small increments.
    C. When you are feeling blame or criticism, talk to someone else first to become more loving and centered and then talk to your partner.

4. Persist
    A. Continue giving him the support he needs to support you. Don't expect him to always remember.
    B. When he resists conversation, persist in asking him to listen even if he has little or nothing to say.
    C. Overcome the tendency to give in and not communicate with him. Patiently persist in practicing these skills.

One of the biggest obstacles to practicing the four skills for women and the four skills for men is not understanding that men and women essentially speak different languages. A man could be growing in his skills slowly but surely, but when he fails to listen or respect her feelings, she feels it is hopeless. In a similar way, a woman will be progressing in supporting her male partner, and then when she forgets to pause and prepare and he feels blamed, he may automatically assume that nothing is working.

Through understanding the different languages we speak it is much easier to recognize that our partners do love us and that they, in their own way, are doing their best. In the next chapter, we will explore a variety of new skills and strategies for translating what women mean when they speak "Female" and what men mean when they speak "Male."

CHAPTER 7

Men Speak "Male" and Women Speak "Female"

It is obvious to a woman when another woman is upset and needs to talk in order to feel better. It is also obvious when her talking has been successful in releasing stress. To men, none of the above is obvious at all. It is as if men and women secretly speak different languages with a whole series of complex and different verbal, physical, and emotional signals. Here's a graphic example:

Bob and Marge: Before

Bob and Marge have been married for six years. They love each other very much but just don't understand this basic difference between men and women. When Marge comes home from work feeling overwhelmed, Bob can tell she's upset.

"Marge, what's wrong?" he asks, trying to be friendly and supportive.

Sighing deeply, she answers, "Everybody wants something from me; I feel like I have to do everything!"

Bob immediately feels frustrated. He is trying to help, but he hears her blaming him for how she feels and begins to get defensive. "What do you mean you do everything? That means I don't do anything?"

"No, I am not saying you do nothing. I am saying I feel like I do everything. That doesn't mean you do nothing. It's just how I feel. Can't I express my feelings without you taking it personally?"

Bob reacts, saying, "Listen, if you say you do everything, then that means I do nothing. If you say everyone wants something from you it means that I want too much from you."

"But I didn't say you wanted too much from me," Marge countered. "I said I felt like everybody wants something from me. I wasn't singling you out. I was just expressing the feeling that I can't be everything to everyone."

Bob, getting angrier, says, "Sure, sure. You do it all. And I do nothing. You know what I think? I think it doesn't even matter what I do. It's never enough. No one could make you happy."

"Why can't I just express my feelings without everything being about you?" Marge demands. "I'm not saying it's your fault. I just want you to let me talk."

"Right," replies Bob sarcastically.

"I knew I couldn't talk to you." Inwardly, Marge is deciding to never again discuss her feelings with Bob.

"You *can* talk to me," Bob calls after her as she storms out of the room. "Just don't be so negative!"

Why We Argue

At this point, Bob feels blamed and unappreciated, while Marge feels even more overwhelmed. As in most arguments between men and women, Bob doesn't understand that Marge just needs to talk about her feelings in order to feel better. Like most men, he makes the mistake of taking her literally and trying to correct her. He has not yet learned the advanced skill of listening without feeling blamed.

Like most women, Marge expects Bob to understand that she wasn't blaming him, and doesn't even realize that there are advanced relationship skills she could apply to prevent him from feeling blamed or unappreciated.

When a man is unskilled in correctly translating what a woman means, it becomes increasingly difficult for him to be a sympathetic listener.

When a man is not skilled in correctly translating what a woman means, it becomes increasingly difficult for him to be a sympathetic listener. He cannot tune in when he feels his efforts are unacknowledged and unappreciated. Although her overwhelming feelings may have little to do with him, he takes them personally.

Instead of understanding what is happening and using an advanced relationship skill to remedy the situation, Marge feels like giving up. Bob's natural resistance to listening to her feelings signals to her that she is not loved and will never get the support she needs. This only compounds the problem and increases her feelings of being overwhelmed and isolated.

Bob and Marge: After

After retraining in advanced relationship skills, Bob has learned to dodge Marge's emotionally charged words and not feel blamed. Marge, in turn, has learned to prepare him for her feelings and thus make it easier for him to dodge the bullets. Now, after much practice, their conversation sounds like this:

"Marge, what's the matter?" Bob asks.

Marge pauses to think about how to prepare him so that he won't feel criticized, then says, "Thanks for asking. (pause) I had a terrible day. (another pause) I just need to talk about it, and then I'm sure I'll feel better, OK?"

"Sure." Bob is now prepared. He knows he really doesn't have to do anything to make her feel better. This allows him to relax and listen without having to think about solving her problems.

"Everyone wants something from me," Marge tells him. "I feel like I do everything." Once Marge has set the stage and prepared Bob, she doesn't need to edit her feelings and can freely express them. Free expression is essential if she is going to let go of her frustrations.

This time Bob is not frustrated because he understands she just needs to talk. He easily dodges the bullets of frustration and simply listens. When she pauses, he invites her to say more with a warm, sympathetic "Hmmm."

"Today," Marge tells him, "I was supposed to finish the books when Richard called. He still hasn't paid his bills, so I had to go to the bank and make a wire transfer."

"Humph!" Bob responds with empathetic annoyance.

"And," Marge goes on, "there was so much traffic. It didn't used to be that way. Everything's happening too fast. There's too much to do for too many people and no time. Everybody's rushing. It's crazy out there!"

Bob shakes his head in agreement.

"And," she tells him, "when I finally got back to work, there were fifteen—fifteen!—messages on my voice mail. I just don't have the time to run around doing errands for everyone."

"Hummp!" Bob validates her irritation.

"I mean, I handled them but . . . it's just all too much."

"It's awful," Bob exclaims, moving closer to her. "Marge, you give so much of yourself. Let me give you a hug."

After the hug, Marge takes a deep breath as if she just let go of a heavy weight and exhales slowly. "I really needed that! I am so glad to be home. Thanks for listening." Marge is careful to acknowledge his help.

Throughout their conversation, Bob remembers not to minimize or argue with her overwhelmed feelings. Instead, he skillfully supports her by focusing on her female side and not keeping her in her workday male mode by trying to help her resolve her problems. To the best of his ability, he is trying to talk her language.

The Benefits of Improving Communication

Through updating and improving their communication skills, Bob and Marge not only avoided arguments but were able to solve the real problems: Marge feeling overwhelmed and over-worked, and Bob feeling defeated and unappreciated. With a basic grasp of "Female," Bob was able to nurture Marge's female side, while Marge was able to appreciate Bob more.

Marge was able to release her overwhelming feelings by being able to talk about them in an uninhibited manner, in "Female." Bob was able to feel appreciated because he had pro-vided Marge with the emotional safety and support that she needed in order to feel better.

Although Bob was not his family's sole provider, he could still feel needed and appreciated in his new role as a skilled lis-tener. Although Marge was not happy and fulfilled when she got home, she was happy to see Bob, and soon after their con-versation she was much happier and very appreciative of him. Without focusing on solutions to her problems at work and at home, Marge was able to release her feeling of panic and begin to return to her female side.

Most couples today are not fluent in each other's language. When they talk, they experience increasing frustration instead of fulfillment. The relationship becomes another of the woman's burdens rather than a way to find release from them. For the man, the relationship increasingly signals his defeat rather than giving meaning to his life.

> Quite commonly the relationship becomes another of the woman's burdens rather than a way to find release from them. For the man, the relationship increasingly signals his defeat rather than giving meaning to his life.

When we consider these new stresses on relationships and family life, and the absence of traditional support systems, it is no wonder that it's so hard to stay together and it explains why millions choose to be single. Neither sex is being nurtured and supported in the ways that matter most because they are speaking different languages.

> Today, neither sex is being nurtured and supported in the ways that matter most because they are speaking different languages.

Breaking the Language Barrier

As we've discussed, it no longer has to be that way. For instance, male frustration could be helped if at the end of an emotional talk, women could say any combination of the following:

"Thanks so much for listening."
"I just needed to get that out."
"I'm sorry it was difficult for you to hear."
"You can forget everything I just said."
"It doesn't matter as much now."
"I feel much better."
"Thanks for helping me sort this out and letting me talk."
"This conversation has been really helpful for me to get a better perspective on things."
"I feel so much better now, thanks for listening."
"Wow, I sure had a lot to say. I feel so much better."
"I feel so much better. Sometimes I just need to talk about things and then my mood changes."
"I appreciate your patience in helping me to sort things out through talking."

Any of these comments would be heaven to a man and would make him feel warmly appreciated. This is because in "Male," his native language, they have a special and positive significance.

What's Obvious to Her Is Not Obvious to Him and Vice Versa

When a woman says in a friendly tone, "It's OK," or "It's no big deal," or "It's all right," or even "Forget it," to a man, it makes it easier in the future for him to listen. It also makes him remember what he did to upset her and try in the future to make things better.

When a man begins to see how willing a woman is to forget the things that upset her, his tendency is to remember more and be more considerate in the future.

When a woman says, "Thanks for listening. I know it was difficult to sit through," a man tells himself in "Male," "It was tough, but I can handle it!" The next time she is upset, he will be much more willing to listen because he's confident he can cope, and he knows he will be appreciated.

When, after sharing her feelings, a woman dispenses with her feelings by saying, "Now that it's out, it doesn't matter as much," his "Male" reaction is, "That's sweet of her to say, but I know how much it mattered to her. Next time, I'll try to be more sensitive."

When Women Can't Talk "Female"

For a woman to restrict herself by only talking the way a man does goes against her instincts. It eventually prevents her from coping successfully with stress and disconnects her from the warm, open, loving, and feminine feelings that allow her to trust, accept, and appreciate life.

> For a woman to restrict herself by only talking the way a man does goes against the grain of centuries of woman-to-woman support and eventually prevents her from successfully coping with stress.

It is very helpful for men to remember that women are instinctually suited to communicate as a means of sorting out their thoughts, clarifying their priorities, and exploring their feelings. As we have discussed, this is because early on in history women learned to cope with life's problems through talking all day and into the evening with other women. A woman's security was assured through talking and forming alliances and friendships. Just the act itself of talking brings up an instinctual feeling of security.

With this increased security, she begins to think more clearly and can sort things out much more effectively and in a loving way. In a very real sense, talking for women is like a pump that generates greater clarity. Without the opportunity to share freely, something very important to women is lost. Through helping her to speak "female," he gives a precious gift.

> **Without the opportunity to share freely, something very important to women is lost.**

Why Men Don't Talk

For a man, it is the opposite. Silently achieving a goal generates an instinctual feeling of security. While doing seemingly meaningless tasks, like waxing the car or driving a golf ball, a man can silently sort out his thoughts and concerns; he can clarify his values and priorities as well as develop a plan of action.

He can forget the stresses of his day and begin to relax back into the joys of his relationship and the comforts of his home. This silent inner process gives him a sense of security.

A hunter's survival and security were ensured by moving quietly, and then successfully achieving his goal. Hunters spoke "Male," a language of few words. Silence is a man's birthright.

When a woman feels free to talk, she feels greater security. Sharing about her problems and feelings is an automatic and natural expression of the way her brain processes information, and the way her nurturer/ancestors survived. Nurturers spoke "Female," a language with an infinite vocabulary. Talking is a woman's birthright.

Through understanding this crucial difference, men and women can more lovingly and effectively support each other.

Silence is a man's birthright, while talking is a woman's. Through understanding this essential difference, men and women can more lovingly and effectively support each other.

How Men React to Feelings

When a woman says she needs to talk, most men feel that they are being told they are doing something wrong. When she talks about problems, a man mistakenly assumes that he has failed her and that she will never be happy. When she wants to talk about the relationship, he does not know that she is just trying to find her female self again. He thinks she is only trying to criticize or change him.

That is because he is hearing her remarks in "Male," while she is speaking "Female." Their lines of communication have completely broken down.

A man who misunderstands "Female" reacts in one of three basic ways:

1. He offers a solution. Men don't realize that many times women don't want solutions when they are upset. A woman may just want her partner to listen and be sympathetic, but if he can't be, he should at least listen and not interrupt. Even making a sound like "hmmm" will signal to her that he is considering what she is saying and is trying to understand her.

2. He minimizes her problems. By minimizing the problem, he thinks that it will make her feel better. What he doesn't know is that she is more concerned with discovering her feelings than with the accuracy of her description. He says things like:

"It's not such a big deal."
"We don't need to talk about this."
"It's not that important."

"So what's the point?"
"Well, there's nothing we can do about it now."
"Just forget it. I'll handle it."

3. **He invalidates her feelings.** He mistakenly thinks he is helping her to analyze and correct her thinking but ends up invalidating her feelings. He does not realize that she sorts things out as she talks. He says things like:

"You shouldn't get so upset."
"That's not exactly what happened."
"Don't worry about it."
"I think you are overreacting."
"We have already talked about this."

Non-Goal-Oriented Talking

When allowed to talk in a nonlinear, non-goal-oriented manner (pure "Female"), a woman can reconnect with her female side and can most effectively cope with the stress of working in a traditionally male role all day. If a man offers advice or tries to help her solve her problems, he is actually holding her in her masculine side, which wants to solve problems. He is demanding that she continue speaking "Male." By allowing a woman to talk about problems without the urgency to solve them, he assists her in moving back toward speaking "Female." By simply responding with empathy, sympathy, and understanding, he nurtures her female side. With this kind of support, she is able to throw off her burdens and release her overwhelming feelings. Gradually, her energy returns, and her heart is full of appreciation and love.

If a woman is able to release her negative feelings in this way and not secretly cling to them, it will also assist a man in being more present in the relationship. When a man initiates a conversation it sometimes is particularly helpful because women today are so much in their male sides that they don't even know they need to talk until they are asked. Particularly if she has been burned in the past while sharing her feelings, she will not consciously feel the need to talk. With the clear signal of a man initiating the conversation, she does not have to fear his lack of interest in what she has to share.

Even when she does feel the need to talk, she sometimes doesn't know where to start. The questions and comments below will help her feel safe in opening up.

Questions to Help Her Open Up When He Is Ready to Listen

A man can assist a woman in opening up and letting her know he is ready to listen by asking any of these questions or making any of these comments:

1. "Did you have a bad day?"
2. "How was your day?"
3. "I'm so glad to see you. Let me give you a hug."
4. "Is there anything I can do for you?"
5. "Tell me about your day."
6. "You look good, did you have a nice day?"
7. "You look like you had a great day."
8. "You look tired . . . "
9. "Are you upset today?"
10. "How are you feeling?"

Each statement conveys the nondemanding message that she is invited to talk briefly or at length. If she fires off a quick answer, he should assist her in saying more by responding with any or all of the following four questions:

1. "What happened?"
2. "Tell me more."
3. "Then what happened?"
4. "How did that feel?" or "How does that feel?"

However, if a woman asks a man any of the ten questions above and he gives a curt reply, she should grant him space. If she needs to talk, she should ask if this is a good time.

Signals That He Can't Listen Right Now

If a man is still too stressed by the pressures of the day to hear her, he must give his female partner clear signals. A way he can communicate that he is not yet ready to hear her is by simply saying any the following phrases:

1. "I need to spend some time alone and then I'll be back."
2. "I need to spend some time doing XYZ and then I'll be back."
3. "I'm in my cave right now. I need to XYZ and then I'll be back."
4. "I'm in my cave right now. When I'm out we can talk."

It is important that a man feel free to make these statements. Any negative message can make it harder for him to come out. Some common messages a woman mistakenly gives verbally or with a look are as follows:

1. "But why now?"
2. "But we haven't spent any time together."
3. "Why can't you be there for me when I need you?"
4. "All you think about is yourself!"
5. "Did I do something wrong?"
6. "How could you leave me now?"
7. "You are spending too much time away."
8. "You don't love me!"
9. "I can't handle this. I feel so abandoned and rejected."
10. "I knew it. You don't really care about me."
11. "But you have already been to the cave this week."

Avoiding any of the above messages can give a man the freedom and support to pull away when he needs to so that he can come back sooner. Many times, after a man has pulled away he wants to come back, but he remembers her negative comment or message and is not sure that he will be welcomed back. Then he has to deal with the problem of whether he has to apologize for pulling away when this is something he needs to do. Having to cope with the fear of her rejection when he comes back definitely prevents him from coming out until it becomes very clear that all is forgotten and forgiven.

Helping a Man Duck and Dodge

During a difficult conversation, there are many little comments or "softeners" that a woman can make to help a man duck and dodge so he can hear her feelings without becoming argumentative. Here are a few examples:

Don't Say:	Do Say:
1. "I strongly feel that . . ."	1. "I am not completely sure about this but I feel like . . ."
2. "I am sure that . . ."	2. "I don't really know if this is true for you, but for me it feels like . . ."
3. "I don't think that's right. I feel like . . ."	3. "It's not that I have this all thought out. It's just a feeling. I feel like . . ."
4. "No, that's not what I mean. I feel like . . ."	4. "I haven't really thought about this, but for this moment I feel like . . ."
5. "I disagree because . . ."	5. "I have another way of looking at it. I feel . . ."
6. "I don't agree at all. I feel . . ."	6. "I don't know what's right, but I feel like . . ."
7. "That's not true! I feel like . . ."	7. "Based on my experience, I feel . . ."

Statements like these assure a man that his mate's words and feelings aren't written in stone. They remind him that the action of sharing feelings is a work in progress. Thus a man can most effectively dodge criticism and avoid taking his partner's momentary emotions as facts.

Each of the above examples is equally useful for a man to apply as well. Many times a man will speak his ideas with such certainty that a woman feels he is not open to hearing her point of view. When a man uses softeners, it helps a woman feel free to share her perspective.

When a Man Withdraws into His Cave

Commonly, when men pull away into their private caves, women mistakenly think that something is wrong and try to pull their mates out. Misreading her mate's needs, the woman thinks he is wasting time and begins to criticize him.

The more women try to get their men to come out of the cave, the longer they will remain in it. A man is able to emerge from the cave only when he has substantially forgotten the problems of his day. When his wife is waiting at the door with more problems, he just won't come out. And it is her resistance to his being in the cave that actually keeps him there.

> The more women try to get their men to come out of the cave, the longer they will remain in it.

Three Steps to Draw a Man Back

To gradually draw a man back to the family is a crucial element of a woman's new job description. Here are the three basic steps they should take:

Step 1. Give him lots of alone time and let him see that you don't mind. Encourage him to spend time with his male friends by not getting upset or feeling hurt when he expresses the desire to do so.

Try to avoid crowding him or being critical. Remember that giving unsolicited advice is generally taken as criticism in the "Male" language. Whenever possible, tell him how much you appreciate his efforts to succeed at work.

If possible, act as if his going into his cave is no big deal. When he returns and begins to be affectionate, be sure to let him know how good it feels.

Step 2. Ask him to do specific little things for you, and express your gratitude when he carries them out. For example, don't complain that he doesn't spend enough time with you. That's an accusation and will put him on the defensive. Instead, ask him to take you to a specific restaurant or movie on a specific day. Don't leave it to him to figure out where and when to go. Make it as easy for him as possible.

Let him repeatedly experience success in fulfilling you. That way, he will gradually associate pleasing you with releasing stress. Eventually, when he wants to de-stress he will begin thinking of little things he can do for you.

Step 3. This third technique is the most important and requires the most skill and practice: at chosen times, ask him to listen to your feelings. At such times be careful not to offend him or give him the impression that he is not doing enough. By preparing him to not feel blamed and appreciating him afterward for listening, you allow him to learn slowly to bring his awareness back to the relationship.

Talk about problems and feelings. If he begins to be frustrated, remind him that you are not asking him to solve your problems and only want him to listen. Without feeling the pressure of problem solving, he will relax and become an increasingly better listener.

Even if a man knows that you are using advanced relationship skills with him, he will still be grateful. Keep in mind that men want to be in relationships. These three steps are just common sense when a woman understands how her partner's needs are different. Just as she needs his support to listen to her feelings so that she can forget her problems, he needs her support to remember what is really important to him.

> Just as a woman needs a man's support to listen to
> her feelings so that she can forget her problems, a
> man needs a woman's support to remember what is
> really important to him.

What to Do When a Man Is Upset

While women directly process their feelings through talking,
men need to do something while silently thinking about their
feelings. Only after first thinking about his feelings will it benefit him to talk about his feelings.

Generally speaking, a man will feel the need to talk mainly
when he thinks it will help convey information to solve a problem. If someone has offended or hurt him, he may feel the urge
to talk to convey that what this person did was wrong and that
they should change. When a man talks while angry, he is generally heavily invested in being right.

> When a man talks while angry, he is generally heavily
> invested in being right.

A man greatly misunderstands when a woman who is upset
wants to talk because he mistakenly believes that she is saying he
is wrong and should change. Why? Because when an emotional
man feels the same need, he *is* blaming and accusing. Men must
learn that when a woman shares feelings, no matter how angry
and accusing she sounds, she is really asking for empathy.

With this new understanding, a woman can appreciate the
wisdom of *not* persisting in trying to draw a man out when he
doesn't want to talk. Not only should she not question him, she
should take special pains to postpone conversation gracefully
even if he *is* willing to talk while emotionally upset.

> Sometimes when a man is angry, a woman should
> take special pains to postpone conversation.

The Wisdom of Postponing Conversations

The old advice that warns couples never to go to bed upset or angry can make a lot of trouble today. When a man is angry, I strongly recommend that a woman give him lots of space and let him sleep on it. Wait till he has cooled off a bit before talking together about what is bothering him.

However, if a woman is upset and a man is centered enough to listen without getting upset, then it is advisable for him to initiate a conversation, ask questions, and draw her out by making it safe for her to talk. The old adage about not going to bed angry was mainly for men to understand about women. A woman didn't need to apply it because when her husband was upset he usually went off to deal with his feelings alone.

Men today are more in touch with their female tendencies, and when they are upset or angry they sometimes want to talk. It is important for women to understand the wisdom of postponing these kinds of conversations, particularly if you have previously had negative and painful arguments. This skill of postponing is another skill your mother could not teach you.

What Do You Say When a Man Is Upset?

If a man is upset and wants to talk, a woman tends to assume that he will calm down through talking. This is true only if she agrees with what he says. Remember, men want to be right when they talk and are upset at the same time. If she is not prepared to agree with what he has to say or at least appreciate his points, then it is important for her to postpone the conversation.

Most women would not consider postponing a man from sharing his feelings because they would not want him to postpone them if he could listen. If a woman postpones another woman, it is rude. If a man can possibly listen and postpones a woman, it is rude. But if a woman feels that she can't agree with or at least appreciate his points when he is angry, then although it may feel rude to him, it is very important that she postpone him.

If a woman feels she can't agree with a man when he is angry or at least appreciate his points, it is crucial for her to postpone talking with him.

How she handles the postponement is very important. She should not be accusatory because it will only inflame him. What she should do is briefly validate his feelings and then postpone discussion. Then, without saying anything else, she should walk away as if what she is doing is perfectly normal and everything is fine. This is an advanced relationship skill which allows him to save face and cool off.

What a Woman Shouldn't Say:	What a Woman Should Say:
1. "I can't talk to you when you're angry."	1. "You have a right to be upset. I need some time before I can talk."
2. "You don't care about me. Why should I talk to you?"	2. "I want to hear your feelings, but I need some time to sort out my own."
3. "You just want to be right! You don't hear what I say."	3. "Let me take some time to appreciate what you said, and then I can talk about it."
4. "You don't understand!"	4. "I need some time to think about what you are saying."
5. "I can't believe the way you are speaking to me!"	5. "I understand that you are upset, and I need some time before I can talk about this."

Women should remember that, unlike themselves, men feel better by taking time to cool off and think

things through. Asking a man questions when he is
upset and angry will tend just to make him angrier.

The Best Time to Talk with a Man

The best time to talk with a man is after he's had a chance to
think about a problem, has released any negative feelings, and
has reconnected with more positive ones. If, after spending
time by himself, he still seems upset, a woman should definitely not press for a discussion. Wait till the next day to ask
him casually if something is going on that he wants to talk
about. If he says "It's nothing," but isn't being warm and loving, the chances are that he needs a little more time to feel
accepted and appreciated for what he does for her before
beginning to come back.

Just as a cold may no longer be contagious but still produces
symptoms, a man may have already resolved his feelings and
solved his problems but needs to be loved and appreciated
before his warm feelings reemerge.

A man may already have made closure with his problems but wants to be loved and appreciated before
his warm feelings reemerge.

Reassuring Sounds

In learning to speak "Female," one of the most supportive
things a man can do is to be an alert listener prepared to offer
simple gestures of support and reassurance. These can be as
basic as a hug, eye contact, an occasional nod of the head, or
sounds from him that translate into calm and soothing coos of
understanding in "Female."

When a woman talks, these are some of the sounds that
make her feel heard by a man. Each sound is accompanied by a
short translation.

He Says:	She Hears:
1. "Hmmm"	1. "I am thinking about that."
2. "Oh"	2. "I am amazed by that. Now I can understand."
3. "Ahhuh" or "Umhuh"	3. "I am following you, I am right here with you, keep going."
4. "Huh"	4. "I think I am getting it, tell me more."
5. "Mmmm"	5. "I am so sorry that happened, I feel really bad about that."
6. "Hunnh"	6. "I can't believe that happened. You don't deserve to be treated that way."
7. "Ooo" (as in *soon*)	7. "I am shocked. That must have really hurt."
8. "Ouch"	8. "I empathize with your pain."
9. "Wow"	9. "Really, that actually happened?"
10. "Auool"	10. "That's too bad, I feel so sorry."
11. "Hmmph"	11. "What they did is wrong; you don't have to put up with it."
12. "Wooo"	12. "That's exciting, how interesting!"

These various sounds should be expressed primarily when she pauses. Practicing them can help a man duck and dodge. Instead of offering solutions when she pauses, he can focus on making a reassuring sound.

If a man is not used to making these kinds of sounds, it may feel very contrived at first. Once he sees that it works, it will, however, gradually become more automatic and natural.

When a Woman Has Strong Feelings

Sometimes when a woman has strong feelings, she talks to discover what her feelings are. If her partner is a good listener and practices ducking and dodging and not interrupting, she can get it all out. By noticing when she is feeling upset, tired, or overwhelmed and then initiating a conversation by asking questions, it can help her a lot.

Here are questions a man can ask to initiate a conversation. They are:

1. "Looks like you've had a long day."
2. "What's the matter?"
3. "What's going on?"
4. "Do we need to talk about something?"
5. "How was your day?"
6. "Are you upset with me?"
7. "Did I do something to bother you?"
8. "Is there something we should talk about?"

In most cases, she will say something like "Oh, it's not you. There is just so much going on," and then continue to talk about it. Even if she was a little upset with him, she will quickly tend to dismiss those feelings because he has initiated the conversation. When she feels supported, she can be very generous with her love. If a woman agrees to talk but is overwhelmed, having trouble getting to her feelings, or directing her negative emotions at him, here are five basic "disarming" questions a man can use to draw her out and deflect her verbal bullets:

1. "How do you feel when . . . ?"
2. "How else do you feel when . . . ?"
3. "Tell me more."
4. "What would feel good to you?"
5. "What do you need to feel supported by me?"

Requests like these impress a woman as supportive. When she doesn't feel the responsibility for initiating conversation, she can much more efficiently move through her feelings.

A Woman's Need for Downtime

After a woman has expressed her feelings, she may not even know exactly what she has said until some minutes later. That's because she is working things through as she is talking. She is in a process. Once she has finished, she then has a chance to look back at what she has shared.

Generally speaking, if a woman is upset and shares her feelings, it takes her about fifteen minutes to reflect on what she said. After such consideration, she begins to appreciate a man's strong support.

However, if a man says something in "Male" (which is bound to be provocative) during that fifteen minutes, it can undo all the good he did. It will be as though he gave a gift and then took it back. And to a woman that is worse than not giving it in the first place.

That fifteen minutes is a very vulnerable time for a woman. It is a time for her to reflect on what she has said. If a man is trying to tell her that she is wrong, or if she feels she has to defend herself, then it is very hard for her to see her mistakes and release any negative feelings she is holding on to.

How Men Learn from Their Mistakes

In a similar way, when a man makes a mistake and a woman is on his case to remind him, he is not free to reflect on his error and plan to learn from it. When a woman corrects a man's behavior, he instinctively moves to defend it by returning to his cave where only "Male" is spoken.

Women generally feel a strong urge to correct a man's behavior. Instinctively, they will offer advice or criticize his decisions or behavior, not knowing that they are preventing him from making the inner adjustments he needs to make.

How We Influence Each Other

When men and women begin to understand their differences in a new and positive light, learn each other's languages, and practice advanced relationship skills, they are able to draw out of their partners the best they have to offer. As a result, both men and women are more fulfilled. A man is greatly fulfilled because he feels successful in supporting his partner, and she feels fulfilled because she has created a relationship in which to grow and thrive. They may still speak different languages, but harmony grows as they begin learning how to correctly translate and convey important messages.

As we have discussed, when a woman can understand a man's behavior and is able to express a greater acceptance of him, over time he begins to change and become more attentive. Her nondemanding attitude draws him out into the relationship like a magnet.

When a man begins to duck and dodge by correctly interpreting his partner's feelings, he is able to listen to her with greater empathy and comprehension. At the most basic level of her being, she feels seen, heard, understood, and supported. Her feminine spirit soars. As a result, she is able to be more loving and accepting of her man. As he increasingly understands her, he quite naturally begins to share more with her.

While these skills may seem unnatural in the beginning, in time they will become very automatic. They are merely the extensions of social and language skills we have already been using for centuries. In the next chapter, you'll understand why men forget things and women remember every detail of men's mistakes.

Why Men Forget and Women Remember

June: "I hate having to nag him to do things, but he says he'll do something and then he doesn't. It's easier just to do it myself. He says he forgets, I say he is just lazy."

Bob: "Every time I start to think things are getting better in our relationship, she gets upset and brings out the laundry list of things that I don't do. It's so frustrating. She never forgets anything."

Bob and June complaints are quite common. One of the major complaints I hear from women in relationships is that they feel forgotten. On the other hand, one of the major complaints I hear from men is that their mates never forget.

Before learning new skills for solving this common pattern, let's first understand it a little better. Once a man gets married, although he loves his partner, quite commonly he begins to focus more on his work. She, however, generally feels ignored and neglected. Once a woman is married, because she feels more secure, she automatically begins to express her feelings more freely. A man generally feels blamed because he does not instinctively understand her need to talk about feelings and the relationship.

Through understanding these different experiences in a new and positive light, many marital complaints can be overcome. A man's predisposition to work outside the home to support his family explains why a woman feels forgotten, and a woman's predisposition to talk about problems to create intimacy explains why men feel nagged and blamed.

With more insight and the application of advanced relationship skills, these natural tendencies can be redirected in ways that will get us the immediate support we need. Without this new information, both men and women, assuming they are not loved, react in negative ways.

To a woman, it seems like a man doesn't care about her when he forgets her or forgets to do things he never forgot to do at the beginning of the relationship. A woman can't readily understand this tendency because when she cares about a man, she doesn't put him second to work. She continues to do the little things, and when she does forget she feels awful.

Likewise, a man can't readily understand this tendency to remember the minute details of a mate's mistakes because when he cares about someone, he works hard at forgetting the incident completely. He feels blamed when she talks again about problems he thought were handled.

> A man feels blamed and defeated when a woman
> remembers, while a woman feels unloved and
> neglected when a man forgets.

What Men Say When Women Remember

These are some more typical comments from men about women who remember their emotional upsets in great detail and persist in talking about them:

Tom: "Ever since I lost money in that investment, whenever I plan to spend money, she brings it up. It makes me want to hide my financial decisions. When we talk about finances, she treats me like I'm incompetent. I want her to give me a break."

Jeffrey: "When I'm driving, she'll tell me to slow down and remind me of my lousy driving record. She just doesn't let up. So what if I have *one* ticket? I don't need another mother."

Bill: "When she's overwhelmed, she isn't just upset about one thing, it's more like everything. She brings out a list of ten to twenty things that haven't been done. Just listening to her makes me feel like giving up."

Gary: "When she gets upset she'll bring up things I did years ago. It just isn't fair. I don't feel like she is reacting to the man I am today. She's still afraid of my anger, and I haven't gotten really angry in years. She just doesn't forget."

Jim: "When we talk it seems like she brings up the same issues again and again. Why can't she just forget? Why beat a dead horse?"

How Men Feel When Women Remember

As we have already explored, women talk about issues to heal and release them. Men, however, don't, and so when a woman brings up her feelings to deal with them again, he takes it the wrong way. These comments represent a common feeling that men share when they do not understand a woman's need to remember her emotional wounds and talk about them again and again. Men feel that if they make a mistake, it will never be forgiven. It seems to them that just when they start to feel good about themselves and the relationship, their mates throw their deficiencies in their faces. It is hard for a man to continue caring about a woman's feelings when he feels so defeated.

When a man does not understand how to dodge female feelings, he inevitably becomes bitter and is convinced that his partner clings unfairly to his every mistake.

When a man doesn't understand how to dodge female feelings, he becomes bitter and is convinced that his partner clings unfairly to his every mistake.

A man also holds on to things and remembers them, but when he cares about someone, he tries to work on forgiving and forgetting in the privacy of his cave. He releases his resentments before he comes out to talk. He doesn't readily understand a woman's need to talk out loud in order to forgive and forget. When she expresses her frustrations, disappointments, and concerns verbally, he mistakenly assumes that she is withholding her love until he changes even more to please her.

When a woman expresses her frustrations, disappointments, and concerns, a man mistakenly assumes that she is withholding love until he changes to please her.

With a deeper understanding, however, a man can learn to dodge and reinterpret her remembering things. With advanced relationship skills, he will see it as a positive signal that she is getting to a deeper level of emotional resistance, where she can finally let go and experience greater love and acceptance for him.

What Women Say When Men Forget

While it is difficult for men to cope with a woman's memory for things that play on her feelings, it is equally difficult for women to cope with a man's lack of memory and motivation to do things. When women feel forgotten or neglected, here is what they usually say:

Maribeth: "I don't understand why he procrastinates so much. When he comes home, he just watches TV and there's always so much to do. I hate having to remember everything."

Carol: "Ever since he got the promotion, it's like he's forgotten me. He doesn't even realize when we don't go out for a while. He expects me to organize our social life. I want to take turns."

Mary: "I can't believe he's so successful and yet so spaced out. If he's talking while driving on the highway, he forgets to make the exit. When he works late, he'll even forget to call. I don't think he cares about me anymore."

June: "When he's home, he doesn't even look at me or say hello anymore. He only talks to ask for things or tell me something that happened to him, he doesn't ask about me. He used to, but now, when I talk he doesn't even bother to listen."

Ingrid: "No matter what I do, he acts like it is OK. I can stop talking to him, I can be mean, I can start yelling and he ignores me. He acts like I don't exist. No matter what I do, he forgets it like it didn't happen. I feel like he's a corpse; there is no love or passion. I would rather he yell at me than this."

How Women Feel When Men Forget

Women simply can't understand how a man could love them and forget them. They're utterly confused that he can remember the minute details having to do with his job, and forget the simplest things he has agreed to do in the home and in his relationship. He may forget to call when he is late, he may forget to make reservations or schedule times to go out, or he may just forget to empty the trash. Although to a man these seem like small things, to a woman they are much more important.

When he forgets to do something for her, it is as if he forgets her. When he minimizes her requests, she feels minimized. It is hard for her to believe that he loves her when he continues to disappoint her by forgetting things.

When he forgets to do something for her, it is as if he forgets her.

To varying extents, a newly married man begins to step up his focus on being a good provider. As he begins to devote more time to his work and less to his relationship, a woman commonly feels ignored, deprived, minimized, resentful, neglected, and unloved.

When a man begins to understand the importance of remembering to do the little things, then his memory begins to expand.

This process takes time, but when a woman understands that it is not just her husband, but most men who forget, then she can be more patient.

There are advanced skills for a woman to assist a man in remembering more, but before she is willing to use them she needs to remember that his forgetting is not about how much he loves her. Unless she understands this first, she will just get angry when practicing the new skills. It will begin to feel as if she is trying to get him to love her. This is not the case at all. A more positive and accurate way of looking at it is that he loves her but doesn't instinctively know how important it is to remember to do the little things. With the right motivation, he can and will remember.

How to Dodge Her Lists

It is nearly impossible for a man to feel successful in a relationship when his partner is constantly bringing up laundry lists of the various things he has either forgotten to do or has done wrong.

To dodge her complaint lists, it is extremely helpful for a man to know how a woman's mind processes feelings differently. When she is emotionally upset, her method of weeding out negative feelings is to remember and talk about what has bothered her in the past. By remembering and talking, she frees herself of cares.

A woman weeds out negative feelings by remembering and talking, which frees her of her cares.

When a man hears a woman sharing lists of problems, he gets frustrated because he thinks she is demanding that he solve them or at least make amends for them. Unlike his mate, he feels that what's done is done, and there is nothing he can do about it. Men tend to forget past mistakes and move on. That's what their fathers taught them to do.

Men tend to forget past mistakes and move on.

What He Can Do

There is something men can do that their fathers didn't know about. When a woman talks, a man can duck and dodge by remembering that she is actually not blaming him when she talks. She is trying to release herself from the grip of negative feelings.

To dodge and not take it personally, he has to remember, "This is not about me, it is just her way of releasing any negative feelings about me; soon she will remember how wonderful I am."

Instead of feeling as if he doesn't have a chance when she brings things up, he can practice remembering, "This is my chance to help her forget by remembering *with* her our past. I will get the support I need when she is done."

Without these insights, it is hard for a man to dodge. He doesn't instinctively understand that for her, her lists are a legitimate process of letting go. By speaking it out loud she is not reinforcing it. Instead, she is gradually letting go of it. It is only reinforced when he argues with her or reacts as if she is trying to punish him with it. If she has to defend her negative feelings, then she can't release them and begin to remember his good qualities.

When a Man Has No Complaints

Quite commonly, men in relationships often appear to have no complaints at all. They act as if everything is fine when it is not. Their only complaint is that their mates have so many complaints. They truly believe that their so-called "positive attitude" is helpful when, ironically, it is a major contributor to their problems.

Women generally find this "positive attitude" intimidating. It's hard to talk about problems when he's acting as if there are none. She wonders if she's overreacting or if something is wrong with her for wanting more from their relationship.

This self-defeating pattern is a true vicious cycle. The more he acts as if everything is OK, the more she feels ignored and inadequate. The more she feels that she won't be heard, the more overwhelmed and upset she gets. The more upset she gets, the more he—in a misguided attempt to support her—gives her a lot of space and acts as if everything is OK, making her feel even more neglected.

A woman needs to talk. When she can't get her partner's positive interest, she automatically shifts to get his negative attention, and stops caring about being nice. Since she needs to communicate, if all else fails, she will start an argument to engage his attention.

> If a woman can't get her partner's positive attention, she will shift to the negative and start an argument to engage his attention.

Why Women Throw Darts

Without motivating a man to listen attentively through pausing and preparing him, a woman has little recourse except to start throwing darts.

When I ask women in my seminars, "How many women will actually throw little darts, or make annoying statements to engage a man in an argument, just to get some kind of reaction?" men are amazed that almost all of the women will raise their hands.

You see, from the common male perspective, men think that they are doing women a favor by not complaining about the problems in the relationship. Men have lists too, but their way of dealing with them is to keep stuffing them or pushing them off to the side. They believe it's a good thing not to bring up their negative feelings or point out hers.

> Men think they are doing a good thing by not bring-
> ing up their negative feelings and ignoring their
> mates'.

All Men Are Not Dysfunctional

A woman panics when a man ignores her negative feelings. It
happens so often that single women begin to feel that all the
available men are dysfunctional. Women who have been married a long time think the problem is their husband's. In my
seminars, it is actually a relief for women to see that so many
other women experience this pattern in their relationships.

Women either assume that a man is psychologically impaired
from his childhood and in a state of denial, or they begin to
doubt themselves and think that they themselves are victims of
a dysfunctional past. Even if these conclusions are partially true,
they are not the major reason a man ignores a woman when she
is upset, nor are they why a woman gets more upset.

This pattern is the result of a fundamental misunderstanding
between the sexes. A psychologically healthy male, without an
understanding of female psychology, will ignore an upset
woman and believe he is being polite. Although this attitude
seems positive and helpful to him, he unknowingly and uninten-
tionally is invalidating her feelings and making matters worse.

Women Are Normal Too

It is also perfectly normal for a psychologically healthy female,
without an understanding of male psychology, to get more upset
when she believes that she is being ignored and having her feelings trivialized. As she learns more about how men operate and
masters advanced relationship skills, she will gradually be able to
cope with assisting him in remembering and in fulfilling her.

As a man begins to listen more and understand his woman's
feelings in the correct way, he will automatically begin to keep
her needs in mind. This is cause for hope.

The innate male ability to contain feelings and process them on his own can be a great boon to women. Because of it, he possesses the potential to focus on her feelings without getting upset at her when she is upset. This calm and solid support is, rightly, treasured by women.

The solution to men ignoring a woman's feelings is not trying to open him up to his feelings. It is giving him proof of the value of focusing his attention on her feelings and letting her talk.

As men realize that this kind of support is really what women need most, they can become world-class listeners. Using advanced relationship skills, men and women suddenly find themselves communicating better.

How Men Learn to Open Up

Even if a man was emotionally wounded in childhood and is literally in denial, he should be encouraged to continue containing his feelings while learning to guarantee his partner's security when she opens up.

Personal therapy can be very helpful to some men, particularly if they have a more developed female side and talk easily about their feelings. For most males, however, the most important gift they can receive from a marriage counselor is to learn how to make it safe for their partners to share. It is crucial that a man not get so in touch with his emotions that he overpowers his female partner's feelings.

As a man learns to listen, support, and eventually understand a woman's feelings, he will *automatically* begin to open up to his own and then to share. He will gradually develop his feminine side while simultaneously strengthening his masculine side.

> As a man learns to listen and support his partner, he will gradually develop his feminine side while simultaneously strengthening his masculine side.

Women, Not Men, Need to Open Up

Most women married to or involved with inexpressive men misguidedly try to get them to open up when they should be doing the opposite. They should be attempting to get these men to help *them* open up.

Women who try to get men to open up should instead be attempting to get these men to help them open up.

Real progress is made when a man learns to make it safe for a woman to slowly open up. No progress will be made if she mistakenly thinks he has to open up first.

Instead of focusing on changing him, a woman should be focusing on changing herself. She is sabotaging the relationship by assuming that if he were to open up first, she would follow. The answer to this universal problem lies in opening him up to the idea of listening, respecting, and understanding her feelings. Her efforts are better spent by focusing on pausing and preparing a man to listen better instead of trying to get him to open up and share feelings.

Instead of focusing on changing him, she should be focusing on changing herself.

When Men Start Making Lists

Men don't understand that it is a woman's nature to make lists, and that she needs to talk in order to feel better. They take her list of complaints personally. Although for weeks he may act as if everything is OK, when his wife eventually explodes with a list of problems, feelings, and complaints, he will suddenly make his own lists. For every item on her list, he will have an item on his list.

This is what he's feeling:

"I try to love you by minimizing my complaints and criticisms. I am happy to do this, but if you don't do it for me, then I might as well pull out *my* lists. When you see that I have at least as many complaints, you'll understand how loving I was for not telling you about them. Maybe now you'll appreciate me instead of complaining all the time." This tactic is absolutely counterproductive. So is the following one:

She says: "I feel upset when you don't turn down the TV."

He responds: "I understand how you feel. The other day I was trying to work, and you had your radio turned up."

This kind of "understanding" only makes it more difficult for her to feel heard and supported. As a result, she will become even more insecure about sharing and relying on him: after all, for days he behaved as if everything was OK and then suddenly opened fire on her with a barrage of negative feelings and complaints.

Tit for Tat

Although the "tit for tat" approach may sometimes work between men and Mafia members, it never works between men and women—to men's astonishment.

When a man "ambushes" his partner, his ultimate purpose is to not feel blamed. If he senses his partner is painting him negatively, he tends to do the same to her. Misguidedly, he is attempting to maintain the image that he is still worthy of her love. He is trying to tell her, "OK, if you have to put up with me this way, I also have to put up with you that way. Since we have both suffered equally, let's call it even," *or* "If you are going to make me wrong for this, then I will make you wrong for that. Since we are equally wrong, then let's forget it."

Let's put it this way: If we were business partners and you came to me and complained that you had lost ten thousand dollars and that I was making more money, and I responded by saying I had also lost ten thousand dollars, then we would be even. Both of us would be happy, and all would feel fair.

When women complain, men similarly want to even the

score. In some cases, a man will even try to beat his partner at her own game. To him this is like saying "I understand that you lost ten thousand dollars. I also lost ten thousand and, in addition, I lost another five thousand. I'm such a great guy that I am still willing to call it even." Not only does he match her complaints, but he ups the ante.

When women complain, men instinctively want to even the score.

Why Men Resist

When I at first explain to men the futility of "tit for tat," some resist. They feel it's unfair to expect a man to have to listen without defending himself. However, once these men are presented with a solution that works, they begin to release their resistance.

Men bring up lists either to get even or to at least level the playing field. Women, however, bring up lists in order to feel understood so that they can find release and put the lists behind them. Once a man learns to duck and dodge and then experiences that she does release her complaints, he then automatically has no reason to complain. The only reason he wanted to complain back was so that she would release her complaints. If, however, listening will achieve his goal better, then he is happy to make the shift.

Men bring up lists either to get even or to level the playing field. Women bring up lists in order to feel understood and achieve release.

If a woman listens quietly to a man's list, he will not be pleased. He wants her to either apologize or promise to do something about his beefs. When a woman shares her lists, even though to him it sounds like she is demanding change, she really just needs to be heard.

Changing the Pattern

Like many men, I felt it was only fair that if my wife complained I had a right to complain back. In one day, however, with the right understanding, my pattern permanently changed.

Bonnie had been upset about various things and asked me to listen. Trying to duck and dodge, I listened attentively for about fifteen minutes. I was bruised many times yet was able to contain myself, but for the wrong reasons. I was telling my inner self, Don't say anything, just listen, soon you will have your turn.

On the surface, I was doing everything right. I listened without arguing or interrupting. I even asked an occasional question to draw her out more. I kept my gut reactions to myself.

For Bonnie's every complaint, I privately had a counter complaint. For her every upset feeling, I had an explanation for why she didn't need to get so upset. For her every emotional expression like "I always" or "You never," I had a correction. But I didn't let them out.

I could hold it all in because I kept telling myself that I would soon have my turn to correct her feelings and "let her know the truth."

When she was finished, I said, "Is there anything else you want to say?"

"No, that's it," she said.

Making sure to do everything by the book, I told her, "Now I understand why you're so upset. You have a right to be upset. I also have a lot of feelings to talk about. Would this be a good time to talk about them?"

Taking me completely by surprise, she answered, "Well, since you asked, this isn't a good time."

"How dare she not listen to my feelings!" I fumed to myself. "I listened to hers."

To this day, I thank God that I didn't explode. Instead, while trying to restrain myself, I asked, "Why is this not a good time for you?" I was thoroughly prepared to argue the validity of my point of view.

Basking in the Sunshine of Love

I will always remember her response. She said, "All I can tell you is that if you were to tell me your feelings right now, I would feel like you had just taken away this wonderful gift that you gave me. Instead of listening to your feelings, I would rather bask in the feeling of being heard. I care about your feelings, but I would rather hear them later."

Her response totally took me off guard. She wanted to *bask*!!??? In the sunshine of my love? I didn't feel very loving. And the part about taking back a gift? I didn't feel like I had given her a gift. Could it be that her feelings really had changed from negative to positive?

Sure, I didn't interrupt, sure, I tried to understand, but I was not feeling warm and loving, I was furious. I wanted to correct her feelings. How could she really appreciate me for listening? How could she feel I had given her a gift?

What amazed me most was how much of my rage went away when I got the message that I *had* given her a gift and that she was appreciating me.

I saw in that moment that my need to correct her feelings came from believing she was rejecting me. I wanted to solve the problem by correcting her so that she would not be upset. I wanted to argue because I didn't feel appreciated. I was afraid that if I didn't change her mind, she would *stay* upset.

Realizing that I had already achieved my goal of wanting her to feel good about me, I no longer felt the need to match her list of complaints with my list. I could get her love and support by just being there for her without making her feel wrong or bad for needing to share her feelings.

Although much of my frustration lessened, I still intended to share my feelings in response.

I said to her, "When would be a good time to talk about my feelings?"

"Tomorrow," she proposed. "By then I'll really be able to hear what you have to say."

"Agreed."

During the next fifteen minutes, as I reflected on this unique conversation, I noticed that my wife was humming a happy song. She really was basking in the sunshine of my love. She was feeling very supported.

Although I had not been feeling very loving, my actions had been supportive and respectful. Her appreciation of my support instantly diminished my rage by at least 50 percent and made me feel more loving.

Making Mashed Potatoes

It was hard for me to believe that Bonnie could be so happy when a few minutes before she had been complaining about her life in a way that made me think happiness would forever escape her. About ten minutes after the end of our talk, she called to me from the kitchen to ask if I would like mashed potatoes for dinner. Mashed potatoes are my favorite food, and she generally makes them when she is feeling very loving.

By making a loving gesture, she was telling me, in effect, "You gave me a special gift, and now I want to give you something special back." As I heard her humming happily, I was also starting to feel happier. Instead of feeling like I had just been beaten up, I was feeling successful. By basking in her warm appreciation and love for me, my own chilly feelings began to thaw. It was a new experience for me.

> You don't have to be right to be loved, just do the
> right thing.

I consciously experienced being loved without having to be right. I didn't have to defend myself. I realized that by just listening to her feelings, I had helped Bonnie listen to herself. By clearly hearing herself, she could make the shifts and corrections she needed. I wasn't required to correct her, she could do it independently. By getting out of the way, I allowed her to recall once more the good things in her life and appreciate me.

The next day she said, "I'm ready to hear you talk about

your feelings. Is this a good time?" To my surprise, I had very little to say. I had forgotten all my grievances. What was bursting to come out the day before was not really a big deal if I was feeling appreciated.

What I did say I said in a very calm way, and she was able to really hear me.

Why Men Get Upset

From that day on, when Bonnie would get upset, I practiced ducking and dodging much more effectively. I could contain my feelings much more easily. Instead of saying to myself, "Soon I will have my turn to talk," I now say, "Soon she will be so grateful to you, soon she will think you are so wonderful for listening, soon she will be basking in the sunshine of your love and remembering what a wonderful guy you are. Tonight's going to be a night to remember."

The Irony of Feelings

When I tell this story in my seminars, the women always relate. They affirm that when a man counters her feelings with his angry feelings, it is much harder for her to feel heard. It is OK if he is angry. She just doesn't want to have to deal with it right away.

By letting go of the tendency to respond to a woman's feelings in a "tit for tat" manner, a man can succeed in making it much safer for her to share her feelings. As she feels safer, the intensity of her feelings lessens, making it easier for a man to duck, dodge, and delay his need to argue back.

> By letting go of the tendency to respond to a woman's feelings in a "tit for tat" manner, a man can succeed in making it much safer for her to share.

Cooking Lasagna

After expressing her emotions, a woman needs time—about fifteen minutes—to cool down and reflect on what she said. In a sense, this is her cave time. She has a private chance to correct her misplaced or misdirected feelings. During this short time of reflection, she begins to appreciate the gift the man has given.

One woman in a seminar compares this time to cooking lasagna. After you remove it from the oven, she observed, it still needs to release steam and "set" before it is ready to be eaten.

In a similar way a man can do all the right things and listen to her for the right amount of time, but if he doesn't let her feelings "set," then she doesn't have time to release her negative feelings and appreciate him for listening.

When a Man Forgets

By making only a few changes in the words she uses, a woman can still be honest but can express her feelings to a man in a much more accessible and supportive way. Quite commonly, when a man forgets to do something, a woman's reaction is to say, "You didn't listen."

It is hard for him to accept or agree with this message, because from his side his experience is that he heard her request and then forgot it. Telling him that he didn't listen just creates resistance.

When a man forgets something, it doesn't mean he wasn't listening. It means he has forgotten. To complain that he never listens is counterproductive, inaccurate, and alienating. The real message a man needs to hear is that he *has* forgotten again what she requested, but she loves him just the way he is and would really love it if he would remember more in the future.

Most of the time, when a man forgets something it is not because he was not listening to her at the time when she made the request. He forgets because he was distracted at the time when he was supposed to remember.

When my wife asks me to return a video, I hear her request, but I may forget to return the video because I am thinking about the problems at work at the time when I am supposed to remember.

Blame Never Works

I do not bring this point up as a reason for men to blame women when they say "You don't listen." Blame never works. I am, however, suggesting to women that women avoid using this term. And that's not always easy.

Communication is so important to women that if they are unhappy, the first comment off their lips shouldn't be taken literally because it is the product of having to speak and listen all day in "Male," an alien tongue. It is sheer frustration pouring out. A man's new job description is to dodge these kinds of comments and not feel blamed. He has to learn enough "Female" to have some idea of what she really means. It would be equally counterproductive for him to correct her and defend himself.

From a man's perspective, however, phrases like "You don't understand" are very hard to dodge. They are like hand grenades hurtled by space invaders.

When my wife occasionally says in frustration, "You never listen," I give her poetic license and dodge. I don't have to verbally disagree with her or start an argument to prove to her that I *do* listen. Instead, to prove to her that I do, I listen to what she really means. By sincerely trying to hear her in her native language, I remind her by my action of listening that I do listen. To argue about it would just make things worse because we wouldn't be understanding a word either of us was saying.

When your wife occasionally says in frustration,
"You never listen," give her poetic license and dodge.

By understanding a man's tendency to forget and why he does it, a woman can more clearly appreciate the times when a man does listen. If every time he forgets something she thinks he wasn't listening, then she will feel more ignored and neglected than she really is.

If every time he forgets something she thinks he wasn't listening, then she will feel more ignored and neglected than she really is.

A Man's Instinctual To Do List

When a man hears something that is not *instinctually* prioritized at the top of his internal to do list, he will tend to forget it.

If she asks him to pick up the laundry on the way home, because doing laundry isn't a part of his instinctual makeup it is much easier to forget. Asking him to sharpen the cutting knife would be easier to remember. Sharpening knives, carrying heavy boxes, and putting out fires (handling emergencies) require courage and physical strength, things that he more deeply identifies with.

Even if a request is near the top of his internal to do list, if something else more urgent or more instinctual comes up, he will tend to forget the items of lesser instinctual male priority. Any kind of urgent crisis has instinctual priority.

Most of this happens automatically. He doesn't say to himself, "I'm really busy today, so I'm going to forget to bring home the milk." It's simply that when he focuses on one thing here, he forgets the other things there.

When a man is consumed with a deadline or is worrying about his next paycheck to provide for his family, details like emptying the trash, picking up milk from the grocery, returning calls, buying concert or theater tickets, making reservations, picking things up, moving things, scheduling time to be together to talk, fixing things, calling the electrician, and running errands just disappear into the lost files of his male mind.

It's not that he doesn't care about his wife and family. On the contrary, he cares too much. Providing for and protecting his wife and family rank higher on his instinctual to do list than anything else.

Women don't relate to this because they tend to remember things at home even if they are focused on a project at work. The more stressed a woman is, the more details she automatically remembers. However, she will sometimes forget important details but it is because she is remembering too many things.

The more stressed a man is, the more focused he is on a single goal.

The more stressed a man is, the more focused he is on a single goal. A man's tunnel vision causes him to forget certain details that his wife doesn't easily forget. In essence, women think of many things at once, while men concentrate on one thing at a time.

Why Women Remember the Details

It is hard for a modern woman to intuitively grasp this difference when she is also a provider. In spite of her pressures, her instincts motivate her to handle the day-to-day details. When he says "I forgot because I was thinking about work" or "I forgot because I was trying to relax and forget the problems at work," it doesn't make sense to her. She simply doesn't understand what he's talking about.

Even with the contemporary pressures of paying the bills, women don't forget as easily as men because the home and family has always been their domain.

When a woman gets married, this tendency to remember the details only increases. It is as though some primal memory says "OK, in a few days he is going out on a hunt and won't come back for days. It's all up to you. You must remember everything."

In a similar way, when a man is married his tendency to focus on work increases. It's as if the hunter in him is saying "All right, now it's up to you. You have to do it all by yourself.

You have to go out, make the kill, and bring it home. They depend on you. Don't let them down."

As he focuses more on work, his tendency to forget the domestic details increases. When a woman is always remembering and worrying about the details and always keeping track of things, a man tends to worry less about those things and worries more about other things more directly related to his job.

The Nature of Partnerships

This kind of compensation is natural in any kind of partnership. In my business partnerships, the people who organize the seminars I teach worry about all the details of organizing, and I worry about the details of teaching. The more I trust them to handle the problems, the less I have to think about those details. I am free to focus more on teaching.

In the ancient relationship between men and women, men didn't worry about the details of raising young children and managing a home because that was what the women primarily handled. In a similar way, women didn't worry about or even know about the details of the men's work.

In a marriage, often the more a woman remembers the details of day-to-day life, the less he remembers. This principle can easily get out of hand, particularly when a woman unconsciously starts to mother a man. The more a woman remembers what he should be doing, the less he remembers. The more she worries about the money, the less he worries. The more she worries about the kids, the less he worries. The more she worries about his health, the less he worries. The more she worries about his time away from the relationship, the less he even notices. Whatever she worries about, he will tend to compensate for by being less worried.

If a man misplaces his keys and his wife always knows where they are, his tendency to feel responsible for remembering where they are will decrease. He will actually start to forget them more often instead of simply assigning a spot and always putting them there.

Remembering the Time

One night when Bonnie and I went to the theater, she asked me as we were getting into the car if we were late. I didn't think so, but I really wasn't sure. I didn't really know because she usually takes more time to get ready than I do. Before going out, as a standard procedure I play with Lauren until she is ready and then we go. I generally trust Bonnie to be ready in time, and she usually is.

When she didn't know if we were late, I could suddenly feel a part of me waking up and saying, OK, John, if she doesn't know when she is late or not, then you better handle that one in the future.

I am not implying in any way that it is a woman's fault that a man forgets. I am saying that she does have a very definite influence on what he forgets. By being aware of that power over him, she can begin to skillfully use it to help him remember more instead of forgetting.

Why Women Stop Asking

A woman will feel personally rejected when a man forgets to do some task. When he treats her requests as unimportant, she feels he is saying that she is unimportant.

It is hard for her to ask again because it makes her feel in an inferior, more unworthy position. It is as though she were having to beg for crumbs. It is an awful feeling, similar in distastefulness to how a man feels when a woman mothers him by reprimanding him for forgetting her requests.

Just as a man needs to work at ducking and dodging such comments, a woman needs to work at pausing, preparing, and persisting if she is to assist him in successfully supporting her. The amazing relationship between men and women is that when a woman succeeds in helping a man support her, then not only does he feel loved, but so does she.

What a Woman Can Do When a Man Forgets

When a man forgets to do things, instead of giving up and doing it for him, a woman should first pause. Next, in a noncritical way she can express her love skillfully by "preparing" him to do it another time. By not giving up and persisting in using this approach, she will eventually get what she wants.

> **It is not as romantic if she has to ask him to do things for her, but she will get what she needs and he will forget less.**

It is not as romantic if she has to ask, but she will get what she needs and he will forget less. It is important for her to know that once he tastes the added pleasure of doing things and having her appreciate them, he will remember things to do without even needing to be asked. As he begins to anticipate her needs, the romance will then increase and it will all be worth it.

When I first describe this, some women panic because to them it sounds as if I am saying that they have to nag him. What I am suggesting is the complete opposite. Preparing and nagging are very different.

Preparing Versus Nagging

Preparing a man so that he will remember something involves responding to him in a particular loving way when he forgets. How a woman reacts to his forgetfulness is crucial. Nagging a man only reinforces his tendency to forget. Pausing, preparing, and persisting will help him to remember.

Nagging a man is repetitively complaining to a man that he is not doing something. Each time a woman feels she has to nag, she increases the intensity of her dissatisfaction to let him experience the importance of her request. She mistakenly assumes that if she gets more upset he will then remember the next time. Nothing could be farther from the truth.

A woman assumes that he will remember how upset she got

because when a man gets really upset with a woman, she doesn't forget. Anytime a man is upset about something, a woman seems to always remember.

Men and women are very different in this way. A man successfully copes with stress by solving his problems *or* by forgetting them. When a woman is upset about something that he has already done and there is nothing he can do about it, then his way of coping with the stress of her negative message is to eventually forget it. The more a woman nags a man, the more he will forget what he needs to do in the future.

What a Man Remembers

Men primarily remember positive messages. When the memory of his wife's voice is pleasing, friendly, and trusting he can then easily remember it, but when she is repeatedly negative, he blocks her out. The more upset she gets, the more he tends to forget what is important to her.

Without this information, a woman just becomes increasingly frustrated with him because he doesn't remember. This only increases her frustration because she feels that he doesn't listen. The problem is not that he doesn't listen, the problem is that he quickly forgets.

When a women reacts in a negative way to his forgetting things, not only does he continue to forget her requests but he is unable to understand why she is getting so upset with him. For example, when a woman gets mad and nags a man to return the video, her frustrated tone of voice doesn't make sense to him. He dismisses it as an irrational reaction.

He doesn't remember all the times he has forgotten, and so when she gets really upset he thinks she is overreacting. Also, he doesn't know that she is mostly upset because she has to keep asking him to remember. He assumes it is because the tape wasn't returned.

He doesn't easily recognize that the frustration in her voice when he forgets the video is for *all* the other times he has forgotten things. This frustration becomes dramatically less when a woman experiences the fact that she can immediately start getting the support she needs. With this new hope that she doesn't have to be his memory, a woman can relax more.

Recovering the Lost Files

A man forgets a request when it is conveyed in a negative way or when its domestic nature does not rank high on his internal instinctual to do list. This forgotten request, however, is not completely lost. It is just stored in a different place. With a little help from his partner, a man can automatically remember what he normally forgets.

When my computer crashes and my screen freezes, I have a special program called *Thunder 7* that protects me from losing my writing. Even if the information I have been writing has not been saved, I can still recover it by going to a special folder. In that folder is my lost file.

In a similar way, men also have a lost file folder. By applying new skills, a woman can help a man to access his lost files so that he can easily remember the things she requests even after his mind crashes or freezes to recover from the stress of work.

This means that after a stressful day at work and a man is driving home, as his mind is seeking to forget the demands and pressures of work, a gentle, soothing, and loving voice inside his head reminds him to pick up the milk on the way home. This is his wife's voice emerging from the lost files.

Preparing a Man to Remember

This skill is easier said than done, but once mastered, a woman will enjoy its benefits for the rest of her life. It requires that a woman postpone getting what she wants so that she can patiently support him in learning to remember. After a few months of practicing this, she will begin to reap tremendous benefits.

She is required to ask him to do something that she normally

would but this time she should also expect him to forget. By
expecting him to forget, she doesn't get upset when he forgets.
This request should be something simple like returning a video,
bringing home milk, picking up clothes from the cleaners, emptying the trash, or moving a box.

When he forgets to do what he has agreed to do, she should
be prepared to not react in an upset manner. She should say
briefly, in an easygoing tone as if he has never forgotten anything before, any of the following phrases:

"Did you get a chance to return the video?"
"Did you happen to pick up the clothes from the cleaners?"
"I know how busy you are, did you remember to empty the
trash?"
"Did you get the milk?"

Make sure the question is brief and simple. Don't say "Did
you remember to empty the trash? Tomorrow is trash day, and
we shouldn't miss it again. We don't have room for it all. It has
to go out tonight, or we will have to wait another week. I
already have too much to do and can't do it." All this makes
him feel nagged or forced into doing it. He may do it, but the
next week he will forget.

After asking him, for example, "Did you return the video?"
be ready for him to say no, and then respond in an accepting
manner. Use any of the following phrases. He will never get
tired of hearing them. They are:

"It's OK."
"No big deal."
"It's all right."
"No problem."

Any of these phrases will be sweet music to his ears. Men
are always saying these phrases to each other. Women don't use
them as much because they don't instinctively know how powerful they are. Women use them in the beginning of a relation-

ship because he hasn't yet let her down by forgetting things. But as the relationship progresses, it is suddenly not OK for him to forget. This just causes him to forget more.

How Men Respond to Their Friends

If a man forgets to do something for a male friend, his buddy will commonly say "No problem." This kind of support is friendly, but it also ensures that he will get the support he needs the next time. Women don't understand this. A woman assumes that if a man says "No big deal" or "No problem," he will definitely forget the next time. She has no idea that it works the other way around.

The less pressure a man feels to do something, then the more inclined he is to do it, particularly when he is seeking relief from the pressures of the job. At work a man responds to pressures, but at home he responds best to this nonpressured, friendly approach. At work his motive is primarily money; at home it is love.

What Motivates a Man

When a woman repeatedly asks for support in a pleasing, nondemanding tone, then when a man needs a break from work his attention suddenly goes to her. He remembers her request, and he remembers how good it feels when she appreciates him.

Instead of being motivated by the fear of punishment, he is motivated in a healthy way by the anticipation of pleasure. When a woman is pleased with a man, then he is pleased. It takes time, but a man gradually learns to associate remembering her and her needs with pleasure.

It takes time, but a man gradually learns to associate remembering a woman and her needs with pleasure.

Asking As If for the First Time

After she lets him know in a pleasing way that it is OK, she should then ask him again to do the task. This time, the tone of voice is very important. She needs to ask *as if she is asking for the first time*.

Each time she asks in this particular way it becomes increasingly clear to him how many times he has forgotten. Through his remembering that he has forgotten without her directly pointing it out he gradually builds a bridge connecting him to his lost files.

I was personally amazed by my inner reaction when my wife, Bonnie, began using this skill. When I would forget to empty the trash, she would just put it out in the center of the kitchen. When she noticed me walking around it but still not remembering to empty it, she then applied this new skill.

She acted like it was perfectly normal to forget the trash and said to me the second time, "Oh, when you get a chance, would you empty the trash?" I said sure and went back to watch TV. Then an hour later she said, as if she were saying it for the first time, "Oh, while you're up, would you empty the trash?"

I still remember my reaction. I suddenly remembered that this was her third request and she was still being so nice. I thought, She is being so wonderful, I'll do it now. After I emptied the trash, she made a special point of noticing and thanking me. After many years of being treated in this way and never being taken for granted or just expected to do things, she rarely has to ask me. I am so conditioned to feeling her love and acceptance when I empty the trash that when I get home, after giving her a big hug and listening to her for a while, many times I will check to see if the trash needs to be emptied.

How to Strengthen a Man's Memory

Each time a man forgets to do something and a woman reacts in a nondemanding way, he will suddenly remember all the times he has forgotten. It is amazing. If she does not remind him of how many times she has had to ask, then he remembers all on his own.

If, however, she remembers for him and says "I have asked you three times," then his memory weakens and the next time he forgets.

By repeatedly remembering what he has forgotten without having to feel guilty, a man's memory for doing the little day-to-day things in life is strengthened. It is easy for him to remember how many times he has forgotten because each of those times she practiced reacting in such a pleasing manner.

Using this new approach a woman is, in effect, pleasing her man and waiting on him as women have done for centuries, but this time she is doing it with a very different twist. She is waiting on him and pleasing him so that he will wait on her more of the time and more successfully please her.

When a woman asks for more in small increments *as if she is asking for the first time,* she is ensured of the fact that he will gradually do more for her. Even if he doesn't feel in the mood to do more for her, if she has asked several times and each time in a nice and pleasing way, then he feels that he owes her one and will happily fulfill her request.

Men Are Fair

Men are very fair. When a woman is accepting of his forgetfulness or mistakes, he feels that he has received a gift of love. Not unlike a woman in this regard, when he receives a gift, he wants to give back. If she keeps asking in a nondemanding tone and keeps accepting that he forgets, he will eventually feel so loved that he will want to do more for her even without being asked.

In the behavioral sciences, it has been repeatedly demonstrated that lasting behavior modification occurs through positive reinforcement. Negative reinforcement is the weakest form of education. By appealing to a man's need for love, a woman can gradually help him place her requests, needs, and wants at the top of his internal to do list.

This change occurs over time as a man experiences that by

remembering her needs and doing small things for her he is greatly appreciated. As he experiences repeatedly that anything he can do to make her feel understood and heard allows her to be happier and able to love him more, then emptying the trash suddenly becomes as important as accomplishing more at work. Remembering to pick up the milk becomes as important as bringing home the bacon.

> When a man repeatedly experiences being appreci-
> ated for doing little things, remembering to bring
> home the milk becomes as important as bringing
> home the bacon.

The more a man experiences being rewarded with her love when he does little things for her, the more he will want to do these things for her. His mind will be freed from the compulsions to achieve more and do "big things" like buy a bigger house, drive a nicer car, or take more expensive vacations. While those things are also appreciated, what is more important is that she feels heard and loved, not isolated.

A Modified Approach

When a woman discovers on her own that the man has forgotten something, she needs to modify her approach slightly. When she knows the trash has not been emptied, she should not pretend that she doesn't know and ask him if he emptied the trash. Instead, what she should do is just ask him again to empty the trash.

She could briefly say "When you get a chance, would you empty the trash?"

It is not necessary to first point out to him that he forgot. By "asking again" it is already implied that she knows he forgot. He is grateful that she is not making a big deal out of it.

It is important for her to use an accepting tone of voice that says "It's OK to forget to empty the trash. I know you are busy. When you get a chance, would you empty it? I trust you will get around to it." With this kind of support, a man is much more motivated to do more in the relationship. More important, she has hope that she can eventually get the support she needs most.

Bringing Home the Milk

My favorite story about how I started remembering my wife's requests has to do with bringing home the milk. Three days in a row, each morning she asked me to bring home milk. The first day on my way home, I forgot. When I got home, she asked, "Did you pick up the milk?"

The first day, I just brushed it off and in a neutral way said, "No, I forgot."

She then said in a very accepting way, "Would you pick up some tomorrow?"

I said, "Sure."

The next day when I forgot again, she said in a friendly way, "Did you happen to pick up the milk?"

This time I said, "Oh, I forgot." I automatically had a greater sense of concern and regret. She was being so kind about it that I didn't have to make mental excuses to justify why I forgot. It is precisely this freedom to make mistakes that allows a man to become more conscientious.

She said as if she were asking for the first time, "Would you pick some up tomorrow?"

I said, "Sure. No problem." Inside I felt much more resolved to do it and grateful that she was so accepting.

The next morning, our three daughters were sitting around the breakfast table complaining.

Lauren, the youngest, said, "Mommy, I am tired of oatmeal. I want cereal with milk."

Bonnie said, "We can't have cereal because there is no more milk."

Lauren said in response, "Why don't we have milk?"

Bonnie then said, "I don't know, but maybe your daddy would pick up some milk today on his way home."

I was so relieved. She could easily have said, "We don't have milk because your father forgot to bring it home two days in a row. I asked him, but he just didn't listen."

I am sure that somewhere inside she had those feelings, but she chose instead to be positive and support me.

Needless to say, that day I remembered the milk, and to this day when I look in the refrigerator I look to see if there is milk. If we are getting low, I am happy to get some.

Doing Small Things Makes Big Changes

When bringing home the milk became as important as bringing home the bacon, I noticed that my life began to change dramatically. Not only was my wife so much happier, but I was changed as well.

One day while making my daughter Lauren's lunch, I felt a wave of successful feelings. It was as though all my ambitions had been realized. I felt so content with myself, my work, and my life.

It completely surprised me. By just making Lauren's lunch, these feelings of tremendous success and accomplishment came up. What amazed me was that it had nothing to do with my work.

At that point in my life I was not yet a best-selling author and my seminars were far from being sellouts. For years I had felt tremendous disappointment and frustration because my ambitions had not been fulfilled. On that day, however, even without having achieved the success I was hoping for, I suddenly felt successful.

I realized that the admiration I received from my wife for being a good husband and father was just as important as the admiration I might get some day if I was very successful in my work. From that day on I have been clearly aware that it is not only the outer successes that make me feel good. It is primarily the love and appreciation that I feel coming from my loving wife, family, and friends that fills me up.

Working hard and doing my best is certainly a big part of feeling good, but what makes it all worth it is the fulfillment it brings others and the love I get in return. Until that moment in my life, like many men, I didn't know how important love was.

In the next chapter, we will explore the natural changes that occur in a relationship, and learn how to cope with these changes so that love and intimacy can continue to grow. Women will discover what happens to the man they love over time, and how to bring out the best in him.

CHAPTER 9

What Happened to the Man I Love?

Without an awareness of advanced relationship skills, it is much harder for married couples to grow together. In most cases, they tend to grow apart or stop growing. They may love their partners, but the romance is gone. They feel powerless to bring back the feelings they shared during courtship.

In her quiet moments, a woman questions what happened to the man she loved, while her husband wonders where is the woman he fell for. Although this questioning seems very discouraging, the true answers to these questions are not depressing at all.

The man she loves is still there. He just needs her assistance in coming out. The woman he fell for is right there; she just needs his assistance to open up so that her soft, feminine love can begin to shine again.

As both men and women begin to experience that they are not powerless to get what they want, it is as though miracles happen overnight.

After taking my seminars, couples who have been married for many years repeatedly share how amazed they are when the old romantic feelings begin to come back. They are so grateful to feel again the love that was buried in their hearts.

How Men Change

During counseling sessions and in my seminars, women are very expressive of how men change in the course of long-term relationships. These are some common complaints.

Jane: "Bill is rarely affectionate with me anymore. The only time he touches me is when he wants to have sex. I feel used. If I'm just a sex object to him, then I don't want to have sex."

Judy: "Jim used to think ahead and plan dates. I felt really special. Now he waits till Friday night and asks me what I would like to do. I hate it."

Mary: "When I got dressed up, Tom would notice me and compliment me on how I looked. Now he doesn't even notice. If I ask how I look, he just says fine. It doesn't make me feel very beautiful."

Colleen: "When we first met we used to have long conversations. Now we don't talk at all. There is just nothing to say. I feel like I am dying of thirst in a desert. It is not just Steve, but I don't have anything to say either. I feel like the love is gone."

Georgia: "Before we got married, Roger would do all sorts of things for me. He emptied the trash, carried boxes, he even washed my car every two weeks. Suddenly he stopped. It makes me feel like I am not important to him anymore."

Sushi: "When I had a problem, Rick used to be so sympathetic; now when I complain about anything, he gets upset with me. It makes me feel like he doesn't care."

Lisa: "Sam used to find me when he came home from work; now he either goes straight to the TV or he plays with the kids. I feel taken for granted. I don't feel loved or special anymore."

Joyce: "When we were dating and I went to Henry's apartment, it was always cleaned. He picked up after himself. Now that we are married, he leaves a trail behind him wherever he goes. I don't want to be his mother and pick up after him. I resent it."

Louise: "Nick used to look at me when I talked; now he just looks away. I feel like what I am saying is not important to him.

He used to be so much more attentive. When he gets a call for work he comes alive, but when I talk he seems distracted."

In each of these examples, the woman mistakenly assumes that the man is pulling his love away and retaliates in kind. As a result, he really begins to pull *his* love away, and more difficult problems begin to emerge. This tragedy occurs because a woman doesn't understand a man's natural changes, nor does she know how to get the support she needs.

Men are not the only ones who change. Although women tend to be more expressive about it, men also complain that women change. Most women are very unaware of how they change in ways that make a man feel unsupported.

As we explore what a woman can do to bring out the best in her man, it may begin to sound as if I am saying that it is all up to the woman. I am not. For best results, teamwork is required. In the next chapter, I will then explore what men can do.

It isn't imperative for your partner to practice these skills along with you; in many cases, if only one of you applies them, the relationship will still dramatically improve. Positive changes occur more quickly, however, if both partners are aware that they are in job retraining. Taking turns reading sections of this book to each other can make a tremendous difference in speeding change along.

Why Men Change

A man's behavior may shift in the various ways described above, and yet to a woman's surprise, he may still love her with great affection. As we will see, in some cases he actually loves her more. A woman misunderstands these behavior changes because from her perspective she is getting less of what she needs most.

Men make changes much more innocently than women can imagine. They make them primarily because they do not understand what women really require in a relationship.

With new insight, a man can give his mate the support she

wants. As a woman begins to understand what is really going on with him she can join him in applying advanced relationship skills to assist him in supporting her more successfully. Without understanding why a man changes, many women feel completely frustrated and powerless to get what they need from men.

When Men Are Goal Oriented

A man's orientation to intimate relationships is much more goal oriented than a woman's. His actions in the beginning of the relationship are the steps he takes to achieve his goal. Instinctively, he touches her affectionately, buys her flowers, calls her from work, plans dates, looks at her when she talks, notices how beautiful she is, listens intently to her stories, and behaves in other ways to say that he cares.

Practically speaking, he is on the hunt. His goal is creating an intimate relationship with the woman he has chosen as his mate. He is fully focused. Once he has achieved that goal, his hunter's instincts shut down.

Instead of regressing, he progresses. Instead of buying flowers, he shares his complete income. Instead of calling from work, he comes home each day. Instead of planning dates, he plans to live his life with her. Instead of giving affection, he gives sex. Instead of just looking and listening to her when she talks, he feels a greater responsibility for her and tries to solve her problems.

Instead of taking the time to do little romantic things, he takes the time to earn money so that she can eventually do whatever she wants. Instead of telling her how beautiful she is or that he loves her, he wears a wedding band that he feels says it all. This man has little awareness that the things he did in courtship are important requirements for intimate growth and keeping the passion alive. He doesn't realize that what he did to win her is still necessary to keep her happy.

Once a man attains his goal, he is no longer focused on repeating the things he did to *get* there. Instead, he focuses instinctively on doing what it takes to *stay* there. Like his ancestors, he concentrates on being a good provider.

> Once a man attains his goal, he is no longer focused
> on repeating the things he did to *get* there. Instead, he
> instinctively focuses on doing what it takes to *stay*
> there.

As a man learns that the steps that got him into the relationship are the same steps that keep romance alive, he is more highly motivated to provide the emotional support modern women require. With a woman's cooperation, a man can shift into giving her what she wants. But unless she validates his process by understanding how he can make the shift back into first gear, she will resent having to wait as he learns.

Climbing the Ladder of Success

For a man, a relationship is similar to the process of climbing the ladder of success. He will do whatever it takes to get to the higher rungs of the ladder. He is willing to wait in long lines, run errands, take orders, and work longer hours because he knows that one day when he has "made it" he won't have to continue doing what he did to get there. In a way similar to the early stages in a man's career, courting is the time when a man "pays his dues."

> For a man, a relationship is similar to the process of
> climbing the ladder of success. He is willing to do
> whatever it takes to go higher.

At work when a man ascends to higher rungs he finds himself with new jobs and responsibilities corresponding to the higher levels of trust, recognition, and appreciation he has earned. He has outgrown what he did to get there. He has paid his dues. He still works hard, but his duties are very different.

Marriage compares to getting to the ladder's higher rung.

Without understanding a woman's perspective, a man mistakenly feels that he's being taken down a peg each time she expects him to do the things he did when they were courting. It seems to him that she's demoting him back to the bottom of the ladder.

Each time she expects him to do the things he did when they were courting, it seems to him that she's demoting him back to the bottom of the ladder.

A man may be at the top of the corporate ladder and still go home to a mate who expects him to go all the way back to starting at the bottom again. If he doesn't understand the validity of her continuing need to be courted, it will indeed feel as if the ladder has been knocked out from under him by the woman he works so hard to provide for.

Does this mean that she will never get what she wants? Not at all. Once she understands his changes from this new perspective, she can relax and realize that her husband probably loves her a lot more than she thought.

When she begins seeing the effects of advanced relationship skills, she will be assured that she can eventually get the loving support he gave so freely when they were first in love. By her helping him to be successful in fulfilling her, they both become much happier. Working together as a team, they create a wonderfully mutual support system that does justice to the special love they share.

By rewriting her job description, retraining, and using advanced relationship skills, a woman can most effectively assist a man in doing the things he used to do, and eventually even more. To sustain her trusting and accepting attitude, however, it is essential that a woman understand in greater detail the perfectly innocent reasons a man has when he stops performing certain loving behaviors.

With this data, she can jump-start him in the right direction. Eventually, doing the things he used to do will become as automatic for him as they used to be. Let's now explore in greater detail our women's comments on how men change:

"He Only Touches Me When He Wants Sex"

In the beginning of their relationship, Bill was very affectionate with Jane. He held her hand in public, stroked her hair, gave her hugs, and wrapped his arm around her when they walked together. He couldn't keep his hands off her. She loved it.

Once they started having sex, all that changed. After a while, he only touched her when he was "in the mood." Bill didn't instinctively understand Jane's need for affection. For him, touching was something you did before you had sex. To do it idly would, in a sense, be going backward.

For him, touching is something you did before you had sex. To do it idly would, in a sense, be like going backward.

What Jane didn't understand was that when Bill touched her before they started having sex, it was *because* he was not allowed to touch her intimately. When a man is dating a woman, to a great extent he has to practice restraint. He can make physical contact with her hands, arms, and hair but respectfully holds back from touching where he would most like to.

Why Men Stop Touching

Once a man is given the green light to touch a woman in a sexual way, it is hard for him to go back to when he couldn't. The impulse to touch in order to be affectionate becomes fainter. When he gets to enjoy the intense pleasures of sexual touch, nonsexual touch pales by comparison.

Once they are having sex, his instinct is to only touch her as a prelude to sex. So he stops touching her when sex isn't a possibility. To get all turned on by touching her and then not have sex would be frustrating to him.

When a woman complains or feels neglected by a man, it is hard for him to validate her feelings. From his side, he is the same guy and he loves her the same as always. When she tells him things have changed, he doesn't relate. When she complains that he only touches her when he wants sex, he doesn't instinctively understand why that is so upsetting.

When she wants just to touch him, he will tend to get the wrong idea and want to have sex. For him, touch means sex; when she cuddles in bed, he assumes it is a sexual invitation. After a while, she stops wanting to cuddle because he misunderstands what it means to her.

Why Men Don't Understand

Most men don't realize how important nonsexual touch is to a woman because since late adolescence a man has been more concerned with the sex than a woman has. For a young man, simply having a place and the opportunity to have intercourse is enough to arouse him. It's a matter of biology and hormones.

Before puberty, both boys and girls feel a need to be touched and cuddled. However, when a boy reaches puberty, this need to be cuddled is dramatically reduced.

When boys are around thirteen, there is a massive increase in testosterone and a decrease in their need to cuddle. Their need for sexual contact suddenly becomes much stronger than the need for nonsexual contact.

Meanwhile, a girl's need for cuddling remains active and strong throughout her life. Although it is difficult to prove, many experts claim that a woman needs to be touched ten times a day to experience high self-esteem.

Studies reveal that a woman's skin is actually ten times more sensitive to touch than a man's. Perhaps this increased sensitivity explains her great appreciation and need for affectionate nonsexual touch.

Once a man understands this difference, he can realize why his partner wants more or why she is dissatisfied when he only touches her in a sexual way. When a man is aware of a woman's sensual needs, he is suddenly much more motivated to touch in a nonsexual way.

**When a man is aware of a woman's sensual needs, he
is suddenly much more motivated to touch in a nonsexual way.**

With this new insight, Bill immediately started touching Jane many times a day. Jane supported him by letting him know each time how much she liked it. She let him know that he was doing the right thing by making a little noise like "mmm," or by just sighing, or by simply relaxing into his touch.

If he forgot to touch her, they agreed that she would remind him in a nondemanding way by simply touching and gently stroking his arm. In time, however, she didn't even need to remind him. He would initiate touching on his own.

How Men Really Change

From this example, we see how men most effectively change.

1. In the beginning Bill touches as a way to get closer to finally having sex.
2. Once they start having sex, he begins to touch Jane less.
3. With her encouragement and positive reinforcement, he starts touching her again.
4. He has learned a new relationship skill, nonsexual touch-ing, and now touches not because he is "required to" but because he wants to.

Generally speaking, unless a woman was deprived of appro-priate touch when she was a child, she does not need to learn the skill of nonsexual touching. She does, however, need to learn, through patience and persistence, how to prepare a man to learn it. Without an understanding of why a man needs to learn, she will not be able to support him gracefully.

Bill learned to touch Jane nonsexually in three distinct stages. They are:

Stages of Change

1. At first he was primarily doing it because he knew she would like it.
2. After a while, however, he began to discover that he enjoyed it just as much.
3. In a very real sense, his own cuddling hormones had been reawakened.

While at first it was a conscious decision based on remembering what *she* needed, touching gradually became a satisfying habit for him. Bill didn't even have to think about doing it. Over a much longer period of time, the habit became completely reflexive. In this third stage of change, not only did he really enjoy touching her in a nonsexual way, but he found that a part of him also needed the contact and benefited from it.

Women who don't understand this transformational process commonly feel that "I don't want him to touch me unless he wants to. I don't want him doing it just for me." After understanding how men change, they can easily encourage and support him in this process.

Four Ingredients for Change

A man can most effectively shift a behavior or learn a new skill when all four of the following ingredients are present:

How Men Change

1. The change or new skill makes sense to him.
2. He doesn't feel blamed for not doing it before.
3. He tests the behavior and repeatedly experiences that it works. He gets positive reinforcement each time.
4. She asks for his support in a nondemanding manner when he forgets. Each time she asks "as if for the first time."

Given these four ingredients, in time a man's positive behavioral shifts will automatically become second nature. What at first is a conscious decision eventually becomes an automatic reaction. And, by supporting his wife's needs and respecting her feelings, his own female side is awakened and nurtured. For example, if a man isn't "into" nonsexual touching but does it to please his mate, who appreciates it, in time he will inevitably "get into" it. By getting into his own female side, he is finding greater balance in himself.

By supporting his wife's needs and respecting her feelings, his own female side is awakened and nurtured.

This same principle of change applies to *all* the ways in which a man stops courting a woman. Whatever he used to do, he can and will do again when given the correct support. Let's look at another example from our list.

Why Men Stop Planning Dates

Judy was frustrated because when they were courting, Jim used to plan dates, but after they married he gradually stopped making plans. This shift or change is very common but has little to do with how much a man loves or cares about his partner. He could love her completely and still not plan dates.

The explanation is simple. In the beginning he *had* to make plans in advance to guarantee that somebody else didn't ask her out. He had no idea that his planning a date in advance was so important to her. He was doing it simply to ensure that they had their special time. Once they lived together, that kind of planning no longer seemed necessary, so he stopped. Judy was disappointed and thought that he didn't care as much.

When I talked to Jim, he was surprised that Judy was upset. He thought he was being considerate of her feelings by always asking her what she wanted to do. Sometimes he didn't even ask her but waited for her to decide.

If she asked him what he wanted to do, he thought he was being nondemanding by saying, "I don't really care where we go. I just want you to be happy."

This kind of passivity is fine occasionally, but if repeated, it is a real turnoff. When Jim reacted as if he didn't really care where they went, Judy felt that he didn't care about her. She appreciated that he cared about her feelings but didn't like being solely in charge. She wanted him to take the initiative at least half the time and plan their dates in advance.

When Jim began to make this shift, he really didn't care much about where they went. But as he initiated more dates and saw how much his wife appreciated it, he started to get more involved.

Judy was pleased because she could relax more and worry less about that aspect of her life. When the woman feels fully responsible for a couple's social life, it's hard for her not to treat her partner like a child.

When the woman feels fully responsible for a couple's social life, it's hard for her not to treat her partner like a child.

Without a man's help, women have difficulty in shifting from the mother mode into the lover mode. When a woman feels taken care of in this way, she is momentarily released from those mothering urges that make her always feel responsible for everything.

How Jim Changed

With Judy's help, Jim's transition was easy. He only needed to understand the situation differently to become highly motivated.

In the past, he would make plans and suggest places to go, but she always wanted to do something else. Instead of continuing to suggest another "wrong place," he simply asked her preference. As a result, he stopped planning their dates.

To support Jim in the shift back, Judy learned to practice advanced relationship skills. Her objective was to help him be successful in planning dates. She would prepare him by indirectly letting him know what to suggest.

She would say things like, "There is a new play at our theater, I heard it was really good."

This was a clear signal for him to say, "Hmmm, that sounds like a fun thing to do. Would you like to go?"

Then she could say, "Sure."

Both Jim and Judy were inspired by a story I tell in my seminars about how Bonnie helps me to be successful in supporting her.

Eating in Stockholm

While teaching a seminar in Sweden, my wife, Bonnie, my daughter Lauren, and I went sightseeing in the old town section of Stockholm. In my very goal-oriented way, I was very focused on getting to as many points of interest as was possible in one day.

Around lunchtime, Bonnie said, "Well, I'm starting to feel hungry, maybe we should stop and have lunch."

As soon as I heard her say she was hungry, I immediately stopped and said, "OK, let's find a restaurant. How much time do we have before you need to eat? Is this like one minute, five minutes, or ten?"

"Five minutes would be fine," she replied casually.

I have learned that when a woman is hungry, part of my job description is to stop everything and get her fed. When her blood sugar drops, she is definitely not as much fun to be with. When Bonnie is hungry, I stand at attention and say, "Right away." So that day, when she mentioned "the food word," alarm bells went off in my head. I immediately began looking for a restaurant.

Unless a man experiences equally intense blood sugar drops, it is hard for him to make the connection between a woman's hunger and her moodiness. For me personally, as with the ancient hunters, it is very easy to forget about food when I am in pursuit of a goal. By understanding that Bonnie is different, I am now quick to respect her hunger.

Up until this moment I had been so focused on the cathedrals that I hadn't noticed any restaurants. Suddenly, I was seeing them everywhere.

"That looks good." I pointed to one across the courtyard. "Would you like to eat there?"

She checked it out and said, "It does look good, but I'm not sure."

I saw another restaurant across the street that looked good. "We could go to that one. It looks much better."

"It does look better," she said, then after a pause, exclaimed, "Oh, but look at that one! It looks very interesting."

Her tone of voice told me that this was the one, so I immediately said, "It does look good. Let's go there."

When we arrived at the restaurant, we both had a good feeling. She felt heard, respected, and taken care of. I felt successful in taking care of her.

The good feelings even continued. When she liked the food, on an emotional level I could take the credit. In this very simple way we had some fun and created some romance. She was able to say, "Thanks for taking us to such a wonderful restaurant," and I proudly felt, yes, I did that.

Advanced Skills for Making Decisions Together

To create this loving moment, we both cooperated. Bonnie knew that I really didn't care where we ate and that I probably wasn't even hungry. But instead of just taking charge and leading us to where she wanted to eat, she skillfully involved me in the process in a way that made me feel successful.

While this interaction of picking a restaurant seems small, it is precisely this kind of positive experience that involves a man in the relationship and inevitably makes a woman feel nurtured and loved. By creating a loving moment that would become a treasured memory, she was also preparing me to make decisions with her in the future.

When couples can successfully make lots of little decisions together, it is much easier to make the big ones. When couples have "big problems," it is really the result of a lot of little problems that they didn't resolve or successfully solve together. I have found that when love seems lost in a relationship, it can be reawakened when a man shares with a woman the process of making a decision and a woman helps a man feel successful in that process.

> When love seems lost in a relationship, it can be
> reawakened when a man shares with a woman the
> process of making a decision and a woman helps a
> man feel successful in that process.

Throughout history, women were nurtured by spending their days in cooperative actions with other women. Today, because the competitive work world does not nurture this feminine side of her being, she craves it in her relationships. At the same time, she also hungers for an autonomous man who doesn't need to be taken care of but who in turn takes care of her.

To fulfill a modern woman, a man has to do more. He is required to be the leader, but must also include her in the process. When making decisions, she doesn't want him to depend solely on her, nor does she want him to ignore her. A woman wants her partner's involvement. She doesn't want him to decide without her input, and she doesn't want to do it alone.

How to Best Learn a New Skill

While this advanced relationship skill is difficult for the man, it can be learned. Just as with any skill, in the early stages he needs lots of successful practice.

The early stages of practice need to be designed so that a man's success is ensured. Women need to remember that there is no greater motivator for a man than success. The more successful a man feels in the decision-making process, the more involved he gets in trying to understand what her needs are while at the same time respecting his own.

There is no greater motivator for a man than success.

My favorite example of this comes from a world-champion bowler. He tells the story of how he learned to bowl. As a child, when he was first learning the sport, his father made sure he never missed a pin. His dad owned the bowling lanes, and when his son would throw the ball, if it looked like he was going to miss the pins, his father would set a bowling pin down in the path of the ball. As a result, the boy never missed. This repeated success motivated the young boy to practice more, and built the confidence of a world champion.

The Power of Positive Reinforcement

When I was a child, my mother used to listen to me talk about my ideas for hours. She would never correct me or imply that she already knew what I was talking about. She would patiently listen with rapt attention. She greatly appreciated my ideas even though they were still rather unformed. As a result, I felt that I had something important to say.

Based on that support, I began giving lectures when I was eighteen years old. Lecturing was a particularly difficult challenge because people expected me to appear old and wise when I looked like I was twelve. When I came out to speak, people assumed that I was attending my father's presentation.

At my first advertised public lecture, on developing your full mental potential, I was so nervous, I fainted. The audience thought I had died.

I eventually overcame my fears and went on to give talks to thousands. Without doubt, my courage to speak publicly came from my mother's support and belief in me when I was young. Her unconditional acceptance and appreciation gave me a special strength and belief in myself that overcame the obstacle of my youthful appearance.

This same principle applies to men in relationships. When a man feels successful in applying a new skill, he will be motivated to continue learning and giving.

When a Man Is Not Successful

When a woman doesn't practice the art of helping a man succeed, he either gives up trying to fulfill her or sacrifices his own needs so that she gets what she wants. Neither approach is healthy.

> **When a woman doesn't practice the art of helping a man succeed, he either gives up trying to fulfill her or minimizes his own needs so that she gets what she wants. Neither approach is healthy.**

A man either thinks "No matter what I suggest, it doesn't matter, so why bother?" or he thinks "There is no way we can both have what we want, so as long as *she's* happy I'll just do what she wants."

The problem with the first option is that he stops being involved in the relationship. No longer motivated to directly express his love, he tries to be a better provider at work. If he feels unable to provide more from work—which is the case in our present economy—part of him starts to die. He becomes increasingly passive. When he goes to his cave, he doesn't know how to come out.

The problem with the second option is that after a time a man loses touch with what he wants and resents being in the relationship. When she wants more, he gets angrier without knowing why. To ensure the growth of love in a relationship, it is important that both partners get their needs met, even if it means compromise or postponing one's immediate needs.

How Bonnie Helped Me Be Successful

In the restaurant example, Bonnie was able to help me be successful through a variety of advanced relationship skills.

By letting me know in advance that she was hungry, she made it very easy for me to pick the right restaurant.

As a result, I was more involved with her while we ate. I felt as if I were providing a special meal for my loved ones. After we ate, Bonnie and Lauren thanked me. Both felt happy and taken care of, while I felt appreciated and more successful.

When a woman hasn't been taught these skills, her options are more limited. She will tend to react in one or more of these four common ways:

How Women React to Problems

---

1. She will talk about the problem.
2. She will share her feelings about the problem.
3. She will solve the problem on her own.
4. She will patiently wait for him to solve the problem.

These options are all expressions of common sense and love. She cannot instinctively understand why with a man they could be counterproductive in a relationship.

When a woman talks about a problem, a man often hears only the complaint and feels criticized. When a woman shares her feelings about a problem that she wants solved soon, a man feels controlled, as if she were demanding him to do it. When a woman solves the problem without his involvement, he remains disengaged; intimacy lessens. When she waits for him to solve the problem, she may wait too long and begin to feel resentful. When he senses her resentment, he feels unappreciated and doesn't want to solve the problem. Let's explore these reactions in greater detail.

1. Talking About the Problem

When Bonnie talked about the problem, she was careful not to sound critical, so she was centered and casual in her request. She said offhandedly, "I'm starting to feel hungry. Maybe we should stop and have lunch." Her easygoing tone of voice made it easy to respond to her request.

Many women make the mistake of sounding upset as a way to get a man's attention and let him know that the matter is important. This technique works when dealing with pets and children, but not with men. When a woman intensifies her feelings about a problem, he tends to minimize the problem.

Sometimes a woman will use the casual approach but will quickly give up when the man doesn't respond. As we discussed before, at those times it is especially effective for her to persist in asking in a casual way instead of in an intense way. Instead of getting his support by magnifying the dilemma, she should magnify her appreciation for her mate for helping solve it.

These are some various ways to persist in a noncritical or demanding way. She could say any or all of the following phrases to persist in her request and eventually get a more positive response:

Don't Say:	Do Say:
1. "We have walked all day and haven't eaten anything."	1. "I can't wait to eat. Let's look for a restaurant."
2. "All this walking just makes me hungrier, and we still haven't stopped to eat."	2. "I'm in the mood for soup and a salad. I bet these restaurants are really good."
3. "There is more to a vacation than seeing the sights; we also need to eat."	3. "There are so many restaurants here. I can't wait to eat."

Don't Say:	Do Say:
4. "These cathedrals are fine, but I can't go any farther unless we eat first."	4. "I'm having such a good time. Let's go to one of these restaurants."
5. "If we don't stop, I am going to drop. We haven't eaten all day. I need to stop."	5. "I think I have about five minutes before my blood sugar drops. Let's look for a restaurant."
6. "Don't you care about anything else? We need to stop and eat."	6. "This is so much fun. Let's find a restaurant and eat. I can't wait any longer."
7. "I can't wait any longer. We have to stop and find a restaurant."	7. "Oh my goodness, how time flies when you are having a good time. It's already one o'clock. Let's find a restaurant."

With each of these comments, a man feels appreciated for what he has done and he hears the problem without feeling blamed or criticized for it. He is much more motivated to solve a problem when *he* is not seen as the problem.

> **A man is much more motivated to solve a problem when *he* is not seen as the problem.**

How Women Sound Critical

Without knowing how to present the problem in a positive way, a woman in Bonnie's situation could have just talked about the problem and unknowingly sounded critical. She could have said any of the following examples:

What She Says:	**What He Hears:**
1. She says: "It's already one o'clock and we still haven't eaten. We need to eat."	1. He hears her saying: "Don't you care about us? All you think about is yourself and how many cathedrals you can see in a day. You let it get too late. We are not having any fun and it is all your fault."
2. She says: "I can't look at another cathedral. I have to eat something first. Let's stop and eat."	2. He hears her saying: "I didn't enjoy the sightseeing. I wish we hadn't seen so many cathedrals. You blew it."
3. She says: "I am tired of looking at cathedrals. I need some food or I am going to drop. Let's find a restaurant."	3. He hears her saying: "You have ruined my day, you push too hard, we didn't do what I wanted to do, and I wish I hadn't spent this day with you."
4. She says: "We are walking too much. We need to stop and eat."	4. He hears her saying: "We should not have walked so much. If you were more considerate, you would have stopped much sooner. Now the day is ruined."
5. She says: "We didn't eat any breakfast and it's already one o'clock. We have to stop and eat."	5. He hears her saying: "You made a big mistake. You should have taken us to breakfast. We are not having a good time because of you. We will always remember this terrible time, and it's your fault."

Although she is innocently talking about the problem, to a man, particularly on an emotional level, it may sound like she isn't appreciating what he has been doing for her. Instead of focusing on solving the problem, he feels an urgency to defend himself.

Fortunately, in Sweden, Bonnie was able to use advanced relationship skills and talk about the problem in a positive way. If she had not, I would have tried to duck and dodge, but lunch would probably not have been as nice.

2. Sharing Feelings About the Problem

When a woman shares her feelings about a problem that she wants solved, a man quite often feels controlled. The more emotional she gets, the more he feels that he *has* to do what she wants in order to please her. Her need is no longer a request but a demand. His support is no longer a choice or a gift but an obligation. When she shares her feelings along with the request, it sounds to him like he has to do what she wants or she will remain unhappy.

Sharing feelings and stating a request at the same time makes it much more difficult for men to listen. When a woman needs to talk to feel heard and understood, she should talk about her feelings. But if she wants his assistance in immediately solving her problem, she shouldn't mix it with strong feelings. It is very important for men to understand the clear distinction between when she wants solutions and when she just wants to be understood.

If a woman wants a man to learn how to listen patiently to her feelings without trying to offer solutions, it is important to leave her feelings out when she really is seeking a solution.

If a woman wants a man to learn how to listen patiently to her feelings without trying to offer solutions, it is important to leave her feelings out when she really is seeking a solution.

When Bonnie wanted to eat, instead of sharing her feelings she focused on assisting me in solving the problem. Instead of intensifying her emotions, she minimized them enough to speak in a casual and easygoing manner when she said, "I'm starting to feel hungry, maybe we should stop and have lunch."

How Women Sound Demanding

Without knowing the value of this approach, many women instinctively begin sharing their feelings before asking a man to do something. A woman in Bonnie's situation could have unknowingly sounded demanding by saying any of the following phrases:

What She Says:	What He Hears:
1. She says: "I can't keep going on like this, I am starving, I need to eat."	1. He hears: "You failed me again. You ruined everything. You better get me to a restaurant or I will be even more upset with you."
2. She says: "I feel exhausted, I need to eat. We are trying to do too much in one day."	2. He hears: "You did it wrong again. *You* are trying to do more than I can do, and now my day is ruined. You better get me to a restaurant or I will be even more upset with you."
3. She says: "I am sick of looking at cathedrals. Why can't we just slow down? We have seen enough. I need to eat."	3. He hears: "You blew it again. You wasted the whole day and wore us out. I don't want to do anything more today. I am finished for the day. You better get me to a restaurant or I will be even more upset with you."

What She Says:	What He Hears:
4. She says: "I feel so rushed. We are always in a hurry to see more. I just want to slow down. I am hungry, I want to stop and eat."	4. He hears: "Your rushing ruined everything. You better get me to a restaurant or I will be even more upset with you."

When a woman expresses her true feelings in this way, it is very hard for a man not to feel blamed and controlled. He feels that if he doesn't solve the problem immediately, she will be more and more upset with him. Instead of supporting her out of love, he is motivated out of fear of punishment—not a healthy motivation.

As a man understands a woman better, he can begin to dodge her feelings by understanding that she doesn't intend to be demanding. As a woman understands a man's perspective, it becomes easier for her to choose an approach that is more supportive of him.

3. Solving the Problem

Quite commonly, women react to a problem by simply taking charge and solving it on their own. This, too, is normal and healthy but doesn't promote intimacy. A man generally does not object to it, and many times may encourage it. From a male perspective, it is one less thing to keep him from focusing on what he is doing.

He mistakenly assumes "If letting her handle the problem makes her happy, then fine." He doesn't know that over time she will resent him for it. He doesn't know that he's missing out on the good feelings of leading her where she wants to go.

When a woman continues to solve certain problems in the relationship, from a man's perspective solving those problems tends to become her department. If she always has the answers, he instinctively focuses on areas where he has the answers and she doesn't. This is the way the masculine work world is run. In business you get paid the most for doing things that most others can't. Jobs that almost anyone can do are not well paid. If Bonnie indicates that she doesn't need my help, I instinctually don't bother.

Bonnie could easily have taken over and said, "I need to eat, let's stop here. This looks like a good restaurant." While this is a positive and direct approach, it lacks the romantic touch. It would have worked well enough, but I would not have been pulled into Bonnie's world and experience. We wouldn't have shared. Throughout lunch I would probably have just continued reading my maps and guidebooks. But because I had picked the restaurant, I was more involved. As she enjoyed the restaurant, I was feeling successful in providing for her and hence much closer.

I am certainly not suggesting that women become incapable of independent problem solving. But as we have discussed before, men primarily feel intimacy and closeness when they are successful in fulfilling a woman's needs.

4. Patiently Waiting for Him to Solve the Problem

Patience is a very important virtue, but it can be counterproductive in a relationship if a woman is not also persistent in letting a man know what she needs in a way he can eventually hear. Just being patient without skillfully doing something to eventually get what you want breeds resentment. Although this passive patience *feels* like love, it becomes toxic when he doesn't solve the problem and she feels that she has given too much.

In Sweden, Bonnie could have tried to be patient and passively waited for me to get hungry. After a few hours of waiting, however, her blood sugar would drop and she would hate me, then hate herself for being so negative. Many women make this mistake.

Although compromise and postponement of wants are important ingredients in a relationship, they are counterproductive for a woman if she doesn't directly and skillfully prepare a man to eventually give her what she needs.

When a women needs more, her primary direction should be to help her mate succeed in giving more so that she is sacrificing less. To sacrifice for its own sake may feel like a gift of love but can end up making things worse.

To sacrifice for its own sake may feel like a gift of love but can end up making things worse.

Working Together

By using new advanced relationship skills, Bonnie was able to involve me and enlist my support. Although on an emotional level I took credit for the restaurant, I was also very aware of her contribution to a romantic moment.

She made it very easy for me. She waited until we were standing near the restaurant she wanted me to pick before announcing that she was hungry. Without taking over, she skillfully helped me lead her where she wanted to go. What a great partner she is.

Bonnie also supported me when she indirectly (and I might add, masterfully) suggested where to go. When my first two picks were wrong, she knew she had to do something fast. That is when she said, "Oh, look at that restaurant. *It* looks *very* interesting." Without taking charge or directly leading, she clearly helped me to lead the family where she wanted to go.

Three Strikes and You're Out

Bonnie knew that when a man is suggesting restaurants and a woman says no three times in a row, he feels frustrated. This same principle applies to most cooperative relationship decisions. Three strikes and he is out. He begins to feel that if she is so picky, she should just do it without his help.

Most women don't realize how sensitive men are about this

issue. They have no idea that when they repeatedly resist a man's suggestions, he eventually stops caring and becomes passive. Consequently, when a decision includes her, he lets her make it. Thus, he becomes less involved in the relationship.

> When they repeatedly resist a man's suggestions, he eventually stops caring and becomes passive and less involved in the relationship.

At other times, when he really wants to do something or has a very strong opinion, he will be more resistant to her point of view. He thinks to himself, "Well, I always do what she wants. Now I want to do this, so I don't care what she thinks."

A wise woman knows how to make a man feel successful in the little decisions so that he is much more open to her ideas in the big ones. If at other times she has supported him, he is more tolerant of her objections at the really important times when difficult decisions have to be made. Even if he really wants to do something, and under normal circumstances doesn't really care what anybody thinks, he will want to take her feelings into consideration.

Why a Man Stops Giving Compliments

When Tom and Mary were dating, he always noticed how she looked and gave her lots of compliments. He said things like "You look great tonight" or "I love how you look tonight." When they went out, he would look at her and definitely enjoy how beautiful she was.

After years of marriage, he gradually stopped looking. Mary felt hurt and rejected. After a while she even stopped trying to look beautiful. When she would dress up and other men noticed her, it just made her feel more upset that Tom didn't.

When she did dress up and asked how she looked, his response was generally, "You look fine, let's go. We're late." Soon she stopped asking. Although she was beautiful, she stopped feeling that she was.

This pattern is very common because men don't instinctively realize how important compliments are to women. A key part of courtship has always been telling the beloved how beautiful she is, but a married man assumes that his mate knows he's attracted to her. He assumes that she assumes he thinks she is beautiful because he picked her for his bride. To him it's obvious. To her it is not.

As a woman's body alters with the years, and her relationship goes through changes, she needs lots of reassurance that her partner still finds her appealing. Without understanding this vital need, a man gradually stops complimenting her.

This shift does not take place because he doesn't love her, but because he doesn't know that the action of noticing her and paying her compliments means so much to her.

Tom's Feelings

Tom, like many men, had stopped complimenting his wife because he thought he had already paid her the ultimate compliment by wanting to marry her. Some of Tom's thoughts and feelings were as follows:

She Complains:	He Thinks:
1. When she complains: "He doesn't compliment me anymore."	1. He thinks to himself: "Why do I have to keep telling her? She should already know how I feel about her. Doesn't she believe me when I tell her?"
2. When she complains: "He doesn't notice me anymore, it doesn't matter to him how I look."	2. He thinks to himself: "Why do I have to compliment her every time she wears that dress? I already told her I liked it when she bought it."

She Complains:	He Thinks:
3. When she complains: "He notices other women, but he doesn't notice me anymore."	3. He thinks to himself: "In the beginning of the relationship I looked at her because I didn't know what she looked like. I was getting to know her. Now that I know what she looks like, I don't need to look as much anymore."

Men often stop complimenting their wives because they think they've already paid her the ultimate compliment by wanting to marry her.

Although every man doesn't feel exactly the same, when a man stops complimenting a woman, his reasoning will generally be similar in some way to Tom's.

In counseling he shared the above thoughts and feelings. As a man I could easily relate, but I could also understand the woman's point of view. As I explained to him how women were different, he was very willing "to try" to make some adjustments.

Mary now objected and said, "I don't want him to try. I want him to want to look at me like he used to. I don't feel loved if he is only doing it for me. I want him to compliment me because that is what he is feeling."

At this point in our session, without some advanced relationship skills they both would have sabotaged their relationship. Tom wasn't about to try something new if she didn't want him to. Her resistance just made him feel like giving up before he started.

Fortunately there was another way of looking at the problem. After I told them the following true story, they were able to resolve the issue easily.

You Look Beautiful, You Look Wonderful

Bill and Susan had been married for nine years. Like Tom, Bill had stopped complimenting his wife. Instead of taking it so personally, Susan applied an advanced skill.

One day after getting dressed up she said, "How do I look?"

Bill said, "You look good," and then looked away.

She then said, "Would you do me a favor?"

He said, "Sure."

She said, "When I ask you how I look, would you say that I look beautiful and wonderful?"

He said, "Well, what if I don't feel like saying that? Do you still want me to say it?"

She said, "Yeah, I would really love it."

Bill, in a kind of joking way, said, "OK, you look beautiful and wonderful."

She said, "Thanks, that feels real good."

Almost each day she continued to ask him and each day he responded by complimenting her. After about three months she asked again, but this time his answer was different.

This time Bill said, "You look beautiful, you look wonderful, and this time I really mean it. I am really glad you asked me to do this. I never realized before how beautiful you really are!"

From that time on, Susan rarely needed to ask Bill. He automatically noticed and complimented her. When he did forget, she would just ask and he would give her a big smile and compliment her.

After hearing this story, Mary's resistance melted away. She just needed to understand that by asking for Tom's support in this way, she wasn't begging for love. Instead, she realized that opening up to this process was a means by which she could get what she needed and also give Tom her loving support. Within a few months Mary was beaming. She told me she couldn't believe it, but it worked. Although in the beginning it felt contrived and artificial for Tom, after some time it became automatic and natural.

Why Men Stop Talking

During courtship, men sometimes do a lot of talking. A woman imagines that she has finally met a man who will open up and share. Then they marry, and he stops talking. She is bewildered; she feels that something is wrong or that he doesn't love her as much.

"When we first met, we used to have long conversations," Colleen said. "Now we don't talk at all. There is just nothing to say. I feel like I'm dying of thirst in a desert. It's not just Steve. I don't have anything to say either. I feel like our love is gone."

In fact, Steve still loved Colleen, but he was showing it differently. He assumed that choosing to share his life with her was the ultimate statement of his love. He didn't feel the same need for ongoing conversations that his wife did.

"Why do we have to always talk?" he asked. "Why can't we just be together and do things together? What is there to talk about?"

In the beginning, he talked to let her know who he was. He listened attentively to her to learn about her. Once he knew her and he felt she knew him, from his perspective there wasn't much more to say.

What Steve didn't know is that women experience greater intimacy through talking and sharing thoughts and feelings. Even if Colleen had no particular point to share, sometimes she wanted to talk just to get close. A woman wants to share her victories and her losses. A man can understand the victories, but it is hard for him to instinctively understand her need to talk about losses unless she wants his help to resolve them.

It is hard for a man to instinctively understand a woman's need to talk about losses unless she wants his help to resolve them.

After understanding the differences between men and women, Colleen was still frustrated. "Am I just supposed to accept that we will never talk?" she demanded. "I want conversation. I used to love talking with Steve."

I assured her that they could have conversations again, but that at first they would both need to practice new skills. Instead of trying to get Steve to talk, she began asking him to listen. This one little shift in her direction completely changed their relationship.

How to Get a Man to Talk

Each day, instead of asking him questions about his day, she just told him about her day. To set this up she said, "When you get home, would you give me five minutes of your undivided attention? That's all I need. I just want to tell you about my day. You don't have to say anything. It would make me feel really good. If you would find me when you first get home or when I get home and ask me about my day, I would really love it."

Steve easily said yes to five minutes, particularly if he didn't have to say anything. In the beginning he felt a lot of resistance but he did it anyway. He reasoned that it was only five minutes. They agreed that he didn't always have to do it. If, however, he didn't do it after a couple of days, in case he had forgotten she would say to him, "How was your day?" That was to be a code for "Is this a good time to talk?"

If he was willing to listen, he would say OK and then ask her about her day. Sometimes when she gave the coded message, even though he really resisted listening, he would generally go along with the request because he knew it would only be five minutes and that it was important to her.

Within a few weeks of her appreciating him for his willingness to do this, his resistance went away. After three months of doing this, Steve began to experience the fact that he really didn't have to say anything and she would feel better.

As he began to listen in a more relaxed way, he would sometimes also share about his day. She couldn't believe it, but it really worked. She rarely had to initiate conversations because he got in the habit of listening to her talk about her day and eventually found it to be very relaxing, sometimes as relaxing as watching the news.

Remember, watching the news relaxes men because it allows them to shift focus from work problems to the problems of the world, which they don't feel are their responsibility at the moment. When a man gradually learns to listen to his partner without feeling responsible for solving her problems, hearing her becomes as relaxing as watching the news. What allowed him to eventually remember to do it was Susan's appreciation for his every step in the process.

Why Men Stop Doing the Little Things

"Before we got married, Roger would do all sorts of things for me," Georgia claimed. "He emptied the trash, carried boxes, he even washed my car every two weeks. Suddenly he stopped. It makes me feel that I'm not important to him anymore."

Like many men, Roger had been motivated to do little things during courtship, but when he finally decided that he loved Georgia enough to marry her, he shifted into doing the big things like sharing his income and the rest of his life.

From his perspective, this seemed like a much bigger gift. Ironically, when he was not willing to share his income and life with her, he had been willing to test the waters and do the little things. From his perspective, when a man does little things and it makes a woman happy, it means that when he does the big things, he will be even more appreciated.

> When a man does little things and it makes a woman happy, he assumes that when he does the big things, he will be even more appreciated.

So, when he is willing to do the big things and *it* is not enough, he feels defeated. This pattern is common with men, but it can be updated with a little cooperation and skill.

I recommended that Georgia and Roger start with an easy exercise like emptying the trash. Georgia set the process in

motion by first asking Roger for his support. "I really appreciate how hard you work," she said, "and I know you just want
to rest when you get home. I would really appreciate it if you
would empty the trash three times a week for me. I know it may
sound silly to you, but it would make me feel really good.
Would you do it?"

They created a secret code to help him remember. Three
times a week, when Georgia noticed that the trash was full, she
would put it out in the middle of the kitchen floor. If he walked
around it and still didn't notice it, she would ask in a friendly
voice, "Oh, would you empty the trash?" In the beginning,
Roger grumbled.

She was worried that he would hold it against her, but I
reassured Georgia that these grumbles were a good sign. Then I
explained to her something that every woman needs to know
about men.

What Every Woman Needs to Know About Men

When a man grumbles, it generally means that he is seriously
considering her request. It is his process for shifting gears from
what he was already doing to focusing on a new goal. Being
goal oriented, men find it much harder to shift directions once
they are already moving toward an end. While making this
shift, men commonly grumble.

As I saw it, Roger was opening up to Georgia's request, but
it was taking a little time. It was like opening a door with rusty
hinges that make a lot of noise.

Women do not instinctively understand a man's grumbles
because women grumble for different reasons. If a man asks a
woman to do something and she grumbles but does it anyway,
she will tend to get upset and stay upset for a long time. "I am
giving too much in this relationship." That is what her grumbles mean.

But when a man grumbles, he is thinking, "Do I really have
to do this? Is it really that important? Is it more important than

what I am already doing? What am I doing? What would happen if I did this? Hey, she might really appreciate it. OK, I'll do it. But it better make a difference. Let's give it a try."

If he then proceeds to empty the trash and she appreciates him, his frustration immediately melts away. He is actually in a better mood because he did something to please her.

When Roger first began emptying the trash, he would resist and grumble. When he finished, Georgia would practice appreciating him. She watched with disbelief as his grumbles went away.

As a man begins to anticipate that his female partner will appreciate his every effort in doing the little things, he eventually grumbles less. At a later stage, he actually begins looking for little things to do for her.

When It's Safe to Ask

If a man grumbles, it is generally a sign that he just needs to feel appreciated. He needs to repeatedly experience that his efforts have been worth it. All it takes to satisfy him is for her to acknowledge and appreciate what he did and not ask immediately for more. Ideally she should let him bask in having done something to lighten up her day.

After a few months of emptying the trash in this way, Roger found himself actually looking forward to emptying the trash because it made Georgia so happy.

He was the president of a very successful clothing chain, but he looked forward to emptying the trash. This made his wife very happy. It made her feel more special than his work, which she felt captured most of his attention.

Ripples of Love

As I was writing this section, my wife told me about something outside in the backyard that needed to be fixed after lunch. I quickly figured that it would take only five minutes at the most. Going straight to my tool kit, I pulled out a hammer and told her, "I'll fix it."

She had such a smile on her face. That beautiful glow stayed with me for hours. Although we both love each other, without these little expressions of love, it is hard to experience or *feel* the love. It is like sitting in a warm bathtub or a spa. If you don't move the water you stop feeling the heat, but with a simple movement you feel the ripples of warmth.

It is these simple ripples that make a woman feel special. By my taking that five minutes, Bonnie felt more special than my work. Feeling her loving response to my loving behavior made me feel more relaxed and happy as well.

How to Get More in Your Relationship

The secret of getting more from a man is to appreciate what he is already giving and then ask for more in small increments. Once Roger had experienced the positive influence he created by emptying the trash, Georgia brought up the subject of washing the car.

"Do you remember when we were dating and you used to wash my car?" she asked. "That was really special. It's kind of like emptying the trash. When you do little things for me, it makes me feel more important than your job. I know you love me, but it just makes me feel really happy if you wash my car. Would you do it?"

Just as with the trash, Roger again began washing her car. Although there were a lot more things he wasn't doing, Georgia was hopeful, and their marriage became increasingly intimate. She had the satisfaction of knowing that she wasn't powerless and that over time she would restore to the relationship many elements she'd loved in courtship. She had correctly seen Roger's potential but just didn't know how to draw it out.

The secret of getting more from a man is to appreciate what he is already giving and then ask for more in small increments.

When women ask me how to get their partners to do more, I suggest that they start with things he did while courting her. These are the easiest things for him to learn, since he once did them.

Here's a good way to get started. Write out a list of ten things you'd like your mate to do. Then pick what you think would be the easiest thing for him to do. Generally, I suggest that a woman first work on assisting a man in being a good listener before focusing on other requests.

A woman should first work on assisting a man in being a good listener before focusing on other requests.

Why Men Stop Listening

"When I had a problem, Rick used to be so sympathetic, but now when I complain about anything he gets upset with me," Susie complained. "It makes me feel like he doesn't care." She mistakenly assumed that Rick didn't love her as much as before and couldn't understand why he had changed.

When they were dating, she complained constantly about being a single mother and the unsatisfactory relationship she had gotten out of. Rick had seemed to be so caring and sympathetic. He always listened and validated her feelings with a silent nod or by a soothing touch. She felt that she could say anything and he would understand.

Once they were married, all that changed. If she talked about the problems of being a mother or wanted to talk about the problems in their relationship, he would become frustrated and not want to listen. When she did talk, he would feel frustrated and try to explain away her feelings.

Rick was the same Rick. His love had not changed. Before it had been easy for him to listen to her problems about her ex-lover because he didn't feel blamed. He was glad to listen to the problems she had in other relationships. When she complained about her ex-lover, he felt more assured that she was available to him. No wonder he loved listening.

It was also easy for him to hear her talk about the problems of being a single mother because he imagined that one day he would be able to solve those problems for her.

His feelings were like this: "If she feels supported by me now, wait till we have a relationship. I will really make things easier for her." He had no idea that at the time, his silent support and sympathy were much more important than anything he could provide later.

After discovering that Rick's love was still there, Susie was encouraged to begin practicing advanced skills. By learning to pause before talking and prepare Rick to listen, she slowly got him to change back again and got the support she had enjoyed in courtship.

She let him know in advance if she wanted him to be a sympathetic shoulder to lean on. She asked, "Would you give me a hug?" That was another agreed-upon coded message that meant "I just need to talk. Would you ask me how I'm feeling?"

Rick learned that it is a hundred times easier for a woman to open up and receive his silent support when he initiates the conversation. By asking him for a hug, Susie gave him the clue that she would really appreciate his asking her about her feelings.

Why Men Stop Pursuing

"Sam used to find me when he came home from work," Lisa shared. "Now he either goes straight to the TV or plays with the kids. I feel taken for granted. I don't feel loved or special anymore." Like many men, Sam had stopped pursuing his partner. Once he attained his goal, he automatically stopped his pursuit.

If your goal is to climb a mountain and you get to the top, you stop and relax. Once the chase is over, the hunter stops chasing. Lisa felt that she was no longer special, and Sam simply didn't understand.

From his perspective, pursuit served no purpose in a marriage. When he was dating and came to her house, he would go upstairs to greet her. If she was in the kitchen, he would seek her out. This was because he hadn't seen her in a while.

When Lisa visited him, he would immediately go to the door to greet her because it was his home and she was a guest. Once they married, Sam didn't feel required to meet her at the door because it was her home too.

As a man pursuing a woman, Sam had also been looking for any opportunity to say "I care," so he was always enthusiastic about seeing her. After getting married, he didn't feel the need to keep saying it. He thought getting married said it for him. For him, the chase was over and now he could relax.

The last thing Sam thought of when he got home was that Lisa was waiting for him to find her. He didn't instinctively know, because many evenings he just wanted to be in his cave and *not* be found for a while.

Lisa and Sam were easily able to remedy this situation. Once the dynamics of ongoing pursuit made sense to him, he was much more motivated. After a few months of practice, it became very automatic for him to immediately seek Lisa out at the end of the day.

Bringing in the Groceries

Bonnie and I have a similar ritual. My writing office is in our home. When I am working and hear her car drive up, I immediately save my work on the computer and go find her. It makes her feel special.

When this pattern repeats over time, just the thought of coming home nurtures her female side and reduces her stress. If a man makes this small shift, he will be astonished by the world of difference it makes to his mate. When I share this story with the men in my seminars, they can't believe that there are so many easy ways to make a woman happier.

When Bonnie comes home with groceries, she leaves the trunk of the car open as a little signal for me. I can then notice and offer to bring them in. When a man offers his support, it is much more nurturing than if a woman has to ask.

If a man, however, is not doing what a woman wants, then it is necessary for a woman to ask graciously. After he eventually learns, she will not have to ask as much. The first step in getting what she wants is for a woman to start asking.

In the beginning I would forget to offer to bring in the groceries, so Bonnie would say, "Would you bring in the groceries?" And I would say, "Sure."

After a few months of her asking and always appreciating me for it, it became second nature. Now when she comes home, I automatically look to see if the trunk is open before I go find her. Then, after I give her a hug and ask her about her day, I offer to bring in the groceries.

After five minutes I go back down to my office and start working again, but this time feeling more refreshed because I have been appreciated by my wife. She is also more refreshed. When she drives home, just the expectation of my support and love helps to wash away the stresses of her day.

Why It's So Good in the Beginning

The early stages of a relationship are incredibly energizing to both men and women. Before a woman knows a man, she expects or hopes that he will be the one to fulfill her needs. When she responds with appreciation, it encourages him to think "She is appreciating me so much for the little things I am doing, wait till I do the big things; she will really be happy."

In the second stage of a relationship, he begins to disappoint her by dropping courtship behaviors, and she stops appreciating him so much. Without her appreciation, he gradually becomes more tired and passive, and she feels more isolated and overwhelmed.

With advanced relationship skills, men and women can move beyond the second stage and re-create the relationship they thought they had in the beginning.

Why Men Stop Picking Up After Themselves

"When we were dating and I went to Henry's apartment, it was always clean. He picked up after himself," Joyce moaned. "Now that we're married, he leaves a trail behind him wherever he goes. I don't want to be his mother and pick up after him. I resent it."

Joyce's attitude is common. She feels that Henry used to be neat and now he is not, so it is easy to be frustrated and feel taken for granted. What she doesn't realize is that he has always been that way.

She didn't know because when he was single, he would clean up the mess each time she went over to his apartment. He was not trying to deceive her, only to impress her. Once they moved in together, he didn't realize how important picking up was for her.

When a man doesn't pick up after himself, a woman tends to feel like she is his maid or mother and resents it. Joyce became bitter because she was already washing his socks; at least he could pick them up. By understanding this, Henry was motivated to begin picking up his socks, and Joyce was less bitter when he forgot.

How to Get a Man to Pick Up

Joyce had to retrain herself not to pick up after Henry if she wanted him to do it. When his socks and underwear built up, she would ask pleasantly, "Would you pick up your socks? I'm going to do a load of wash." She went out of her way to not sound critical or demanding.

When he began getting in the habit of picking up, she made a point of noticing and appreciating him. She would say things like "Oh, everything looks so neat. Thanks for cleaning up."

This is an advanced skill that most women don't do enough of. They figure "They're his socks, so why should I appreciate him for picking them up?"

The reason to appreciate him is that he has made an effort

to do something for you. He doesn't mind if his socks lie around until they run out. When he picks them up before he runs out of clean ones, he is doing it for you and deserves your appreciation.

After a few months of doing this, Henry started to appreciate the value of a neater room himself. He was no longer doing it for her but because he liked it. Susie, however, wisely continued to appreciate him. She had learned how feminine and good she felt when she could find things to appreciate about him.

It is hard for women to understand how a man could be so unconscious of what he leaves behind. Taking into consideration a man's goal-oriented nature, it is easier. As soon as a man takes off his socks, he is quickly moving on to his next goal, the bed. His tendency is to not look back. When he wakes up, his goal is to get ready to go. Picking up socks is not needed to get to work (his next goal), so in many cases he just doesn't even see them.

Why Men Stop Focusing on the Relationship

"Nick used to look at me when I talked. Now he just looks away," Louise said. "I feel like what I'm saying is not important to him. He used to be so much more attentive. When he gets a call about work, he comes alive. When I talk, he just seems distracted."

Like many men during courtship, Nick was highly focused on his relationship with Louise. So he was much more attentive and responsive to her needs and feelings. After they got married, however, he shifted.

It was as if his body was home while his mind was still at work. He was either preoccupied with work-related issues or in his cave trying to forget work by watching TV.

Whenever Louise needed his time or attention, he became impatient and resistant. Louise could be understanding until she noticed that when his office called he would suddenly come alive. To her, it was very clear that he loved his work more than he loved her. This pattern is very common between men and women, but with the right understanding it can be corrected.

When a Man Is on the Hunt

In the beginning of a courtship, it is as though a man is on the hunt. He is completely focused on the woman he cares for. Winning her over is his primary goal. He will do whatever it takes to be successful. He will sleep out in the cold, endure blistering heat, risk his life, and silently bear any sacrifice. All his energies and inner resources are focused on one goal: winning her over. This is his way of showing her that he loves her.

His ability to focus intently and do whatever is required makes a big impact on a woman, particularly when she is the center of his focus and the goal of his desires. The problems begin only after he wins her over.

A man's ability to focus intently and do whatever is required makes a big impact on a woman, particularly when she is the center of his focus and the goal of his desires.

Having achieved his goal, a man relaxes and gradually redirects his focus and energy toward a new goal. With renewed vigor, he concentrates on his job so that he can provide for her. He mistakenly assumes that her needs will be satisfied by his earning money. As his energies become focused on work, she mistakenly believes that he cares more about his work than he does about her.

He becomes perplexed that she doesn't feel loved. He doesn't realize how important his focused attention was to her. He doesn't even realize how he has changed.

Even though in the relationship she feels ignored and unseen, he thinks he is loving her. He sees himself as the same man he always was. His focus has just shifted to work. He still loves her and he is still willing to make huge sacrifices for her, he just does them at work instead of directly *for* her as he did before they were married.

How a Man Can Redirect His Focus

To override his instinctual tendency to focus on his work and redirect his focus to her, a man needs a woman's assistance. When she can accept his tendency to focus on work as an expression of his loving desire to provide for her, she can easily motivate him to again begin doing the little things that make her feel so special. By patiently asking him to listen, requesting that he do little things for her, and then appreciating him, she assists him in shifting away from work and focusing more on her.

> To override his instinctual tendency to focus on his work and redirect his focus to her, a man needs a woman's assistance.

As she becomes more skilled in helping him to be successful at home, his attention will automatically focus on doing things directly for her because he has experienced that it's the little things that make a difference.

Through understanding how important it is for a woman to get a man's direct attention, a man can also choose to change this pattern. I have focused on what women can do, because with this awareness she can greatly help a man. There is, however, a technique I used to create a new pattern of making sure my wife felt more important than work.

Balancing Work and Home

I remember back to the first year of my marriage to Bonnie. As with most marriages, it started out very loving, and we were both happy. Then, as months passed, she became increasingly unhappy. In the honeymoon period, she was excited to see me when I got home, but gradually, as routine set in, it was no longer special. We talked less and less. I didn't even notice her shift because it was so gradual and seemed normal. After all, that's what my parents had done.

There is another reason, however, that I didn't notice. Each night when I returned home from work I was exhausted but happy. I was happy because I was successful, earning a good living, and saving money to buy a house. I was doing what I felt a man was supposed to do: I was being a good provider. Meanwhile, Bonnie was trying to be a good and loving wife and not complain. As time passed, however, it eventually became clear that she was not happy.

She said she didn't feel that I loved her anymore. She felt taken for granted and unimportant in my life. With tears in her eyes, she told me that I loved my work more than I loved her and that she could never compete. In response, I tried to explain that I did love her. Although she tried to receive what I said, my explanations only made matters worse.

She said that I gave all my energy to my clients, and that when I came home, I had nothing left for her. She felt like she was at the bottom of my list of priorities. I explained that she was the reason I was working so hard. Without the money, we would not be able to have a life together. I thought she should be happy that I was working hard to secure a home. Although what I explained made sense, I eventually came to realize that being a good provider was only a part of what our marriage required. Like every other woman today, Bonnie needed more.

In the old days, a man expressed his love by going off to war or risking his life hunting or enduring hardship to bring home food. Although his energy was directed elsewhere, it still allowed a woman to feel loved and supported. The new way for a woman to feel loved is for a man to also devote himself directly to supporting her.

The Golden Twenty Minutes

Without Bonnie knowing that I was trying a new technique, I decided to come home an hour earlier each day and devote a fifty-minute hour to her. To make this shift, I pretended that she was my most important and best-paying client. Somehow, by convincing myself that it was my job, I was able to keep my energy up when I got home.

My old habit was to work and, in a sense, collapse when I got home. By pretending that I was making a house call, I was able to make the shift easily.

When I got home, I practiced everything I knew to be more supportive. First I found her, then I offered her a big hug and initiated conversation. Regardless of what she was doing, I would join in and help out. I would cut carrots, clean countertops, empty the trash, or simply hang out wherever she was and talk a little about my day and then ask her questions about hers.

She was so used to my not being interested that at first she had very little to say. Eventually, she really started to open up. After experimenting, I found that she really began to glow after twenty shared minutes. It didn't even take the full fifty. Within days, she started to glow constantly, and felt better and less fatigued.

Since that time, I will occasionally forget to give her the golden twenty minutes, but when I notice that things are getting routine in our relationship or that she is becoming more stressed or overwhelmed, I diligently begin again.

The technique has become second nature. Most of the time, when I get home or she comes home, I immediately find her and spend some time sharing affection, attention, and support.

Relationships and Stress Reduction

As I learned to redirect my attention to the relationship, not only was my wife happier, but I could also relax more quickly from work. Until I learned to make this transition, not only did my wife feel neglected, but without even knowing it I had lost touch with the warm, loving feelings of our honeymoon period.

A man feels much less stress when he is in love. Even if he is working hard, he doesn't get as fatigued by his job. His work does not consume him because he is focused on his relationship.

When a man's focus completely shifts back to work, he

starts becoming more fatigued and stressed. He again feels the pressures of work. He doesn't know that if he consciously redirected his energies into the relationship, he could more effectively forget those pressures and be more energized at home. He doesn't realize that if he could forget work and focus more on his wife's needs and feel her appreciation in response, he would be less stressed and have more energy.

Men do not instinctively understand this because in hunter/nurturer days, if a man merely returned home from the hunt alive, his mate was happy and enormously appreciative. For a modern woman to feel that much appreciation, she needs her partner to focus directly on her emotional needs.

Understanding Our Changes

In many cases when our partners change, it is easy to misinterpret their motives and feel that they don't love us as much. Women commonly feel that they give but are not getting back. With greater insight, a woman's heart can be softened by the awareness that her man is trying to do his best but doesn't really grasp what she needs.

> **With greater insight, a woman's heart can be softened by the awareness that her man is trying to do his best but doesn't really grasp what she needs.**

With a greater understanding of how a man's changes can affect the relationship, not only can a man make things better, but a woman is empowered to create the changes she wants. Besides learning how to interpret a man's changes correctly, it is also important for women to be aware of how they also change in a relationship over the course of time.

In the next chapter, we will explore some of the ways in which women commonly change. Men will learn new skills to draw out of their mates the love they so freely gave in the beginning. Women will benefit by understanding how their changing affects their men.

CHAPTER 10

Where Is the Woman I Fell For?

Just as men shift in a variety of ways, so do women change over the course of a relationship. In most cases, they are completely unaware of how they are contributing to the problems of the relationship. They honestly believe that it is only their mates who are different.

Although these changes are largely unconscious, a man who doesn't understand them may become resentful and truly hold back. Through using advanced relationship skills, he can immediately begin to bring back the woman he fell in love with.

By learning to give his love in specific ways, a man can help his partner cope with and overcome these changes. Without this information, he will tend to react instinctively and, in most cases, he will only make things worse. Even though his intention is to help her love him better, she eventually begins to pull away.

How Women Change

When a woman changes, it doesn't mean that she isn't in love with her partner. Even still, in his quiet moments, a man wonders where the woman he chose to marry has gone. Let's explore some common feelings men have about the ways in which women change. These are some common comments and complaints:

Bill: "In the beginning, Jane was almost always in the mood to have sex. She loved it. Now when I want sex, other things are more important, or she's not in the mood. For a while, I was always trying to figure out when she wanted it and when she didn't. I don't bother anymore. I just wait till she initiates it. I'm not going to beg."

Jim: "Judy used to really appreciate the places I would take her. Now it seems that no matter where I want to go, she wants to go somewhere else. I don't even want to bother."

Tom: "When we were dating, no matter what I did Mary seemed to be happy. She was so easy to please and so appreciative. Now when I do things like call from work or open the car door or make a date, she doesn't react like that. It's like I'm expected to do it."

Steve: "When we were dating, Colleen was always so happy and excited to see me. Now when I come home she is generally complaining about something or is cold and distant. I've been solving problems all day; I don't want more problems when I get home. As soon as I begin to relax, she starts asking me about my thoughts and feelings. Why can't we just *be* together? Why does she always want me to talk? I talk all day. When I get home, the last thing I want to do is remember my day. I'm trying to forget it."

Roger: "In the beginning, Georgia's love was so unconditional. I felt that I could just be me and that was enough. Now I feel like she is trying to change me. She's always telling me what to do. I hate it. She's treating me like a child."

Rick: "In the beginning, Susie was always so happy to have me in her life. I felt like I really made a difference. Now she is always wanting to talk about the relationship. I hate it. Why can't we just enjoy our relationship like we did in the beginning? Why do we have to talk about it?"

Sam: "Lisa used to be so happy with whatever I did. It seemed like I could do no wrong. No matter what I did, it was enough. I used to want to spend time at home. Now when I get home, I'm barraged with a list of 'honey do's.' As soon as I sit down, Lisa starts giving orders. It's like she waits for me to relax. When I get home, I feel like I have to hide from her. I don't want to come home to another boss. I have to go on fishing trips just to get away."

Henry: "In the beginning, she never complained. If I forgot to do something, it was no big deal. It was fun doing things together. Now she complains that I don't do enough around the house. When I do help, she either points out what I didn't do or she doesn't even notice what I did. If I empty the trash or clean up the house, she acts like it's no big deal. If that's the case, why bother?"

Nick: "In the beginning, Louise was so happy to be with me. She was impressed by my competence and my work. Now I feel like no matter how hard I work it's never enough for her."

There is a common theme to each of these examples. In each case, a man feels that his female partner wants more and appreciates less. In the beginning, he felt accepted and appreciated but then, over time, this feeling lessened. Although from his perspective her behavior may not have changed much, her attitude has, and she is much less supportive of him.

With an awareness of how and why a woman's attitude changes, a man can begin to get her to open up again. Let's explore in greater detail what he can do to support the woman he loves.

Why Women Stop Wanting Sex

"In the beginning, Jane was almost always in the mood to have sex," Bill confessed. "She loved it. Now when I want sex, either other things are more important, or she's not in the mood. For a while, I was always trying to figure when she wanted it and when she didn't. I don't bother anymore. I just wait till she initiates it. I'm not about to beg."

Bill didn't understand that for a woman to feel sexual desire, she needs love and romance. It is not enough for her partner to be a provider and protector. She needs him to do the little "magic" things he did in the beginning—to sweep her off her feet again and again.

For a woman to feel sexual desire, she needs love and romance.

During the courtship, a man makes the romantic gestures to open a woman up to having sex. Once they are having sex regularly, he doesn't realize that she still needs to be romanced. Without romance, she can easily become so overwhelmed with day-to-day tasks and duties that sexual desire moves to the back burner.

What men must remember is that when a woman comes home from her "day job," her domestic instincts tell her to start producing again. There is too much to do as a homemaker and mother before she can relax enough to enjoy sex.

By being aware of Jane's tendency to feel overwhelmed, Bill can effectively compensate by initiating conversations so that she feels heard and not alone. With good communication and a little romance from Bill, she can reconnect to her sexual feelings. With continued support at home, a woman will begin to relax more and remember how enjoyable sex can be.

Why Women Become More Difficult to Please

"Judy used to really appreciate the places I would take her," Jim said. "Now it seems no matter where I want to go, she wants to go somewhere else. I don't even want to bother."

Jim doesn't understand that women need variety. Because men are so goal oriented, when they find a restaurant they like, they tend to keep going back. It is a sure thing. Why risk failure by trying something new?

Variety increases a man's chances of failure, while variety lifts a woman out of the boredom of routine. She looks forward to trying new things.

Variety increases a man's chances of failure, while
variety lifts a woman out of the boredom of routine.
She looks forward to trying new things.

In the beginning, Judy could appreciate his choices in restaurants because they were all new to her. It was fun and exciting to discover his hangouts. But, later on, when his choices became routine, she was ready for a change.

As a woman changes and begins to resist her mate's suggestions, he mistakenly believes that she doesn't approve of his choices. Rather than risk repeated failure, he stops suggesting.

How Jim Dodged

Once Jim understood Judy's innate need for variety, he was able to dodge her resistance and not feel frustrated. He eventually learned to anticipate her desire to try something new. Sometimes, he realized, having a good, open conversation about where to go was even more important than where they ended up going.

Judy conscientiously supported Jim by always finding something to appreciate about the places he selected. If the restaurant turned out to be only so-so, she would focus on how nice it was to spend such a special time together, not on the quality of the meal. Without her telling him her opinion in great detail, he got the message and never suggested that particular restaurant again.

Why Women Resist

At the beginning of a relationship, a woman is happy to do what her mate wants and is eager to learn about him. She assumes he'll want to do the same for her. She assumes that at a later date it will be her turn to pick the restaurants and make suggestions about what to do for the evening. When this happens, he feels she has changed. He does not realize that she was just taking turns and letting him make his suggestions first.

Jim learned that he could make room for Judy to get what she wanted and also get what he wanted. Sometimes they went to places he knew they both liked. At other times he would encourage experimenting with somewhere neither of them had been. Instead of worrying too much about the result of their decision, he wisely focused on making the process harmonious.

Why Women Stop Appreciating the Little Things

"When we were dating, no matter what I did Mary seemed to be happy," Tom recalled. "She seemed so easy to please and appreciative. Now when I do things like call from work or open the car door or make a date, she doesn't react the same way. It's like I'm expected to do it."

From Tom's perspective, Mary had changed dramatically. In reality, she was behaving like an ordinary wife. When a woman first meets a man, she regularly expresses appreciation to let him know she is open to having a relationship.

Once they are married, she doesn't realize that he still needs her appreciation. She doesn't grasp how important it is for him to be acknowledged. She assumes her job description is to do things to express her love. What she doesn't know is that he would rather she "do" less for him and appreciate more what he "does" for her.

Men would rather a woman "do" less for him and appreciate more what he "does" for her.

As a marriage proceeds, and the woman begins doing more things for her mate, she begins to *expect* him to do things for her. Before marriage, if he calls from work, she is thrilled. After marriage, if he doesn't call three times a week, she is crushed.

When a man feels he "has to do things," he doesn't feel like doing them. As he does less and his mate does more, her appreciation decreases proportionally.

Resentment Flu

Tom learned to accept that although men need to feel appreciated, sometimes women just have no love to give. They are temporarily empty. At those times, he learned to be patient and persisted in doing lots of little things for her even when she was not appreciative in response. He mastered the advanced relationship skill of giving when she had only a minimum of love to give.

Generally speaking, a man gives when his support is appreciated. If she is not openly responsive to his support, then he easily loses the wind in his sails. This is because he doesn't want to do something if it doesn't seem necessary, useful, or productive. If she is unresponsive to his support, he figures it doesn't seem to help and stops doing it.

A man gives when his support is appreciated.

When a woman feels she is giving more support than she is getting, sooner or later she catches the resentment flu. As soon as he does something nice for her, she reflexively sneezes resentment all over him.

Emotionally, she is saying "So what if you opened the car door for me? I do so much more for you. When you do more, I'll appreciate you."

At such times, a man must bear in mind that his partner is really out of balance and has nothing to give. If he patiently waits while continuing to do little things, he will soon win her over.

Tom learned that if he could support Mary at those times when she could not appreciate him, she would always show him her appreciation later.

If a man can support a woman at those times when she cannot appreciate him, she will show him appreciation later.

Why Women Begin to Complain More

"When we were dating, Colleen was always so happy and excited to see me," Steve said. "Now when I come home she's complaining about something or is cold and distant. I have been solving problems all day. I don't want more problems when I get home. As soon as I begin to relax, she starts asking me about my thoughts and feelings. Why can't we just *be* together? Why does she always want me to talk? I talk all day. When I get home, the last thing I want to do is remember my day. I am trying to forget it."

A woman being courted naturally puts her best foot forward. As the relationship grows over time, she feels it's safer to open up and express her more vulnerable feelings like frustration, disappointment, worry, and embarrassment. A man tends to misunderstand and thinks she is becoming negative.

When Steve learned that Colleen just needed to share her feelings at the end of the day, and that she wasn't blaming him or expecting him to solve her problems, he found it easier to listen to her. And when Colleen was cool or distant, instead of ignoring her, he would hug her and ask about her day. Gradually, she would warm up and talk. Colleen was so appreciative of Steve's new behavior that she found it easier to accept his need to withdraw into his cave sometimes and not talk about his problems.

Why Women Give Unsolicited Advice

"In the beginning, Georgia's love was so unconditional. I felt I could just be me and that that was enough," Roger shared. "Now I feel like she's always trying to change me. She's always telling me what to do. She's treating me like a child. I hate it."

When a woman loves a man, she quite naturally wants him to be the best he can be. Out of her love, she sees his great potential and sets out to help him realize it. She wants to nurture his growth.

Even if a woman is not a mother, the tendency to "mother" her partner grows stronger when she loves him. If she has children, the urge is even stronger. Unfortunately, it is difficult for a woman to nurture a man without mothering him.

When Women Mother Men

When a woman gradually begins to mother a man, she thinks she is being loving and helpful, but she is really sabotaging her relationship.

When a woman gradually begins to mother a man, she thinks she is being loving and helpful, but she is really sabotaging her relationship.

Men want to be trusted to provide. When a woman mothers a man, she withdraws that trust. Instead of allowing him to learn what he needs to learn on his own, she begins to take responsibility for him.

In the beginning of a relationship, a woman generally doesn't mother her man. She sees his potential and assumes that he can and will develop and express it.

But, over time, as she sees him doing things differently from the way she believes he should, she begins giving him unsolicited advice. She thinks she is helping, but in reality she is sending him the message that he can't succeed on his own. He feels that she is trying to change him.

How Women Mother Men

These are some ways in which some women unknowingly begin to turn a man off by mothering him. They are classic examples of the breakdown in communication when a woman speaks in "Female" and her partner listens in "Male."

She Says:	He Hears:
1. When a man gets dressed, a woman will say: "I hope you are not going to wear that."	1. He hears her say: "You can't even dress yourself."
2. When a man buys something for himself, she will say: "Did you shop around first? How much did that cost? You paid that?"	2. He hears her say: "You don't know how to get the best price on your own. You can't make adult decisions."
3. After visiting a man's office, she will say: "When are you going to clean up your office? It's such a mess in there. I don't know how you can think in there. If you cleaned it up, you would get a lot more done."	3. He hears her say: "Not only are you a slob, but without my help you will never amount to anything. I know better than you how you can be more successful."
4. While a man is eating a dessert, she will say: "You've already had a dessert today. I don't think it's good for you to eat so much sugar."	4. He hears her say: "You can't eat that. You should eat what I say is OK. You can't be trusted."
5. While a man is eating potato chips, she will say: "Those are really bad for your heart. You know you shouldn't be eating them."	5. He hears her say: "I know what's best for you and you don't. When are you going to grow up?"
6. While a man is working hard to meet a deadline, she says: "If you didn't wait till the last minute, then you wouldn't have to rush like this."	6. He hears her say: "My way is better than your way. You should listen to me and change your ways. When you are more mature, you will understand what I know."

She Says:	He Hears:
7. When a man buys a black car for himself, she says: "Black cars get dirtier much faster. You should get another color if you are not going to wash it regularly. Are you going to wash it more often?"	7. He hears her say: "You don't know how to pick a car. I know better. If you do pick black, then you have to wash it every week. You will then probably forget, and I will have to remind you."
8. When a man is driving the car, she says: "You shouldn't drive so fast. You could get a ticket."	8. He hears her say: "You don't know how to drive as well as me. You don't even know that you could get a speeding ticket for driving fast."
9. After a man gets a speeding ticket, she says: "I knew you would get a ticket. Maybe the next time you will listen to me."	9. He hears her say: "You need me to tell you these things. I can't imagine how you get along without me. I was right again, and you were wrong. Your problem is that you don't listen."
10. When a man is disappointed about a business loss, she says: "The next time you should take more time to make a decision like that. You should get several opinions."	10. He hears her say: "You made this mistake because you are not responsible enough. You are incapable of making good business decisions on your own. You should do it my way. You still haven't learned."

She Says:	He Hears:
11. When a man is stressed out and needs to be in his cave, she says: "I can see that you're really upset. You should talk about your feelings. You should really open up or get help."	11. He hears her say: "You can't deal with this on your own. You are wrong for wanting to deal with this alone. I know better what is good for you."
12. When a man is leaving for a trip, she says: "Do you have your wallet? Do you have your airplane ticket? You didn't give yourself enough time. What if there is a traffic jam, you will be late."	12. He hears her say: "You can't plan your trips without my help. I don't trust you. You are still a child, and I have to take care of you."
13. When he is fixing the toilet, she says: "You know, if you jiggle the handle, that will help. . . . Maybe you could call the plumber. He will know what to do."	13. He hears her say: "You can't do that without my help. I know more about this than you, so I am going to watch and help you learn how to solve this problem."

In each of these examples, a woman is preventing a man from making his own decisions by giving advice when he hasn't asked for it. This is not support. Even if he needs the input, he will not hear her. When a woman persists in offering a man unsolicited advice, he will gradually turn off to her.

When a woman persists in offering a man unsolicited advice, he will gradually turn off to her.

Camp Director

When my wife begins to mother me, I try to remember that she generally does this when she feels she needs help and she isn't getting it. So I try to view her tendency to give advice and instructions in a more positive way. My affectionate term for it is "camp director."

When Bonnie is in her "camp director" mode, I avoid feeling victimized by her controlling attitude by remembering that I can do something to get her out of it. Once I start taking charge by offering to help, she begins to relax and appreciate my support rather than seeing me as another child who needs direction.

I first realized this when we were packing for a trip. While I was packing my bag, she was packing her own bag and helping our three children pack theirs. She was quite definitely overwhelmed.

She said things to the kids like: "Did you pack your toothbrush? Make sure to pack your special blanket and panda bear. Make sure to bring a jacket and a sweater. It could be cold. We only have fifteen more minutes and then we have to leave! Once you are done, make sure you get something to eat. We still have bagels. You can just put them in the toaster. . . ."

When I came into the room, she continued to talk to me in that same tone. "Do you have the tickets? How much money do you have? Make sure to call your office before we leave. Did you pack a sweater?"

My gut reaction to being talked to like a child was strong resistance. I hadn't asked for her help. I had the tickets, I had enough money, I had already called my office, and I didn't want to pack a sweater. What I wanted was to get away from her. In the past, I would have. This time, because I had a deeper understanding of what women need to be loving to a man, I was able to address the problem more effectively.

What a Man Can Do

When a woman is overwhelmed with responsibility and a man ignores her, she feels even more isolated, unsupported, and therefore responsible for everything, like a camp director. If he stays and gets upset, she feels that he doesn't understand.

I decided to dodge Bonnie's "directions and orders" by making her feel less alone. Quite simply, I started repeating her orders. When she said to the kids, "Did you pack your toothbrush?" I would say, "Lauren, it's time to pack your toothbrush. When you're finished, bring your panda bear and I'll pack him."

Passively taking orders would not have helped her from feeling overwhelmed. But by doing self-initiated behaviors and thinking up more things that needed to be done, I released her from feeling totally responsible.

At some point, I looked over at Bonnie and without her even being aware of it, she straightened up, took a deep breath, and started to relax.

In simple terms, when I was not directly helping, she went too much to her male side and became camp director. By bringing some take-charge male energy into the room, I allowed her to relax and feel her feminine energy again. Not only was she more receptive and open to being supported, but she was more appreciative of me.

I learned that with my direct support, I could minimize her camp director tendencies. With this new awareness and confidence it became much easier to dodge her orders.

If a car is running out of gas, you don't worry as long as there's a filling station in sight. But if there isn't one, you begin to panic. Similarly, without knowing how to assist a woman out of the camp director mode, most men panic. They fear that they will have to live with being mothered for the rest of their lives when all they really need to do to help her out is to apply these new skills.

When a woman turns into a camp director, at some point it is helpful for a man to walk up to her and touch her or offer to give her a hug. Touch always helps center a woman back to her female side. By nurturing her female side with touch, it helps her to find balance.

Then, after touching her, he can start offering to do things to help out. The more active she sees him being, the less alone she feels. The more he begins to think of things that need to be done, the more she can relax. When she begins to feel "adult" support, then she begins to be more aware of how she sounds to him and can remember to not mother him or give unsolicited advice.

How to Stop Unsolicited Advice

If a woman doesn't understand how and why men are offended by unsolicited "motherly" advice, there are ways in which a man can inform her so that she will stop it. As with any behavioral change, the art of getting a result is knowing how to ask.

> **As with any behavioral change, the art of getting a result is knowing how to ask.**

At another time, when she is not correcting him or giving advice, he should casually or gently let her know that he doesn't like unsolicited advice. If he wants her to remember this request, then he should repeatedly let her know this at times when he is not upset with her and she has not just done it.

He could say "By the way, you know the other day when we were packing and I came into the room? It was uncomfortable for me when you started telling me what to do. I felt like you were treating me like a child. When you can remember, I would really appreciate it if you wouldn't do that."

Even though he makes the request in this gentle and calm manner, he should not expect her to say "Oh, I am so sorry, I did the wrong thing again." Instead, he should be prepared for her resistance.

She may say "I can't worry about your feelings when I have to do so much" or "How else am I supposed to get your help?"

He could reply with "I know it must be hard. Whenever you can, (pause) I would really appreciate it."

He should be very brief, clear, and not argumentative. It doesn't matter if she resists. Resistance is almost always a sign that his request is being seriously considered.

The more she is supported in resisting and can talk about her resistance, the more she will remember the request in the future. If he argues, she will not open up to the validity of his request and she will not remember.

Planting the Seed of a Request

Asking for a behavior change is like gardening. You wait for the right time of the season and then plant the seed. Once the seed is planted, you don't keep digging it up. You just water it and wait for it to sprout.

In a similar way, if you want your partner to make a shift, ask her during the right season, which is never when you're upset. Then, once you plant the seed, don't dig it up.

This means that once you make the request, don't argue with her to make her do it. Just assume that she needs time to consider the request and that she will do her best. By not arguing with her, you can be assured that for days she will think about your request and try to do it whenever possible.

Here is another example of how a woman could resist and a man could skillfully dodge an argument and assure her support.

1. He says: "I would really appreciate it if you would not talk to me that way. It makes me feel like you are talking down to me."
2. She says: "I can't do that, you expect too much of me. Sometimes I just need to express how I feel."
3. He responds with: "I know it must sound difficult. All I ask is that you consider it. I mainly just want you to know why it is hard for me to listen at those times."

If he makes a request, not a demand, she is more likely to consider his request and, over time, try to support him in it.

This amazing technique of gently asking for support also

works with men. As we have explored before, if a woman can ask a man to do things without demanding, he is much more likely to remember to do them. If he was resistant to her request and she doesn't argue but only asks him to consider it, then he will automatically over time become much more open to fulfilling her request.

Women and Mothering

It is very difficult for a woman with children and/or a career outside the home to shift from the role of mother to the role of lover.

Whether or not a woman is actually a mother, the tendency to behave like one is instinctual. For that reason, it is hard for her to discern the differences between nurturing her male partner with love or mothering him with love. One kind of love is supportive and the other is toxic.

One woman shared this revealing statement: "All men just want to be mothered. They are like little babies who need to be appreciated for whatever they do."

Although to a man this kind of statement is completely insulting and demeaning, it was not intended to be. She didn't mean to be demeaning. She just didn't realize that her attitude insults masculinity. If she were to continue expressing her love in such a mothering way, her partner would resent her and she would eventually resent having to be a mother to him.

To appreciate a man for what he does is to nurture his masculinity. It is to give him the emotional support that he needs. It is not mothering him at all. Since children also need this kind of loving appreciation, a woman may mistakenly assume that a man is being a child if he also needs it. This is a major mistake.

How Men Misunderstand Women

In a similar way, a man misinterprets by assuming that a woman's need to talk about feelings in order to feel better indicates inferior intelligence. He doesn't understand the crucial role that talking plays in her life.

**A man misinterprets by assuming that a woman's
need to talk about feelings in order to feel better indicates inferior intelligence. He doesn't understand the
crucial role talking plays in her life.**

A man misinterprets her feelings and thinks she must be
incapable of solving her problems and assumes that she is either
incompetent, emotionally disturbed, or simply a being of lesser
intelligence. None of the above is true.

A man may make these judgments because he does not
understand that a mature adult woman needs to talk about
feelings if she is to cope with stress and feel intimacy in her
relationships. In a similar way, women don't realize that a
mature adult man needs to feel appreciated for the things he
does.

To clearly understand the difference between giving a man
emotional support and mothering, we will explore in greater
detail just what mothering is.

The Role of Mother

The role of mother requires a woman to take responsibility for
the well-being of others. A mother instinctively guides, directs,
educates, feeds, loves, and disciplines her children, who are
dependent on her to grow up in a healthy way. As a marriage
partner, a woman is also required to support a mate but should
not feel responsible for him. His well-being and fulfillment are
not part of her job description. When she guides, directs, educates, and feeds him without his expressed permission, she is
mothering him.

It is important for women to realize that treating a man as a
child is not only offensive to him but weakening and counterproductive. This is a very subtle distinction, but once recognized
it is as wide as the Grand Canyon.

What a Man Needs

A man needs a woman's love but not her mothering. He needs her to appreciate his efforts, decisions, struggles, intentions, and the results of his actions. When he makes mistakes or appears incompetent, he needs her to forgive and forget. When she can forget, he can more easily remember. When she releases responsibility for him, he can more effectively feel responsible for himself. He needs her to trust his loving intention and his abilities to learn things on his own.

When a woman mothers a man, she treats him like a child. As a result, he may indeed behave and react like a child when he is with her. Even men who seek out mothering women eventually react by being passive, overly dependent, overly sensitive, and rebellious. They grow in self-doubt, not in confidence. Consequently, their partners become still more overbearing.

> **Even men who seek out mothering women eventually react by being passive, overly dependent, overly sensitive, and rebellious.**

A man cannot remain attracted to a mothering woman. After a while, his passions will be redirected to other women. My own mother was aware of this when she explained to me why she thought my dad had affairs. She said, "He wanted a wife, but I became a mother."

In a similar way, a woman loses much of her attraction to a man when she feels she has to mother him and may easily be swept off her feet by the romantic expectations of being with another man who is not so dependent on her.

What a Woman Needs

For a man to fulfill a woman and assist her in not mothering, she requires a particular type of love and support. She needs to repeatedly experience that he cares for her as much as she cares for him. When his behavior becomes more work-focused and she believes he cares less, she begins to care "more" and mothers him.

This is why romance is so important to women. Romantic behaviors like buying presents, bringing flowers, opening car doors, physical affection, and planning getaways all clearly demonstrate and say that he cares for her. To a woman, romance is a way she can slip out of the mothering role and feel taken care of.

When a woman feels unsupported by a man, she begins to mother him. When she cares for him more than she feels he cares for her, then automatically her mothering instincts get activated.

> To the extent that she feels she can't trust or depend
> on him, the more she feels that he depends on her
> and she has to mother him.

If a man becomes too dependent, in her eyes he is no longer a provider but is someone she has to care for. If she can't depend on him, she begins to mother him more. It is OK for a man to need a woman, but when he needs her more than she can depend on him, her tendency is to begin mothering.

To counteract this tendency, a man must do certain things that most dramatically assist her in feeling taken care of. Particularly by satisfying her need to be heard, she can appreciate that she is cared for by him. If he initiates conversations and gives her lots of empathy, she will see him not as a child but as an adult, an equal she can depend on to be there for her in time of need.

The Climate for Mothering

Whenever the climate of a relationship is conducive to mothering, the female tendency to mother increases. For example, if a woman is cooking, cleaning, washing, or shopping for a man, her mothering tendencies intensify. In the beginning of a relationship she is not doing a lot of domestic things for him and so she doesn't mother as much. But as time passes she gradually changes.

The resolution is not to avoid doing things for him. It is for him to do things for her that she will really appreciate. We now know that this does not take an enormous amount of change on a man's part. By becoming a good listener and slowly but surely doing a little more around the house, he can make her feel that she's being taken care of.

By giving her the support she needs, he builds trust. He doesn't have to be perfect. He just needs to show repeatedly that he cares. When a man offers unsolicited support so that a woman feels she doesn't have to ask for it, she is greatly freed from the instinct to mother.

> **When a man offers unsolicited support so that a woman feels she doesn't have to ask for it, she is greatly freed from the instinct to mother.**

A woman can also help remedy the situation by taking responsibility for communicating her needs in an adult manner, using the advanced relationship skills I have outlined. By helping her partner be successful in supporting her, she engages in non-mothering adult behavior. Instead of being responsible for his needs, she is more responsible for her own.

When Women Are Providers

Mothering is harder to avoid when a woman is a provider. When she is not financially dependent on a man for support, she quickly begins to feel that she is giving more than he is. She doesn't know why, but she no longer is turned on to him. For this reason, it is important that a woman feel she is getting support equal to what she is giving to her mate.

As a woman makes more money, a relationship can be successful only if she is aware of how much she still needs her mate emotionally. The less physically dependent she is, the more emotionally dependent she needs to become. By making a deliberate effort to allow her man to listen to her feelings, she will begin to realize that—with the extra work stress in her life—she needs him more than ever.

Unless they increase their understanding, women who make

more money than their mates tend to find them less sexually attractive and feel that they "have to" mother their partners. As this predicament is not the fault of either partner, so must both parties be involved in its successful resolution.

A woman must help her man be more successful in fulfilling her emotional and romantic needs. A man must realize that underneath that tough exterior is a very vulnerable woman needing his emotional support but sometimes too proud or scared to admit it.

When a man provides a strong woman with the emotional and romantic support she needs, over time he becomes more empowered in the relationship instead of weakened.

Why Some Women Stay Single

Single women who have to provide for themselves must be careful not to give the impression that they are too self-sufficient to need a man. If this is the case, they will always be alone and will learn the hard way that they do indeed need the emotional support a loving man can offer them.

A man is drawn to where he is needed most because it is there that he will be appreciated most. A man feels secure in a relationship when he feels accepted, appreciated, and trusted just the way he is.

Why Women "Marry Up"

Traditionally, women have always "married up." I'm not referring to social class, but to the fact that they usually marry men they view as more competent than themselves in certain ways. This factor is imperative for a relationship to survive.

Unless she sees her man as more competent in some ways than she is, she will always feel responsible for him.

Like it or not, that's how it is. A man needs to feel appreciated. A woman needs to feel she can appreciate a man. When she feels that she is the more competent, she starts to mother, and we've seen how destructive that can be to a relationship.

As women become more competent in the traditionally male work roles, they must begin to recognize what else they need from men. Without this new awareness, women with higher degrees and bigger bank accounts have a much harder time finding and keeping mates.

As women become more competent in the tradition-ally male work roles, they must begin to recognize what else they need from men.

If a woman is highly successful in the business world, that's terrific. Her need for emotional support is even greater. If she can help her partner be successful in giving her what she needs most, then there is hope for their relationship.

Commonly, successful businesswomen are very resistant to helping a man in their relationship. It reminds them of how much they don't want to take care of someone because their work already pulls so much on them. But helping him becomes easier when she remembers that she is not helping a child, but a man who wants to learn how to help her. As she begins to reap the benefits of getting his support, then it becomes much easier to help him without feeling that she has to mother him. It is helpful for her to keep in mind that she is not really caring for him but is helping him to care for her.

When a Man Is More Sensitive

When a man is more sensitive or easily hurt than his partner, she will instinctively become more motherly. The more irritable, vulnerable, or emotionally needy he is, the greater the chance that a woman will make matters worse by mothering. The wisest course for her is to leave him alone when he's in a negative mood. If he wants to talk about feelings, she should gracefully back off and not encourage him to talk about his feelings.

Strong women need to focus on finding their own sensitivities and letting the male partner "be there" for them. This will restore balance. Without a deliberate effort on their part, they automatically lose touch with their own sensitive feelings and needs because the mother in them tells them that they must be there for others.

By suppressing her sensitivities and emotional needs for a man, a woman actually makes him *more* sensitive and emotionally needy. This particular kind of loving support is actually toxic. Her mate becomes increasingly passive, moody, irritable, demanding, or easily hurt by her.

To remedy this situation, she needs to assist him not in feeling better but in helping her feel better. If he pushes her to be there for him, she needs to back off. She can do this gracefully by saying something like "I care about your feelings, but I need some time to think about this. Then we'll talk."

When a man is feeling more sensitive than his mate, he is more on his female side. At such times he will insist on talking about his emotions. Although neither partner is aware of it, his doing so will disturb the balance and lessen the attraction in the relationship.

I am not saying that sensitive men should not share their feelings or complain. I am saying that they should not be more emotionally needy than their mates.

If a man becomes emotionally needy, he should back away and deal with his feelings alone in his cave, in a men's support group, in therapy, or simply talk with his male friends. He should not make his intimate partner responsible for his feelings.

Why Women Want to Talk About the Relationship

"At first Susie was always so happy to have me in her life," Rick grumbled. "I felt like I really made a difference. Now she's always wanting to talk about the relationship. Why can't we just enjoy it? I hate it. Why do we have to talk about it?"

In the beginning of a relationship, a woman does not feel a strong need to talk about it. After all, she is just learning about her partner. As time passes, that tends to change.

Women are hyperaware of how feelings change and so, if her mate starts taking time for himself, she automatically begins to feel insecure. Without understanding a man's need for cave time, when he pulls away she hears the message "I don't want to be with you." Suddenly she faces the possibility of losing what she has and wants to talk about the relationship for several reasons.

For one thing, she is looking for assurance that she is still loved and is important to her man. For another, she wants to talk about whatever problems she perceives there to be so that she can make things better. This reaction, unfortunately, tends to frustrate men.

Instinctively, a man is willing to work on problems at his job but not at home or in the relationship. Traditionally, a man's work was outside the home. It is hard for him to agree happily to talk about the relationship and hunt for problems when he is basically satisfied. When she wants to talk about the relationship, he hears her saying something is wrong and that he is not doing enough.

When Men Go to Their Caves

We have discussed at length that a man's pulling away into his cave is normal behavior. Women must remember that it is not necessarily an indication that there is a problem.

During courtship, a man maintains a separate home, so his need for cave time is naturally fulfilled. When a couple move in together, she observes cave behavior for the first time, begins to resist it, and tries to pull her partner out by talking about the relationship.

When a man resists coming out, a woman panics and thinks there is an even bigger problem in the relationship. She panics because she thought everything was fine. Now she wants him to talk about his feelings more than ever. She mistakenly assumes that he doesn't want to because he is either upset with her or is hiding something. When half an hour later he acts like everything is fine, she feels that he's "in denial," whereas from his point of view, everything *is* OK.

Ironically, the times when he most needs to pull away are the times when she most wants him to talk. As mentioned, I have found that by taking five to twenty minutes several days each week when I first get home, to give my wife lots of attention and support, I help her feel secure. Then when I go to my cave to recuperate from the day, it is easier for her and me.

Honey Do's

"When I get home I am barraged with a list of 'honey do's,'" Sam groused. "As soon as I sit down, Lisa starts giving orders. It is like she waits for me to relax and then she needs more. When I get home, I feel like I have to hide from her. It is not just me, because when I talk to other men they also feel this way about their wives. I don't want to come home to another boss. I have to go on fishing trips just to get away."

Women don't realize that men need to relax and do nothing responsible for a while in order to recover from the day's stress. Particularly when she is overwhelmed, a woman feels that everything has to be done before she can relax. She mistakenly assumes that if she reminds her mate of what to do, then they will both eventually be able to relax.

In this case, men must take charge. By choosing to give their mates focused support when they get home, these men are working to make a woman less inclined to feel overwhelmed and unsupported. Of course, if she continues to ask for more, they have to say no in a graceful way.

How to Set Limits

A woman does not mind a man's limits. She wants him to set them. If he is not good at it, then she feels she again has to figure out on her own what is too much to ask for. She starts thinking too much for him and not enough for herself.

The secret here is for him to set his limits in a respectful manner. Some men just continue to say yes until they feel resentful and get mad at the woman for asking for so much. When a man is saying yes to her requests, a woman sometimes assumes that this is her lucky day and she keeps asking. She needs him to set his limits and only say yes to what he can do without resenting her.

Although in the moment she may not be thrilled with his limit, after a little time passes she will respect it. Without understanding this, a man gets unnecessarily mad at her. He may begin to feel that he "has" to say yes to her or she will resent him. To please her, he feels that he has to say yes. It is comforting to a man to learn that he can say no and that she will also eventually be pleased.

She may not be thrilled that she is not getting what she wants, but she can certainly be pleased by the way he says no. This situation is similar to a woman asking a man for more. He may not be thrilled with her asking for more, but the way in which she asks can make him feel very supported. Likewise, when a man says no, the way he says no can make a woman feel very supported.

How to Say No Respectfully

Let's take some common examples of how a man can say no respectfully. The situation:

1. Susie wants to keep talking, and Sam is growing impatient to get to his cave.	
Don't say: "I can't listen to this anymore."	Do say: "I really want to hear you, but right now I need to take some time for myself. I'll be back, and then we can talk some more."

2. Susie starts asking him to do things as soon as he gets home.	
Don't say: "Look, I'm tired; I don't feel like doing that."	Do say: "I would be happy to do that, but right now I need some time for myself and then I'll get to it. If you want, write out a list; I'll be happy to work on it later."

---

3. Sam wants to go fishing, and Susie feels deserted.

Don't say: "I have to go fishing. I need to relax. It's what I do."	Do say: "I need some time for myself. I'll be back tomorrow around noon. Then we can spend some real quality time together. I very much want to be with you, but first I need to go fishing. Then I can be more present with you."

---

4. Susie starts asking him to do things as soon as he sits down.

Don't say: "OK, OK. I'll do it." If he says yes but resents her, he will begin to feel an even greater need to avoid being home.	Do say: "I'll be happy to do that later, but right now I need to relax. I'll do it in twenty minutes." By giving her a concrete time, he allows her to relax.

---

5. Sam is watching a TV show, and Susie wants to talk.

Don't say: "What is it?" if he is not willing to turn off the show. (He shouldn't try to listen and watch at the same time.)	Do say: "I really want to talk, but first I would like to finish watching this show. Then we can talk." Or he could say: "I really want to talk, but this is a very good show. At the commercial I can give you my full attention."

In each of these examples, a man is asked to say no if that is his limit but also lets his partner know her request is important to him and that he will get to it. As she sees that he's sincere, she becomes much more open to his limits.

Why Women Resist Limits

Many times, when a man first begins to set limits in a positive way, a woman may temporarily react negatively; though the process is working, it seems as if it isn't. This is because he is making it safe for her to express her feelings. Among those feelings is mistrust.

Abruptly, she seems to him to have completely forgotten all the times he has done things for her and remembers in excruciating detail the times she was disappointed. When this happens, men should remind themselves that this too will pass. Once a man validates a woman's feelings, they will change.

The most effective response to resistance is to not get upset with her but in his most understanding tone of voice to repeat his original message. She will appreciate his attempt to remain civil. Let's look at some examples.

Sam says, "I would be happy to do that, but right now I need some time for myself. Then I'll get to it."

Susie could resist by saying any of these phrases:

- "You say you'll do it, but you never do."
- "If you don't do it right now, you'll forget."
- "I get tired of reminding you of what to do. You always forget."

Even if she doesn't verbally express these words, her facial expression and eyes may say it for her.

A man should be prepared for a woman's negative reactions to his setting limits. As she sees that he does eventually respond to her requests, she will resist less.

It is also vital for a man to contain his automatic tendency to argue by pointing out all the things he has done for her. Overcoming her resistance demands that he remain calm and firmly repeat his original message: "I would be happy to do that, but right now I need some time for myself and then I'll get to it."

The Power of Repetition

If a woman persists in verbally resisting a man, he should continue ducking and dodging. He wins by not getting upset. If he gives in and gives up his limit, then he will just resent her for controlling him, and she will resent him for "making her a nag."

To persist in dodging he could simply say "I don't know what else to say." If she continues to persist, he should more clearly set the limit by saying "I want to support you, but right now I am getting upset. I don't want to fight with you. You don't deserve that." Then he should again repeat his original message: "I would be happy to do what you ask, but right now I need some time for myself and then I'll get to it."

A man's power to avoid an ugly argument or power struggle lies in not letting the subject of the conversation shift to all the other things he does wrong. By repeating his first response over and over, he remains centered and focused on his loving intention to support himself and her. By holding on to his caring intention, she will appreciate his strength even if she disagrees with him. Repetition allows him to succeed.

At such times it is enough for her to express her feelings. If he expresses his, the encounter will quickly get out of control and many things will be said and regretted. Even if after a few days, when everything seems forgotten, the woman will be less inclined to trust her partner's love, and he will be less willing to do things for her because he doesn't feel appreciated.

Saying No Is As Important As Saying Yes

Women also appreciate a man's ability to say no in another way: if he can say no, she can too. On a certain level, a woman is attracted to a man with clear limits because it assures her that he will respect hers.

It is much more difficult for women to set limits. Limits are more definite to men. A man just needs to learn how to express his limits in a more graceful, respectful way. Women tend to be more respectful of others but don't know how to say no. When they finally do say no, it is rarely respectful or graceful.

Women tend to wait until they have repeatedly sacrificed for others, and feel victimized, before feeling empowered to refuse. Without this sense of entitlement, it is hard to say no, especially when your nature tells you to say yes.

When a woman is free to share her feelings, she likewise feels more entitled to say no without having to feel resentful and victimized in order to be able to do it. Not only does sharing feelings help her feel more entitled, but it helps her to discover what she wants before it becomes an angry demand.

While courting, a man thinks of his woman as feminine, loving, giving, and gracefully accommodating. She can show him the best of herself because she is getting everything she wants. He gets used to her accommodating nature and appreciates it. But as time passes and he keeps asking for more without equally increasing his support, she starts saying no to the things she used to say yes to—and she does it ungracefully.

Instead of just saying no, she tells him in great detail how unsupported she feels and why he has forced her to refuse him. This is very hard for him to hear and will almost surely spark an argument. Commonly he simply walks away wondering what happened to the woman he fell in love with.

A woman generally does not know how to say no gracefully. These are the basic rules.

- •She should say no simply and briefly.
- •The more words she uses, the harder it is for a man to hear.
- • If he persists in asking for something, she should also stay focused and persist in repeating her original brief message. Here again, repetition makes it much easier to say no in a positive way.

Why Women Take Men for Granted

In the early days of a relationship, women are very appreciative of whatever a man does. After the relationship progresses and they move in together, she grows less so. However, she is probably not aware of it, so when her mate points it out, she misunderstands and resists. Without understanding how men are different, it is hard for her to validate his driving need for appreciation.

When a woman doesn't understand a man's deeper need for acknowledgment, he inevitably feels taken for granted.

"Joyce complains that I don't do enough around the house," Henry shared. "When I do help, she either points out what I didn't do or she doesn't even notice what I did. If I empty the trash or clean up the house, she acts like it is no big deal. If that's the case, why bother?"

Joyce simply didn't understand Henry's emotional needs. She didn't realize that every time she overlooked what he did or focused on what he wasn't doing, she was alienating him.

Through practicing advanced relationship skills, she learned to respect Henry's sensitivities even though they were different from hers. In a very real sense, both men and women have different sensitivities. They are like sacred circles that need to be honored.

Sacred Circles

A man's sacred circle has to do with his actions, behavior, and sense of competence. A woman's sacred circle has to do with her feelings, communication, and her sense of worthiness.

To respect Henry's sensitivities, Joyce learned to focus her efforts as a loving wife on supporting him in the ways he needed most. She practiced appreciating what he did and restraining herself from offering criticism or advice. As she supported his sense of competence, she immediately experienced his increased involvement in the relationship.

Men pull away to recover from the stresses of the day, which to various degrees make them feel either out of control or incompetent. When a woman makes him feel successful in fulfilling her, his need to pull away becomes less. When he is appreciated, he feels more in charge of himself and capable of making a difference. He is automatically motivated to do more.

Henry learned to respect Joyce's sacred circle by honoring and supporting her need to communicate, express feelings, and feel heard. By practicing ducking and dodging and showing that he cared by doing things to help her, he discovered that he could get the appreciation he wanted. With this kind of support, Joyce felt increasingly worthy and entitled to ask for Henry's support in the ways she needed it.

Work and Relationships

As a female partner invests more energy and time in making her man happy, the more she feels he should be doing for her. She automatically begins to complain and nag about what he isn't doing.

Since men are work oriented, he misunderstands and thinks she is saying that she's not happy because he's not providing enough. This is a huge source of pressure on him.

He feels compelled to put in more work hours, but to do that he has to spend more time away, which she also complains about. He doesn't know what to do.

"In the beginning, Louise was so happy to be with me," Nick said. "She was impressed by my competence and my drive. Now I feel like no matter how hard I work, it's never enough for her."

When Nick returned home from working hard, he was met with more requests and complaints. He felt Louise was being unreasonable and demanding. He worked hard and wanted to rest. When she expected more, he experienced all kinds of conflicting emotions.

Nick wanted Louise to be happy, but it seemed to be an impossible task. Like most men, he didn't know how to duck and dodge. Instead, he would ignore her in an attempt to avoid fights. Unfortunately, he just made matters worse because when Louise didn't feel heard, she complained even more.

When Nick finally learned how to listen without thinking that he had to solve her problems, he could take the time he needed to relax. He listened to his wife but didn't feel that he had to respond to everything she talked about.

He also discovered that Louise had an amazing ability to accept the problems at home when she could freely talk about them. When she felt heard, she could appreciate him more. Nick could feel Louise supporting him and appreciating how hard he worked for their family. When he would do a project around the house, she was very appreciative instead of immediately pointing out what else needed to be done.

Eventually, Nick started spending more time at home. He could definitely be more understanding of her desire for him to spend more time with her and less time at work when he understood that more money was not the solution to her happiness.

How Love Changes

The changes we have discussed in this chapter, while more or less inevitable, are not indications of an inability to love or of incompatibility. Through practicing advanced relationship skills, couples can eventually overcome them. Our partners can learn to give us the support they so freely gave in the beginning as we learn to give them the support we used to give them.

This process is not automatic. It has to be studied, learned, and practiced. While growing up, we could not learn how to have a relationship that would work in modern times. The rules for relationships were different then. Our parents didn't know about them, so they couldn't pass them on to us. In the future, advanced relationship skills will become automatic. They will not take so much work as we, the first generation to need and use them, must put in.

The skills our parents used in their generation are not enough to cope with the changing needs of modern times. When women were dependent on men to survive, they didn't mind a man's preoccupation with work. They not only accepted him but greatly appreciated his instinctive tendency to focus more on providing.

When a man returned home, it was easy for him to handle the changes a woman went through because he felt accepted and appreciated. Although traditionally she would clean house, wash clothes, and cook for him, she didn't get caught up in feeling that she was mothering him because she was so dependent on him. It is hard to resent mothering someone who takes care of you and protects you.

Today, all that has changed. As men and women get closer, the chances of intimacy are much greater but so also are the chances for friction. A relationship today can grow in passion or it can easily become routine.

When couples are not skilled in creating lasting intimacy, they inevitably begin to feel increasingly distant and estranged. Divorce is many times the only option they have. Through applying advanced relationship skills they now have another. Each weekend in my seminars, I have repeatedly witnessed thousands of couples rekindle the passion of their love.

When couples do not, however, understand their differences, then they are unable to fully support each other in the most meaningful ways. When a woman does not feel supported in a relationship, she will, over time, naturally begin to move away from her female side and become more masculine. In an opposite way, men can also move out of balance in a relationship.

Even though two people love each other very much, this tendency toward emotional role reversal can kill the attraction in a relationship and can make two people feel that they are not right for each other when, in truth, they are.

The problem of emotional role reversal is so new that most people don't even know it's a problem, and they definitely don't know how to solve it. The inability to recognize and solve this problem is one of the biggest reasons for divorce today. In the next chapter, we will explore how and why role reversal happens and will learn ways to balance the masculine and feminine within ourselves.

Men Are Still from Mars, Women Are Still from Venus

In my relationship seminars, I explain that the differences between men and women make it seem as if we are from different planets. I explore these differences in much greater detail in my book, *Men Are from Mars, Women Are from Venus*.

While thousands of people nod their heads in agreement when I give my examples, there are some who don't fully relate. In fact, it is not at all uncommon for many women to say that they more fully relate to my examples of being a man. They feel that they are from Mars and not Venus. I assure them that nothing is wrong, and that even though society has to a great extent influenced them to become more masculine, they are still from Venus.

There are many factors that influence a woman having a more developed masculine side or a man having a more developed feminine side. Quite commonly, if a girl bonds more closely with her father or if she was raised in a very male-dominated household, she will tend to more fully develop her masculine side. Likewise, if a boy bonds more closely with his mother or if he is raised in a very female-dominated household, he will tend to more fully develop his female side.

Generally speaking, though, a woman becomes more masculine when she has not witnessed a woman being feminine and also being respected. Likewise, a man becomes more feminine when he has not witnessed a man being loving and also being strong and powerful.

Cultural backgrounds and certain ethnic groups also have characteristics that are more "masculine" or "feminine." For example, Germans and Swedes tend to frown upon open displays of emotion or talking just for the sake of talking instead of trying to make a point, whereas Italian families are much more emotionally expressive.

Sometimes the different feminine tendencies don't show up in a woman because when she is single and rather isolated, she has become the Martian and takes care of herself. Once she is in a relationship, many traditional female tendencies begin to emerge.

In other cases, a woman will become more masculine or Martian because in her relationship over time she experiences that it is not safe to be feminine.

For example, the feminine need to talk more may cause too much frustration or make her look weak. Rather than appear too needy or cause conflict, she automatically begins to suppress her feminine side.

Men sometimes also feel that they are from Venus. Creative men in particular experience both their male and female sides. These men generally are attracted to women who are more on their male side. Again, the formula holds true: differences attract.

In some cases, these men didn't have positive role models for expressing masculine power. They do not know how to assert themselves and set limits, but also be loving and caring. To fulfill the woman, they are willing to sacrifice their needs. Not only are they personally weakened, but when they become more feminine, women lose their attraction to them and leave. By using advanced relationship skills, these men can automatically begin to develop their masculine sides while also respecting their feminine sides.

Emotional Role Reversal

When a man is more on his female side or a woman is more on her male side, he or she is experiencing an emotional role reversal. As we discussed earlier, this term does not in any way imply psychological neurosis. It is merely an imbalance.

> When a man is more on his female side or a woman is more on her male side, he or she is experiencing an emotional role reversal.

To improve relationships, balance must be reestablished. To create ideal relationships, both the male and female sides of each partner must be nurtured.

When couples are not skilled in supporting each other, a woman will automatically begin to close down to her female side, and a man will withhold his instinctive desire to support from his male side. She feels "I will not give of myself anymore because I am not supported," and he feels "Why should I be giving of myself when it doesn't make a difference?"

To sustain passion we need to be aware of this reflexive tendency. With effort, skillful planning, deliberation, and the exercise of advanced relationship skills, we can forge relationships that nurture our whole beings.

When a Man Is on His Female Side

When a man is operating too much from his female side, the antidote is for him to do things that will immediately allow his mate to nurture his male side. He should look to her for appreciation and acknowledgment. When she supports him in this way, and he can more quickly reestablish balance, she benefits as well.

If a man is on his female side, applying advanced relationship skills may not at first feel natural. His female side will say "Why do I have to duck and dodge and make it safe for her? I want her to make it safe for me! I want to talk too."

By overcoming this resistance and learning to listen first and "contain" before expressing his own feelings, a man exercises and strengthens his male side. When his male side has successfully supported her female side, it is then productive and healthy for him to allow her to be there for his female side. After he has nurtured her female side and she has nurtured his masculine side by appreciating his support, then it is fine for him to look freely to her to nurture his female side.

If a man has a more developed female side, he will feel a pull to be nurtured by his mate's masculine side. He will feel a greater need for her to be there for him. He will get upset when she doesn't want to talk or work on the relationship. He will complain that she is not there for him in the relationship. He will ask lots of questions to get her to talk more. He will want her to listen and understand his feelings and offer sympathy and help him in various ways.

How a Man Can Get the Support He Needs

A man's female side has legitimate needs, but to allow them full access in a relationship will tend to push a woman to her masculine side. Such a man can better support the needs of his feminine side by going to a men's support group, spending more time with his male friends, doing personal growth work, or looking to God for this kind of support.

Requiring his partner to support his female side puts an enormous strain on the relationship. A woman is already needing more support to connect with her female side; she can't find her female side and also be the man for his female side.

A woman is already needing more support to connect with her female side; she can't find her female side and also be the man for his female side.

When a man looks to a woman primarily for this kind of support, not only does he push her to her masculine side but it may even weaken him. Unable to talk with other males about their problems, many men complain to their wives. This creates even greater imbalance.

After a while, as he talks more and more she will talk less and less. A man needs to be careful not to "whine" too much with his wife or she will begin mothering and her desire for him will flicker and dim. As a general suggestion, a man should not express more sensitivities than his mate. If he is more sensitive, he will need to toughen up a bit by nurturing his male side more.

Sensitive Men

When a woman says she wants a sensitive man, she really means that she wants a man who is strong but is sensitive to her needs. Quite commonly, women are turned off when a man becomes more sensitive than she is. Briefly, in the beginning, it may seem very attractive, particularly if she is on her male side, but very quickly, if it persists for too long, she becomes increasingly annoyed.

A man needs to be careful not to look to a woman to fulfill his feminine needs. Ideally, a man should look to a woman primarily to nurture his male side and not his female side. His male side is nurtured every time he feels appreciated, accepted, and trusted. The more nurtured he feels, the stronger and tougher he will be, but at the same time he will grow more sensitive to her needs. This strength and sensitivity to her needs is what women really appreciate, and it makes him feel both strong and loving.

If he happens to be more sensitive than she is, it may take a few years to balance out and find his masculine strength in the relationship. In the meantime, he should not burden her with his sensitivities. For example, if his feelings are hurt or if he feels more emotionally needy, he should then talk with men friends and not look to her primarily to support his need to talk and share feelings.

A man achieves balance in a relationship primarily through successfully supporting the female. When a man succeeds in supporting her, then to a great extent his own female side is automatically nurtured. When she is happy, he feels happy because indirectly his own female side is automatically supported. When a man loves a woman and feels a deep connection with her, it is then as though her female side becomes his. Through fulfilling her female side not only is his male side appreciated but his female side is also nurtured.

When a Woman Is on Her Female Side

When a woman feels responsible to nurture a man's female side, it actually puts her out of balance. For example, when he expects her to listen more to his feelings, it has the effect of turning her off not only to him but to her own female side. Automatically, she begins to become more masculine. Advanced relationship skills are required to assist women in returning to their female side.

A woman feels most nurtured when her female side is directly supported. A woman achieves balance through successfully supporting her male partner in supporting her. If she can create a climate in which to receive the support she needs in order to be happy, her male side is also simultaneously developed.

In this way a woman is able to assert her male side to solve the problems while safeguarding her female side through being directly nurtured by her partner. On the other hand, when she directly supports her male partner's female side, she overlooks her own, until one day she wakes up angry and resentful that their caring and understanding are no longer reciprocal.

When a woman is too much on her male side, the antidote is creating relationships in which her female side blossoms. If she works in a traditionally male role all day, she will have to make deliberate efforts to overcome much inner resistance in order to do this.

How She Can Get the Support She Needs

When a woman on her masculine side gets home, she may want to go to her cave. She is definitely not in a communicative mood. She feels a much greater need for space than her man does. She needs to solve problems and can't waste time talking about them.

Since her male side wants to be appreciated, accepted, and trusted, she resents it when her partner gives her advice or doesn't recognize all that she does. In most cases, she would rather do things herself. She definitely feels that her partner isn't giving her the appreciation she deserves as a provider.

It is definitely not healthy for a woman and man to compete for appreciation in a relationship. To support her male side she needs to spend time with other women who can nurture her male side's need to be appreciated.

Ideally, a woman should look to the man in her life for caring, understanding, and respect. These qualities of love nurture her female side. As she gets those needs fulfilled and her appreciation for her partner increases, then she can certainly expect that he will overflow and appreciate all that she does as well.

It is definitely not healthy for a woman and man to compete for appreciation in a relationship.

While it is important for women to be appreciated, they should look to their male partners to support their female sides. Women today need a man's support more than ever to be able to return to their feminine sides at the end of the day.

Emotional Role Reversal and Attraction

With so many women in the workforce, it is becoming more common for them to begin a relationship in emotional role reversal. By pursuing him more actively, a woman causes a man to move more to his female side. Rather than feel a responsibility to initiate a relationship, he waits and lets her do the pursuing.

When a woman is on her male side, she tends to be attracted to a man on his female side and vice versa. Many men sense this automatically and move to their female side. This is a trap.

Unless men consciously work to find balance, they will eventually lose their appeal.

When a woman is more masculine, a man tends to become more feminine. Likewise, if a man becomes more feminine, a woman becomes more masculine. If she doesn't learn skills to assist him in nurturing her female side, she will become even more masculine. The more masculine she becomes, the more feminine he becomes.

If a very masculine man becomes more feminine, he is moving toward balance. But if he is already too much on his female side, pushing him farther into it creates greater imbalance.

If he is very feminine and she is very masculine, maintaining attraction requires his slowly but surely developing his masculine side as she develops her feminine side. By developing the male and female sides in tandem, advanced relationship skills promote greater balance and attraction.

Conventional Relationships

In more conventional relationships, the man is more masculine and the woman is more feminine. The attraction lessens over time if the woman repeatedly experiences that she cannot be supported on her female side. Rather than risk the pain of repeated invalidation or rejection, she closes up and becomes in certain ways more masculine.

The same is true for men. Rather than continuing to do masculine things like make decisions, initiate sex, and solve problems for her, when he doesn't feel appreciated he suppresses his male side. In various ways he will automatically become more feminine. Without the sexual polarity, the attraction between partners dissipates.

Although couples may start out very masculine and feminine, over time they begin to reverse roles emotionally. When a man doesn't feel his masculine side being supported, he then automatically begins to go out of balance. Likewise, when a woman doesn't get the support she needs at the office and at home to be feminine, then she also goes out of balance.

Balancing the Masculine and the Feminine

Ironically, men go out of balance because they are not getting the support from women that they used to get in the old days, while women go out of balance because they are not getting a new kind of support from men.

To solve our modern problems, women need to find within themselves the feminine love they used to share, but without giving up the new power they are expressing. A modern man's challenge is to draw upon his ancient courage and risk failure by trying out new formulas for success in order to support the woman he loves in new ways.

When men and women are unaware of the necessary techniques needed to create balance, emotional role reversal automatically kicks in. For both sexes, it commonly happens in distinct stages. We will first discuss what happens to women and then explore how men go out of balance.

Emotional Role Reversal and Doing It All

When a woman returns home from work, her tendency is to stay in her masculine side, particularly if there is more work to be done. Instead of relaxing and talking about her problems, she feels that she faces a new list of problems *that need to be solved*. She either talks about them to get her partner's help to solve them or she doesn't want to talk at all. She feels she has to do it all. To cope with her frustration, she too may begin to withdraw from the relationship and feel a need to go to her cave.

Her experience changes when she is on her female side. When a woman is connected to her feminine side, she is capable of enjoying and appreciating the small details of living. She may be aware of problems, but she does not have to solve them immediately in order to feel good.

When she is too much on her male side, she then suddenly feels an urgency to solve all of life's little and big problems. She feels too responsible for doing "everything" and taking care of everyone. She feels overwhelmed. Instead of feeling loving, peaceful, warm, and happy to be home, she feels, to various degrees, frustrated, overworked, unappreciated, and unsupported. It is then extremely difficult for her to take time out for herself and appreciate life's simple pleasures.

When a Woman Feels Overwhelmed

When a woman feels overwhelmed at the end of the day, she is generally enough in touch with her female side to remember all her problems, but her male side demands that she find solutions and do something. In this state, it is hard for her to relax or even know what would nurture her female side.

When a woman feels overwhelmed at the end of the day, she is generally enough in touch with her female side to remember all her problems, but her male side demands that she find solutions and do something.

When women are feeling overwhelmed, they are so focused on getting things done that they literally can't feel the inner needs and wants of their feminine sides. Each time they finish a task, rather than feel relieved, they begin to feel the inner emptiness and longing of their female sides.

Three Ways a Woman Goes Out of Balance

When a woman feels heavily overwhelmed, she doesn't feel safe talking in a non-goal-oriented manner because she has moved out of balance to her problem-solving male side and can't get back. This tends to manifest itself in three distinct ways.

1. She hungers for more food and overeats.
2. She feels driven to solve domestic problems and rarely relaxes or appreciates her partner's support.
3. She hungers for her partner to open up and talk more and ends up creating arguments.

These reactions are counterproductive to fulfilling her true needs and easily become addictive behaviors that assist her in avoiding the feelings of her unfulfilled feminine side. By avoiding her feelings she may find temporary relief but in the long run the problem gets worse. Let's explore these three stages.

Stage One: Feeling Overwhelmed and Overeating

A woman's most common reaction to undernourishment of her female side is to eat. Eating is an easy replacement for love. Through feeding herself, she can temporarily suppress the painful feelings of insecurity that are emerging from her female side. By numbing feelings, her potential for passion is stilled.

Women overeat to quench the deeper thirst for nurturing and secure relationships. This tendency is technically called a "need replacement." If she can't get what she really needs, the real need is replaced by another need that appears more attainable.

In this case, her need for love is replaced by her need for food. Until the craving for love is satisfied, she will always be hungry. Through eating more she is able to temporarily repress the persistent longings of her female side and find relief. In some cases, she may even fool herself temporarily into believing that she is quite happy and that she doesn't need to talk or share in a nurturing relationship.

Why Women Gain Weight

Quite commonly, soon after a woman gets married she frequently begins to put on weight in excess of the natural gain mandated by aging and childbirth.

This shift takes place not because the relationship has problems, but because marriage itself makes a woman relax and feel more secure. As her female side begins to blossom, it says "Now that I am loved, I can finally come out and be nurtured, supported, and heard." She begins involuntarily to experience emotions and urges that women have felt for centuries but which have been suppressed by modern independent living.

You see, as a woman connects more deeply with her female side, her natural tendency to talk about feelings and problems abruptly emerges. It is as if she is possessed by the spirits of her female ancestors. These alien feelings from her ancient past make her modern self feel that she is overly needy, emotional, illogical, petty, even weak. Many women are embarrassed by these feelings.

In a state of emotional confusion, the last thing a woman wants is to share the origins of that confusion with her spouse. In most cases, she doesn't even feel comfortable sharing these new feelings with other women. She doesn't know what to do because she never saw her mother successfully sharing feelings or problems with her father that resulted in her getting his respect and support. To avoid creating unnecessary conflict or frustrating her mate, she chooses to suppress the need to share these feelings coming from her female side and, as a result, feels a new need to eat more.

The more she eats, the more she is able to keep at bay these strange new feelings and tendencies, but only temporarily. Until she finds a way to fulfill and directly nurture her female side on a regular basis, she will continue to use food as a painkiller.

Why Dieting Doesn't Work

When a woman tries to solve the problem of overeating through dieting, she goes even farther out of balance by moving toward her male side. During a diet, the body feels the panic of famine and craves food even more. The female side is nurtured by feeling secure and supported. The imposition of strict discipline requiring control nurtures and strengthens the male side, not the female side.

Ease, comfort, effortlessness, security, fun, recreation, pleasure, and beauty all nurture the female side. Dieting does not. Recent diet programs that encourage women to *eat more* low-fat foods and exercise at a slow, easy pace instead of depriving themselves are definitely a better approach to losing weight. However, the most effective solution to female weight problems is more nurturing relationships and a less pressured, more relaxed lifestyle.

Stage Two: Women Who Do Too Much

When women are deprived of the support their female side requires to avoid feeling the pain of rejection, they move to their male side and begin exhibiting traditional masculine tendencies. They become increasingly goal oriented, competitive, assertive, independent, and efficient. They take great pride in being logical and rational. In most cases, life experiences or certain messages in childhood have conditioned them to reject feminine feelings as weak, undesirable, and definitely unlovable.

It is hard for these women to see themselves as being lovable to men if they were to be soft and feminine. They work hard to hide their feminine sensitivities and needs. Incorrectly assuming that "femininity" is undesirable, they have no idea why a man would be attracted to "that."

These women deal with their inner female side by becoming hard instead of soft, tough instead of sensitive, and independent instead of dependent. Self-sufficiency is their primary method of coping. They tend to pull away from intimate conversation. In some cases, they even scorn the male support that could eventually bring them fulfillment and prevent them from shifting into the mode of doing more.

For some women, the tendency to "do more" means more domestic perfectionism. Everything has to be in its place, organized, and clean. For others, it simply implies that there is never enough time to relax. If women cannot relax because their male side demands solutions to their problems, passion quickly loses its magic and disappears, and sex becomes mechanical.

Other women do too much by taking on excessive responsibility. They have a hard time saying no when they feel needed. They may even feel compelled to do things that they are not even asked to do. They pride themselves on anticipating the needs of others and "being there" for them.

What a Man Can Do for Her

To support a woman, a man must understand that, deep inside, she longs to relax, let go, and surrender to someone she trusts to care for and support her. This is the true inner need of the female side.

> A man must understand that, deep inside, a woman longs to relax, let go, and surrender to someone she trusts to care for and support her.

However, because she judges her need for help as unacceptable, it is unconsciously replaced by a false need. The replacement need emerges as an urgent calling to fulfill others. She feels as if her happiness is based on providing fulfillment for others instead of getting her own needs satisfied. In a sense, she becomes the responsible and caring man she wishes could fulfill her.

This insight is valuable for both women and men. When a woman is becoming overly responsible, instead of chastising her for doing too much, a man can realize that she needs help in getting back to her feminine side. If he can give her more time and attention and slowly open her up to talking by asking questions, gradually her urgency to do more for everyone subsides.

A Cry for Help

When a woman is "doing too much," it is a cry for help. In a sense, she is sinking. Her only way of asking for support is to endlessly give the support she herself so desperately needs. Without a supportive partner, women on their male side tend to become increasingly self-sufficient and thus decrease the possibilities of having a man support them.

When a woman does too much, her only way of asking for support is to endlessly give the support she
herself so desperately needs.

Women who feel overwhelmed rarely get the support they
need. They do not know how to be vulnerable or to ask for it.
Since they are seen as self-sufficient, help is rarely offered. If it
is, it's rejected. No one is allowed to see the vulnerable part of
her. Everyone is encouraged to regard with admiration the
strong and giving side.

Such women have trouble even contacting their needs and
giving to themselves for a change. There is little a man can do
for them unless he understands that the stronger these women
appear, the more needy they are deep within.

Men with Women Who Do Too Much

Men without a deeper understanding are easily frustrated by
women who do too much. The busier she is, the less time and
appreciation she has for him. He does not feel that he can help
her and then fulfill her.

No matter what he does for her, she is always driven to do
more. On a feeling level, he feels cut off from her. If he cannot
do for her, then he cannot receive her love. He doesn't feel that
he can make a difference in her life. In a very real sense, her
independence and sense of autonomy push him away.

These women do not understand that men love to make a
difference; to be fulfilled a man needs to feel successful in providing for her fulfillment. This is how men experience greater
intimacy with women.

How to Attract Mr. Right

Because it's more difficult for women who do too much to start
relationships, they commonly ask me how to attract a man.

My response is to ask them why they *need* a man. The question invariably takes them by surprise. They give answers like:

"Well, I don't know if I really *need* a man" or "I'm not so sure that I *need* a man."

Others are more deliberate, clearly stating, "I don't really *need* a man, but I want one."

If these women are to secure a lasting relationship, they must first begin to open up to their feminine side, which feels no shame in saying "I need a man."

If women are to secure a lasting relationship, they
must first begin to open up to their feminine side,
which feels no shame in saying "I need a man."

The Magic of Trust

When a woman is in a hurry or desperate for a relationship, she is definitely feeling from her female side, but it's not sufficiently nurtured to attract the right man. Through nurturing her female side something magical begins to happen. She feels her need for a man and trusts that at the right time and in the right place she will find him. This openness can be cultivated by finding fulfillment in her female friendships without depending on a man, yet remaining open to receiving a man's support.

How Men Experience Intimacy

We must always keep in mind that a man bonds emotionally by successfully doing for a woman. A man experiences greater intimacy each time he succeeds in providing his partner with fulfillment. We must also remember that women experience greater intimacy primarily by receiving love and support. This is a very important distinction. If a woman *cannot* slow down and allow a man to nurture her female side, she will have trouble creating a bond in the first place.

A simple example of the advanced relationship skill of slowing down to allow a man to support more can be seen very simply and graphically: a man and woman approach a door. Women who do too much will speed up, politely open the door, and wait for the man to walk through. They give to others what they need themselves, which only reinforces the tendency to give and not receive. To nurture her female side, a woman should practice slowing down to make sure he gets to the door first, waiting for him to open it, walking through, and thanking him. When she lets him open the door for her, she gives him an opportunity to support her successfully.

Rituals for Finding Balance

Through this dynamic, a man is placed in the masculine role of providing, and a woman moves to her feminine role of graciously receiving. It also clarifies her real need, which is to be cared for. She doesn't physically need him to open the door, but when he does, it supports and nurtures her female side. Her femininity needs and thrives on this kind of support in order to find balance.

When a man opens the door for a woman, it is as if he is saying "You are special to me, I care about you, I honor you, I am here for you, I understand you do so much for everyone so I am happy to help make things easier for you whenever I can."

> When a man opens the door for a woman, it is as if
> he is saying "You are special to me, I care about you,
> I honor you, I am here for you."

This loving message is given each time a man goes a little out of his way to show consideration for making his partner's life easier and more comfortable. Actions speak much louder than words.

Stage Three: Women Who Want Men to Talk More

The third most common reaction women have when they experience the imbalance of emotional role reversal is to long for their men to talk more and share themselves in traditionally feminine ways.

A woman in this third stage longs for a man to open up and share his feelings the way she would if she were in balance. It is as though she wants him to be feminine before she can feel safe in being feminine.

These women fully believe that they would be fulfilled if their partners would only open up and be more sensitive and vulnerable. This longing for men to be softer and more sensitive is really a replacement need. It covers the women's real longing to be more sensitive and soft themselves.

> This longing for men to be softer and more sensitive
> is really a replacement need. It covers the women's
> real longing to be more sensitive and soft themselves.

Just as the overweight woman replaces her need for love with the need for food, or the woman who "does too much" replaces her need to be supported with the need to support others, this woman replaces her need to be feminine with the need for her partner to be feminine.

These replacement needs are not deliberate choices but are reflexive reactions that occur when women are required to function like men without the support they need to be feminine.

When a Woman Doesn't Feel Safe

A woman in a loving relationship may feel unsafe because she feels unlovable or because her partner hasn't yet learned how to make her feel secure. Regardless of why she doesn't feel safe, when she can't express her female side, she will automatically move to her male side and exhibit more masculine traits. To find balance, she will begin to crave a more "feminine" partner.

Generally, the man she chooses is already more sensitive and open. In some cases, though, he is originally a less sensitive man, but over time she tries to make him more feminine by demanding that he open up and share more or become more domestic. This reaction occurs because the woman doesn't have a clear picture of how to get the nurturing support she needs for her own female side. She feels driven to support his female side.

Why Women Initiate Conversation

Instinctively she feels "If I can listen sympathetically to his problems and feelings, he'll listen to mine. If I can fulfill his feminine needs, he'll fulfill mine." While this formula works with other women, it does not work with men. By revisiting the distant past, we can understand where this tendency originated.

As we've ascertained, through daily supporting the female side of other women, a woman was assured of their reciprocal support. The tribal code was: "I scratch your back by listening to you, you scratch my back by listening to me. If I am there for you, you will be there for me." This remains one of the basics of female communication.

When a Woman Wants to Talk

I can tell when my wife really has something to tell me because she inevitably asks me lots of questions. For example, when I return from teaching my weekend seminars, she will sometimes be particularly interested in seeing me and asking lots of questions. This is a signal that she has a lot to share. I now understand that after answering a few questions, I am supposed to ask her questions about her weekend.

By cracking the secret feminine code, I have learned to give Bonnie what she's asking for. Before I understood how we were different, the same situation would turn into a major argument.

She would ask me questions about my weekend when she wanted to talk instead of simply telling me what she wanted to share. What I really wanted to do was relax quietly. But I could tell she wanted me to talk, so I would try. When I look back at those times, I can see that it was like pulling teeth. The more she wanted me to talk, the less I wanted to.

After a few minutes of answering her questions as briefly as possible, I felt as if I'd answered her questions (as a gift to her) and then would go relax and watch TV (as a gift for me). Little did I know that this was not what was expected. Now she was even more upset. Not only had I resisted her questions, I wasn't asking her questions in return.

The process only became positive when I could read the signals and begin applying advanced relationship skills. Now when Bonnie asks me lots of questions, I talk a little and then ask her lots of questions. If she is still not talking, I gently persist. Once she gets going, I let her do most of the talking because it is her need more than mine.

Never talking more than a woman as a general guideline counteracts the tendency to go into emotional role reversal. Certainly, on some occasions I will talk more, but when I begin to notice it is happening a lot, I pull back and focus on assisting her in opening up.

What Happens When Men Open Up

When a man opens up more than his mate, he can actually block her from feminine feelings. When a man begins to talk more, share more, and need more in a relationship than she, the woman actually begins to pull away and begins talking less, sharing less, and needing less.

The startling truth that I have discovered only in the past ten years is that the more a woman is dependent on her partner to talk and open up, the farther she gets from her female side. The more successful she is in opening up her partner and nurturing his female side, the less nurtured her female side will be. The more sensitive a man becomes in a relationship, the stronger a woman feels she has to be. Put simply, the more a man moves to his female side, the more a woman will feel driven to her male side. Instead of being more fulfilled, she will begin to pull away. Certainly, some sharing of feelings is fine, but when the man begins to open up more than the woman, she will automatically begin to close down.

With this insight I eventually came to realize that the greatest gift I could give my clients was to help the men be successful in listening to the women. I would also help the women "prepare" them so that listening was not insurmountably difficult. Once a man eventually learned this skill, he didn't get so upset with his female partner's feelings. Suddenly, women were feeling much safer and freer about expressing their feelings. Using this approach, couples quite quickly felt more successful in their relationships.

How Women Begin to Feel When Men Open Up

Let's explore some of the diverse comments made by different women whose partners were more expressive of feelings than they themselves were. While not every woman will relate to each of these, they are very common, particularly to women who have lived with men who are more sensitive.

He Does:	She Feels:
1. He shares how upset he feels when she talks about her feelings.	1. "I didn't realize he was so sensitive. Now I have to be careful all the time. I don't feel safe saying anything to him."
2. He becomes angry and shares his gut reactions to her feelings before taking time to cool off.	2. "No matter what I say, it's upsetting to him. I am afraid to open up with him."
3. He shares openly about all his problems in response to her talking about hers.	3. "He has enough problems. I don't want to burden him with mine. He is just too needy. I don't want another child."

He Does:	She Feels:
4. He complains too much and always wants things to be better.	4. "I really appreciate that he's opened up, but now that I know him, I'm not really that attracted to him. I feel bad about it, but I really don't want to be with him anymore."
5. He shares his deep feelings of insecurity and his need to be loved.	5. "I care about his emotions, but I feel like I can't be me around him."
6. He talks too much about his feelings whenever he gets ticked off.	6. "I feel like I have to walk on eggshells when I am around him. I don't feel heard or understood."
7. He shares his hurt feelings and cries more than she does.	7. "I am embarrassed to say this, but when he cries all the time I can respect his feelings, but I lose all my romantic feelings for him."
8. He gets angry a lot and feels that he has to get it out rather than silently contain his feelings in order to cool off.	8. "When he gets angry, I feel like he is a child throwing a tantrum. Automatically I begin to feel like I have to always please and mother him."
9. He talks about his problems more, or the problems with the relationship, than she does.	9. "I am really glad we are in therapy. He really needs it. I didn't realize he had so many problems. It's not that I'm perfect, I just feel like he needs someone else. I want to leave because I don't know what to do for him."

He Does:	She Feels:
10. He whines and complains about things more than she does.	10. "I resent that he whines about everything. I want to be with a more masculine man. I don't want to be married to another woman."
11. He talks about his needs for more in the relationship and looks to his partner to fulfill his female side.	11. "He is always very attentive to me, but I feel that he is always needing more. When I don't talk, he gets upset, and when he talks, I just want to get out of the room. I listen, but I really don't want to."

None of these women could have predicted that they would feel this way. Like many women, they thought that if their male partner would just open up they would be in marital bliss.

How Women React to a Man's Sensitivities

The way a woman reacts to her partner's vulnerabilities is practically the opposite of how a man will respond to hers. If he hears her feelings *and doesn't feel blamed,* then he cares and connects with his own female side. By listening to a woman share, a man can feel sensitive to her feelings and yet strong and determined to help.

When a woman listens to a man's feelings, she also becomes stronger but resents having to care more for him when she needs him to care for her.

This shift in women can be extremely gradual and hard to detect. As a man opens up, she is initially very impressed and finds his behavior endearing. Unfortunately, she eventually tires of it and turns off to him. Even when she wants to leave him, she will feel that it is "not him but her." In many cases, however, it is because he opened up more than she did and she was simply turned off.

The bottom line here is that women are more fulfilled if their male partners reveal less but help them to reveal more. When a woman longs for a man to open up and be sensitive, she is really longing to open up and become more sensitive and vulnerable herself.

> When a woman longs for a man to open up and be
> sensitive, she is really longing to open up and become
> more sensitive and vulnerable herself.

Three Ways a Man Goes Out of Balance

When a man doesn't feel appreciated in his relationship with a woman or at his job, he begins to shift out of balance in any of the following three ways.

1. He becomes addicted to working more.
2. He feels stuck in his cave and can't come out.
3. He swings way over to his female side and, overwhelmed with feelings, becomes moody or wants to talk about problems.

Each of these reactions is counterproductive. They may bring immediate short-term relief from feeling the pain of not being supported on his male side, but in the long run they only weaken him more. They are addictive behaviors that assist him in avoiding his pain but do little to directly solve the real problem.

Stage One: Overworking

A man's most common impulse when he doesn't feel supported at home is to work harder at the office. As we have already discussed, a man reacts instinctively to a woman's dissatisfaction by trying to provide more money, so he becomes increasingly driven to achieve more and succeed more. No matter how successful he is, it is never enough. He silently criticizes himself for not being better, for making mistakes and not being good enough.

Through repeatedly focusing on his need for success (or his failure to achieve that success), he is temporarily freed from feeling his unfulfilled need to be appreciated by others. He avoids feeling unappreciated in his relationship by asserting his independence and competence at work.

He will convince himself that he doesn't need to be appreciated. This is only because he has not tasted the fulfillment of being appreciated for his every effort and action regardless of the result. Forgiveness, acceptance, and appreciation have not been his experience growing up or while in relationships with women.

When a Man Focuses on Work

In most cases, when a man begins drifting from a relationship focus to a work focus, he doesn't even know that he's missing the appreciation he used to get from his spouse. He may agree with her when she says, "Why should I appreciate him for emptying the trash, it's his trash too." Unaware that he needs to be appreciated for the little things, he seeks to do big things for her that should reap the reward of her favor. But they don't.

Without the daily experience of appreciation at home, a man begins to measure himself solely by the results of his work. Because his hunger for success is really a replacement for his true need to be appreciated, he is never satisfied with his success.

He is in a self-defeating pattern and is spiraling down. The more he focuses on work, the less he does directly for his wife. If he is not doing things directly for his wife, her appreciation will not touch him. Even if she does appreciate him, he can barely feel it. The less appreciated he feels, the more self-critical and dissatisfied he becomes.

This first stage inevitably leads him to the second stage of imbalance. When he comes home, he is unable to shift from the work mode to the relationship mode. He stops coming out of his cave.

Stage Two: He Doesn't Come Out of His Cave

When a man comes home feeling unsuccessful at work, he immediately pulls away from his partner to relax and forget the problems of his day. As we have already discussed, temporarily pulling away is quite normal. However, since he is recovering from the added stress of feeling unsuccessful, it will take him much longer before he is ready to emerge.

But in stage two, he simply cannot forget the pressure. If a man feels bad about his work, it is much harder to feel good, even while pursuing a hobby or watching his favorite team. When the pressure to succeed predominates, the power of his cave time activities to release him from the grip of work diminishes proportionally.

When a man's male side is not sufficiently nurtured by his mate, he has little energy when he gets home. It is as if he is storing it up until he can confront his problems the next day. The masculine energy he used to bring to the relationship is greatly suppressed.

Why He Can't Forget His Pressures

Men experience difficulties in forgetting work-related problems and pressures because their female side keeps reminding them of the problems, while their male side feels incapable of solving them. They cannot easily forget their problems and come out of the cave. As a result, they become addicted to cave time activities in an attempt to forget the problems and pressures of work. Such men tend to be disinterested in what is going on around them.

It is hard for a man like this to connect with his partner because not only is he so preoccupied, he doesn't even have the motivation he once did. He has low energy because deep inside he feels like a failure. Failure is deadly for a man.

Failure is deadly for a man.

A Man's Replacement Needs

In stage one, a man's replacement need is to succeed; in stage two, it is to rest and relax—even though his real need is to be loved and appreciated. He feels as though he wants to be ignored so that he can rest, nap, relax, or zone out by watching TV. While his "vegging out" is a legitimate need, his mate believes that he is just being lazy. That only makes it more difficult for him to hear or be responsive to her requests and needs.

While his "vegging out" is a legitimate need, his mate believes he is just being lazy.

Instead of being assertive, he becomes passive; instead of being interested, he is distracted; instead of wanting to connect, he wants to be left alone. Although resting will bring temporary relief, it does not satisfy his need to be energized by appreciation.

Without an understanding of what their mates require, women unknowingly make the situation worse. They complain that he is not there for them. They do not instinctively focus on appreciating what he does do for them. Even if a man does very little, a woman can still focus on what he *does* do instead of what he doesn't do. In this way, he will be assisted in eventually doing more and getting the appreciation he needs.

The Snowball Effect

Once he gets going, it is like a snowball rolling down a hill, building up speed and growing bigger and bigger. As a man is appreciated for what he does, he will do a little more. When a man is appreciated, he will summon up the energy and motivation to do still more. When he is appreciated for still more, he can continue always to do more. With a woman's love, he can build up his strength to come out of the cave.

When a man is appreciated, he will summon up the energy and motivation to do still more.

Helping Him by Helping Herself

A woman can also help a man by helping herself. Her being happier will even help him to come out. When he sees that she isn't unhappy and blaming him for not coming out, he feels he must be doing something right.

When a woman is happy, a man tends to take the credit and feel good about himself. For example, if he supports her financially, if she goes shopping and returns thanking him for what she bought, he'll feel much better.

When a woman is happy, a man tends to take the credit and feel good about himself.

The downside of a man's taking the credit for a woman's feelings is that when she is not happy, he feels that he's more of a failure and retreats even deeper into his cave.

When men are in this stage, women tend to criticize them for being lazy and unsupportive. By understanding this second stage, it will be much more possible for her to be compassionate and supportive instead of nagging and complaining.

Comparing Men and Women

By comparing a man's second stage to her own, a woman can increase her understanding. Just as it is difficult for a woman to move out of stage two, it is equally difficult for a man.

A woman in the second stage feels compelled to do more. For her to relax and slow down, she needs a lot of support. When she is married or has children, she is even more driven. Almost every woman knows how hard it is to relax and have a good time when feeling overwhelmed and needed by others.

In a similar but opposite way, a second-stage man feels driven to do less. He can easily relax but cannot feel motivated to do more. He is energized by the thought of some recreational activity but becomes suddenly exhausted by the thought of being domestically responsible. He feels a strong need to rest, and do less, while she feels a strong need to do more. Just as she can't do something fun and for herself, that is all he has the energy to do.

Without understanding this dynamic, a relationship can just make it worse for the man. The more he is needed, the more disappointed others who depend on him will be. As a result, he becomes even more immobilized.

With this knowledge, a woman can begin to imagine what her man is going through. In a similar way, men can fathom why women in stage-two imbalance can't just "relax and take it easy."

Moving the Couch Potato

Understanding stage two of emotional role reversal has helped me immensely. At times when I am not feeling good about my work, I tend to stay in my cave for extended periods of time. Even though I would like to come out, I feel trapped.

To get myself out, I remember that what I really need is appreciation. My body is telling me that I need to rest and relax, but my mind now knows better.

So I force myself up off the couch even though every cell in my body is saying rest, relax, don't get up. I imagine I am lifting weights to build up my muscles. When I am out of shape, lifting weights is always a strain and I don't want to do it. But once I do, I feel much better and stronger.

In a similar way, when I am feeling like a couch potato and

I am glued to the couch, I lift myself up and do something physically that I know my wife will appreciate. It can be as basic as getting up to empty the trash. Once I start moving, she can give me some appreciation. Soon my engines start pumping again.

How Bonnie's Support Helps

This technique works especially well because Bonnie takes pains to appreciate my effort. When I do something at home, instead of reacting like "So what, I've been busy since I got home," she will take a moment to articulate her gratitude.

If she doesn't notice what I do, instead of missing an opportunity to be appreciated I can say, "Did you notice that I emptied the trash?"

In response, she will always take a moment to say, "Oh, thanks."

Even if she is resenting me and her guts are saying "Big deal," she makes a point of saying something brief but nice.

Knowing that I can easily be appreciated in my relationship helps me tremendously in coming out of my cave. The repeated experience of appreciation allows me to feel my need for it and then come out and get it. The certain anticipation of her warm responses always helps motivate me to get out of my cave.

If Bonnie takes the time to appreciate me when she is in stage two, it helps her as well. By appreciating me, she is taking a moment to become aware that she really isn't alone and that she does have my support. So she begins to relax. For example, when I come out of my cave to empty the trash, she is not just appreciating me for emptying the trash, she is appreciating me for being her companion, friend, and partner in life.

Her support frees me from getting trapped in my cave. This does not mean that I don't take cave time. When a man is stressed, it is healthy and natural for him to go to his cave. It only becomes unhealthy when he can't come out again.

Twelve-Step Programs

Generally speaking, it is in stage two that a man turns to drinking excessively or other forms of addiction. These elements, of course, only lock him into the cave even more. When a man knows he can spend time with a friend or friends who appreciate him and don't expect anything much from him, it is much easier to leave the cave. This is one of the reasons the twelve-step sharing programs and other sharing programs which validate his adequacy have been so helpful.

When a man is stuck in his cave, one of the ways to bury the pain of not being appreciated is to begin drinking. In a twelve-step program, for example, if he can do one important thing, he will win the appreciation of many others. By abstaining from drinking and showing up, he immediately wins their approval. By continuing to not drink and come to meetings, even if he feels inadequate at work or in his relationships, he feels good about himself because he is not drinking. This is a tremendous help.

Generally speaking, alcoholics in AA are very proud of how many days, weeks, months, or years they have been sober. They wear it like a merit badge, and as the years pass gain seniority. They suddenly have a right to feel better about themselves, and a lot of other people admire and appreciate them as well. They have all been there and understand and appreciate the strength it takes to stop an addiction. This admiration strengthens the male side and counteracts emotional role reversal.

Women also turn to addictions as a result of emotional role reversal. Twelve-step and other sharing programs are again particularly helpful, but for a different reason. The sharing gives women the nurturing that their female side primarily needs.

I do not want to imply that men do not benefit as well by the sharing of feelings. They also have a female side, but before they can come out of their caves they first need to feel that they can do something they will be appreciated for.

One of the many great values of AA for people is that it is a place where they share what they have done or overcome to become sober again. Men get the appreciation they primarily need, while women get the empathy they primarily need.

Relationships and the Cave

When a man is single, there is nothing preventing him from coming out of his cave whenever he feels like it. When he is in a relationship, however, it is nearly impossible for him to come out if his mate resents his pulling away, and sits waiting at the door. Too many women unknowingly make this mistake and actually end up working against their own desires.

It is nearly impossible for a man to come out of his cave if his mate resents his pulling away, and sits waiting at the door.

When a man is in the cave, a woman wants more from him but can sense that if she asks he will resist like a grumbling bear. It doesn't occur to her that like a bear he is hungry for the honey of her love. She believes that if he talks about his feelings, he'll feel better. Needless to say, the more she tries to get him out by suggesting he do things or by asking him questions, the more he resists.

How to Get a Bear Out of His Cave

With this new awareness, she can use the advanced relationship skills that her mother never knew or needed to know to get him out. She can do it by pretending that he literally is a bear.

No one in their right mind would enter a bear's cave while he was sleeping, nor would they try to pull him out.

Instead, you would indirectly draw him out by leaving little pieces of bread outside his door. If the bread doesn't work, you put honey on it. When he smells it, his instincts will tell him to follow the scent. He appears.

Now you begin to sense that he will go wherever you want him to if you leave a trail of bread and honey behind you. If the "bear" is a human male, the bread is the opportunity to do something, and the honey is the appreciation he will get by doing it. Men, like bears, are looking for honey. When they clearly smell acceptance and appreciation, they are motivated to leave the cave behind.

Stage Three: He Wants More Support from Her

When a man's male side is not supported and he feels stuck in the cave, a third reaction occurs. His male side stays in the cave, but his female side comes out. Suddenly, he wants his partner to take care of him, but because he is still a man, he demands it in an aggressive way.

We know that when a man is in his cave, a woman should not try to go in after him. In third-stage imbalance, he comes out all right—but with all guns blazing. He is easily hurt, offended, and provoked.

Like a woman, he feels he is "doing everything" and not getting nearly enough back. He has moved way over on his female side and is generally very verbally expressive.

Whenever a man cannot fully come out of his cave, his female side tends to emerge and take control of the relationship. He will tend to overreact to his mate's mistakes, feel a much greater need to talk about his feelings, become much more defensive of his actions, and will demand apologies when she has upset him.

The Need to Be Respected

In this stage of emotional role reversal, a man's real need is still to be appreciated, but because he is not getting the kind of support he really requires, a replacement need takes over. The true need to be appreciated is replaced by the need to be respected.

This tendency is most clearly exhibited in a more extreme manner by an abusive alcoholic father. Quite often he will tend to demand respect by remarks such as "This is my house, and as long as you live here, you will do things my way. . . ."

Even if he is not an alcoholic, a man in this third stage will from time to time present these kinds of demands. When he does, the most effective steps he can take to stop himself are to cease talking to his partner about his feelings and set about containing them. Talking only makes him more rigid, righteous, demanding, and punishing. These are examples of remarks that indicate that a man must get a grip on himself.

What Happens:	His Gut Reactions in Stage Three:
1. She expresses feelings of frustration or disappointment.	1. "If you can't be happy, then we should just end this relationship."
2. She expresses unsolicited advice.	2. "You know I don't like it when you talk to me that way. Don't do it."
3. She expresses disapproval about something he did or forgot to do.	3. "No one can treat me this way. If you do not change, then I will leave you."
4. She is in a bad mood and unable to be appreciative.	4. "I do everything for you and this is what I get in return."
5. She complains about something he hasn't done.	5. "How dare you treat me this way. I will not stand for it. You are so ungrateful."
6. She disapproves of something he did and gives advice.	6. "I will not put up with this anymore. I do everything right, and you are wrong."
7. They get into a heated argument over something petty.	7. "I just can't stand this anymore. I don't deserve to be treated like this. You will never learn. That's it, I'm finished."
8. She does something to annoy him.	8. "I don't want to be mean, but you make me this way. I have to teach you a lesson."

While the above expressions may accurately reflect what he's feeling, it is lethal to express them to his mate. They are entirely negative, selfish, arrogant, shaming, and controlling and can do nothing to create a climate of trust and openness. If he is at all interested in getting the love and support he truly needs, then he must practice containing these kinds of feelings. Yes, they are his gut reactions but not the reactions of his heart and mind. Before he talks, he should first be centered in his heart and mind, not his guts.

Everyone Needs to Be Respected

A man in emotional role reversal has gone respect crazy. When he gets through making others feel guilty or intimidated, he is only temporarily satisfied. His hunger for respect will grow because his soul is really asking for appreciation. Whenever there is a problem, he has to be right and he is quick to blame and reject others.

In the third stage, a man may want more communication. He demands to know his woman's feelings, yet when she tells him, he argues and wants to share more of his own. Although he is acting like a woman in needing to share, he is still a man and generally wants to be right and is very willing to argue.

These spirited arguments feel good to him but bring only temporary relief. He will continue to feel a strong need to be heard and obeyed. No matter what a woman does for him, it will never be enough.

When Men Get Angry

The difference between men in this stage and a woman who needs to be heard is that when a man feels the strong need to share his feelings he will also want to be right. When a woman needs to share feelings, generally speaking she only requires that she feel heard and validated. She does not require a man to agree with her.

This third stage is greatly encouraged by popular culture. In the last twenty years, men are repeatedly encouraged to get in touch with feelings and to express them. In many cases, they are shamed for not being more expressive of their feelings.

As we have already noted, when a man expresses too many sensitivities, a woman quickly tires of him. And particularly when a man expresses anger, a woman begins to close up. Because she doesn't feel safe in sharing with him, she refuses to talk and closes up. Suddenly *she* is in her cave and *he* is trying to get in.

When a Woman Won't Talk

At my seminar, men in the third stage generally share similar complaints. Let's explore a common example.

Tim was very angry when he stood up to share his story. He complained that he was much more willing to work on the relationship than his wife.

"You say women want to talk," he grumbled. "I want to talk more, but my wife won't talk to me."

The righteous tone in his voice tipped me off to what was wrong. "Has your wife ever said to you that you don't listen and that she can't talk to you?" I asked him.

"Sure. That's all she'll say," he answered. "But it's not true. I will listen. I am the one who wants to talk more. I do all the things you say a man should do. I cook, clean, make dates, and do all the things women are supposed to want, and then she spends all her time in the cave. I have had it."

"Well, that's the reason she won't talk to you. You don't listen," I told him flatly.

He then proceeded to prove my point by arguing with me: "No, you don't understand. I do listen, I am supportive, I listen to her feelings, but I also expect her to listen to mine."

"The way you are talking to me is probably just the way you talk to her," I persisted. "By arguing, you are ensuring that she will not want to talk with you. Even if she was warming up to the idea of sharing with you, your approach would stop her dead in her tracks."

A woman simply cannot feel protected or respected when a man speaks to her in such a righteous and demanding tone, particularly when it comes to talking about her feelings.

Why Women May Stay in Their Caves

When a man is too emotionally demanding or overly sensitive and easily hurt, a woman feels as if she can't trust him to hear her feelings correctly.

She will not feel safe opening up with him when he feels he needs to talk more than she does. The only recourse left open to her is going to her cave.

This means moving more to her male side, because to protect herself from her partner's emotionally charged attacks and demands, she has to become like a man. After a while she will feel so comfortable in her cave that her female side will *want* to stay there.

Why a Man Gets So Upset

When a man is on his female side, it will sound very unfair to him when his partner won't talk to him or apologize for upsetting him. He feels powerless to get what he needs unless she agrees with him and expresses a willingness to change. He does not know how naturally women change when they feel loved.

When a woman feels loved, she slowly begins to open up and is willing to change unsupportive behaviors. When her mate is demanding, she will inevitably resist him, which of course only makes him feel angrier and more demanding.

When a stage-three man is upset, he is basically feeling deprived of the support he wants and deserves. To feel really better, he needs an effective game plan for getting what he wants.

When a man comes up with a workable solution that makes sense to him, he begins to move back to his masculine side, which wants to solve the problem.

When a woman doesn't want to talk and a man does for healthy reasons, this is what he can do:

He should say: "I can tell something is bothering you. What's wrong?"

He should not say: "I am upset and I need to talk with you."

She says: "I can't talk to you."

He should say: "Hmmm," and then just pause and consider how he probably gives the message that it's not safe for her to talk.

He should not say: "Of course you can talk to me. I am the one who is trying to get you to talk. I am the one who is trying to make this relationship work."

If she says: "You will just argue with me. I don't want to even get started."

He should say: "You're probably right."

What is most important is that he should remain calm and accepting. This is the only way to win his partner over. He needs to prove to her that he can duck and dodge her provocations without getting mad. With this kind of safety insurance, she will begin to open up.

He should not say: "I will not argue, I just want to talk!" That would be arguing.

To argue with a woman when she doesn't want to talk just confirms that she can't open up and talk to him. To make it safe for a woman to open up and be feminine in a relationship, he must practice containment. He should contain his feelings so that she can first feel heard.

This does not mean that he should never feel or express his feelings. It means that he shouldn't overwhelm her with more negative feelings than she can handle. Instead of spilling his guts, he should go to his cave and think. After he has calmed down, he should focus on the solution, not the problem. He should come up with a workable strategy for doing something that will get him the appreciation he really craves.

When Men Make Lists

I can tell I'm in stage 3 of emotional role reversal when my female side comes out and starts making lists of all the things my partner is doing wrong. When I start making lists, unlike a woman who primarily just needs to talk about her lists, I want Bonnie to agree with me and promise to correct her behavior.

When I used to express myself in this way, Bonnie felt that she was living with a domineering tyrant. It was the "me" I become when I am not able to be my true loving self. The domineering tyrant is my shadow self.

If we are not feeling loved, we become the opposite of who we are when we are wonderful and loving. People who are very generous become very tight when their gifts are not appreciated. People who are very trusting and open become completely closed when they feel disappointed. When people who are very patient and flexible finally reach their limit, they become impatient and rigid. This is how love turns to hate. As a man or a woman moves into emotional role reversal, their shadow selves make more and more appearances.

If we are not feeling loved, we become the opposite of who we are when we are wonderful and loving.

To create and preserve a loving relationship, we need lots of ways in which to help us keep our balance, particularly when strong winds blow and the earth shakes beneath our feet.

For example, I still sometimes feel like a tyrant, but I do my best to keep these feelings to myself. I recognize at these moments that my male and female sides are imbalanced and do something to recover my equilibrium. Instead of acting out, I go to my cave. From inside my cave, I wait till I want to feel better. Then, to come out, I do something that will ensure my getting the appreciation from Bonnie that I really need in order to feel better. Instead of complaining that I am not appreciated, I do things that will garner her appreciation.

Through the application of advanced relationship skills the pitfalls and dangers of emotional role reversal can be gradually overcome. In the next chapter, we will explore more ways in which men and women can find balance. We will also explore how to sustain the passion in a marriage through maintaining balance and being monogamous. We will explore the secrets of lasting passion to create a lifetime of love.

A Lifetime of Love and Passion

The high rate of divorce is not a sign that people today are less interested in marriage. On the contrary, it indicates that we want more from our relationships than ever before. Men and women alike are dissatisfied because their marital expectations are much greater than in the past. We want a lifetime of love; we want lasting passion with one special person.

Even with the high level of divorce, there is also a high rate of remarriage. If the flame of passion goes out, both men and women would rather risk the pain of divorce than the loss of feelings. We intuitively know that through continuing to nurture a special relationship something much greater can be experienced. Deep inside, we sense that passionate monogamy is possible, but we do not have the skills to fully experience it.

The enormous market for women's romance novels, TV soap operas, and male pornography is not the cause of this dissatisfaction but is actually the symptom of an unfulfilled desire for passion in our relationships.

Generally speaking, when a man's emotional and passionate needs for love are not satisfied, he becomes entranced with sex, while a woman tends to become captivated with romance.

These strong tendencies are not necessarily symptoms of dysfunction but are the natural expressions of a frustrated deeper need for emotional support in their relationships.

Generally speaking, when a man's emotional and passionate needs for love are not satisfied, he becomes entranced with sex, while a woman tends to become captivated with romance.

In Our Parents' Generation

In our parents' generation it was expected that the passion would lessen over time. Lasting passion and emotional fulfillment were not the goal of relationships. Relationships were formed primarily to fulfill our survival needs, not our romantic emotional needs. That's why my mother admired my father for staying with the family although he was having an affair with another woman and had long since stopped considering her romantic emotional needs.

To a great extent, it was just accepted by most that passion would burn out once the honeymoon ended and the children arrived.

I remember vividly that to the teenagers of my generation, the loss of passion after marriage was an accepted fact. Before marriage you couldn't have sex, all you ever thought about was sex, and if you were having sex you did it every chance you had. There were definitely not enough chances. But once you got married and you could have sex whenever you wanted, for some mysterious reason you stopped wanting it as much.

Another Bean in the Bottle

When I was in college, it was quite common for young men to be told this story by the coach or some other authority figure.

"When you men get married, you can expect to have lots of romance and sex. When you get married, get a bottle, and every time you have sex, put a bean in that bottle. After one year, every time you have sex, take a bean out of that bottle. If you can empty that bottle, then you will be real lucky."

This was his way of letting us know not to expect the passion to last in a relationship. In most world cultures, men and women have coped with the loss of passion by having extramarital affairs. The survival of the family was much more important than whether one got laid or with whom.

When Men Have Affairs

In the past, if a man was reasonably discreet about his affairs, a woman would quietly accept them. As I've described, my mother did.

My father and mother continued to love each other, but my father also kept his mistress. Somehow my mother found a way to continue loving and sharing her life with him—even though the romance in their relationship had faded away.

Since contemporary women increasingly can provide for themselves, they want more from a partner than helping to take care of the family. Women today want the emotional support and romance that only monogamy can provide. If her husband needs another woman to be passionate, a woman today would rather start over with another man who wants her passionately.

In reaction to the lack of passion in their relationships, some women have also taken the traditionally male escape route of having affairs. It is only natural, because working outside the home side by side with men creates more opportunities.

For men or women, having an affair is ultimately an attempt to fulfill our need for love. While it may temporarily satiate this need, an affair leads us farther and farther away from being able to have a truly fulfilling relationship with our mates. When either a man or a woman is having an affair, the opportunity to grow together in loving passion is greatly restricted.

A Relationship Is an Investment

A relationship is like an investment. We give to our partner and hope over time to get more and more in return. Initially, getting the emotional support we are looking for may be difficult, but through the years, it becomes easier and easier.

Having an affair is like taking all your savings and blowing them in Las Vegas. You spend it all and you are quickly back to where you started. Whether the partner finds out or not, the effect is there. On an intuitive level, the other partner loses the feeling that they are special. Without this feeling, love and passion cannot grow. It will then take years to recapture that "special" feeling.

Having an affair is like taking all your savings and blowing them in Las Vegas. You spend it all and you are quickly back to where you started.

This does not mean that an affair necessarily ends a marriage. I have helped many couples revitalize their relationships over time as they healed together. Forgiveness is very powerful and can solidify a loving bond forever.

In these cases, the affair was a turning point because it allowed both partners to see clearly and talk decisively about problems that had been developing for years. Through forgiving and effectively communicating about the hurt and being motivated to make necessary changes, some couples are able to start completely over in love and experience greater passion and intimacy than ever before.

The Death of a Relationship

Sometimes it takes the threat of permanent loss to make people appreciate what they have; sometimes the imminent death of a relationship must stare us in the face before we can feel our deep love and longing to live together. Just as a near-death experience will often motivate or inspire a person to greater heights, so also can an affair exert an inspirational influence on the relationship.

This does not imply that we should risk making our mates feel betrayed and rejected in order to bring feeling back into the relationship. There are other ways. Through practicing advanced relationship skills, we can revive the passion even if it has been declared dead.

The Seven Secrets of Lasting Passion

To sustain passion in a relationship, there are seven important secrets. They are as follows:

1. Differences attract.
2. Change and growth.
3. Feelings, needs, and vulnerability.
4. Personal responsibility and self-healing.
5. Love, romance, and monogamy.
6. Friendship, autonomy, and fun.
7. Partnership and service to a higher purpose.

To apply advanced skills in each of these areas, we will discuss each one in greater depth.

1. Differences Attract

The most important aspect of attraction is that we are different. Just as the positive and negative poles of a magnet always attract each other, when a man remains in touch with his masculinity and a woman feels her femininity, the attraction can be maintained in a relationship.

Having to give up who we are to please our partners ultimately kills the passion. By seeking to resolve our differences without having to deny our true selves, we ensure lasting attraction.

Without a doubt, a man feels most turned on and attracted to his partner when she makes him feel like a man. Likewise, a woman is most attracted to a man when he makes her feel totally feminine. By taking the time to make sure that we avoid emotional role reversal, we can maintain the attraction we feel to each other.

**A woman is most attracted to a man when he makes
her feel totally feminine.**

This attraction is not just physical. When passion is sustained, our curiosity and interest in our partners also grow over time. We find to our surprise that we are still interested in what our partners think, feel, and do.

The Importance of Nurturing Gender Difference

Working with our differences is a requirement for keeping the passion alive. If we consistently have to give up or change who we are to please our partners, passion dies. Using advanced relationship skills, we can make small changes that stretch us but do not cause us to deny who we are. Through stretching, we actually connect to more of who we potentially are.

**Using advanced relationship skills, we can make
small changes that stretch us but do not reshape us.
Through stretching, we actually connect to more of
who we potentially are.**

The most important differences that need to be nurtured are our gender differences. For a woman to stay attracted to a man, he must be in touch with and express his male side. It is fine for him to express his female side, but if he suppresses his male side to be in a relationship with her, she will eventually lose her attraction for him.

In a similar way, for a man to stay attracted to a woman she must continue to express her female side. She can also express the qualities of her male side, but if her female side is not available to him, he will turn off.

Emotional Role Reversal Kills Passion

Couples without advanced relationship skills automatically move into emotional role reversal. When a woman moves too much to her male side, it kills passion. Excitement can only be sustained when her relationship helps her connect with her female side. When a man moves too much to his female side, his partner will cease to feel passion for him. She may care for him, but she will not be attracted. Through consciously striving for balance in a relationship, passion can be sustained.

How a Woman Can Nurture Her Female Side

Besides using advanced relationship skills and assisting a man in supporting her, a woman—single or married—must take pains to nurture her female side. Here is a list of the many things she can do:

1. Taking more time each day to share in a non-goal-oriented way about the problems of her day. This is best done on a walk or by having lunch with someone she does not look to for solutions to her problems.

2. Getting a massage or some kind of nurturing body work every week is extremely valuable. Being physically touched in a nonsexual way is very important to relax her and bring her back to a pleasant awareness of her body.

3. Talking on the phone and/or staying in touch with friends and relatives. It is vitally important that she not let the pressures of work and keeping a family and home together prevent her from taking time to talk with friends.

4. Making regular time for prayer, meditation, yoga, exercise, writing in a journal, or working in the garden should be observed with great commitment. Ideally, she should create twenty to thirty minutes twice a day when she can just *be* without having to *do* anything for anyone.

5. Creating a working style that supports her feminine side. Practice enlisting the support of others rather than being too independent and autonomous. Never miss an opportunity

to let a man carry a box for you or open the door. Have pictures of your family and friends around you while you work. When at all possible, surround yourself with beauty and flowers.

6. Getting at least four hugs a day from friends and family members.

7. Taking the time to write thank-you notes for the support you receive from others.

8. Varying routes home from work. Try to avoid the tendency to most efficiently get home each day by following the same route every time.

9. Becoming a tourist in your own town and regularly taking a mini vacation. Also try to get away from the home and enjoy new settings and vacations.

10. Joining a support group or visiting a therapist to make sure you can share your feelings freely without being concerned about your professional reputation.

11. Setting aside one evening a week for yourself. Go out and enjoy a movie or the theater, or stay home and take a long, warm bath. Play beautiful music, light candles, and either read a wonderful book or turn down the lights and fantasize. Take the time to do what you would most enjoy doing.

12. Listing everything that needs to be done and then putting in big letters at the top, "Things that don't have to be done immediately." Take at least one day a month to rest and not solve *any* problems. If you are a mother, take the day off, and get away from your home and children.

To suddenly try to do everything on the above list would, in itself, be overwhelming. Post a customized version somewhere, and slowly but surely begin incorporating these suggestions. Without taking deliberate steps to nurture her female side, a woman today will tend to automatically stay in her masculine side and unknowingly sabotage not only her relationships but her relationship with herself as well.

Ways a Man Can Nurture His Masculine Side

In my seminars, men commonly ask how they can develop their masculine side—particularly if they are not in relationships and don't have a woman to appreciate their actions when they need support.

Whether a man is single or married, there are many things he can do to stay strong. He should pick and choose which suggestions are appropriate for him. Here is a list of twelve:

1. Spend time with other men competing on a team or individually. By channeling your competitive tendencies in a playful way, you are released from feeling so driven by your work. You are automatically released from measuring yourself only by your work. Watching your favorite sports on TV or going to a game has a similar cathartic effect.

2. Go to action movies. It is healthy for adult males to experience violence on the big screen, particularly if it is expressed skillfully and ultimately to protect others. Watching movies like *Rocky, The Terminator,* and *Universal Soldier* is a way for you to feel and redirect your own violent tendencies. When children, however, experience violence on TV or in the movies, it has the opposite effect: it creates more violence in them.

3. Take cave time in your relationships. You should not feel guilty saying no to others when you need to be alone to recharge. You should not feel obligated to talk when you don't feel like it. This does not mean that you should never talk but that you should carefully pick the times.

If you tend to rarely take cave time, then you should do it even though it is lonely and painful. In ancient times, a boy became a man by fasting alone for a week in the wilderness. His aloneness forced him away from his mother, or female side, and he found the man within.

In a similar way, a man doesn't continue to experience his male power unless he takes the risk to put himself in a situation where he needs his strength. Courage grows through doing courageous actions.

4. If you do not have a sexual partner and you want to be more in touch with your male side, then practice self-control and don't masturbate. This suggestion is not moral advice. Masturbation is innocent, but it does nurture the female side, not the male side. Excess masturbation moves a man to his female side.

Practice abstinence from casual or recreational sex if you are not presently in a loving relationship because abstaining from sex is one of the most powerful ways to find male strength if one is too much on the female side. To restrain oneself sexually in this manner dramatically assists a man in connecting with his male side.

If a sexual release is needed, it will naturally occur during sleep. Regular cold showers, exercise, and some form of spiritual discipline like prayer, meditation, or yoga can help transmute sexual needs until you have a loving relationship with a sexual partner. Also, when a man waits in this way, he is much more motivated to find a sexual partner.

Frequenting adult bookstores or theaters, watching videos, or reading magazines that overstimulate you sexually is not advisable if you are practicing abstinence. A moderate amount of stimulation is, of course, fine. Just enough to keep you remembering what you are missing is just enough to keep you motivated.

5. Make sure you exert your muscles every week. Lift weights, jog, ride a bike, climb a mountain, swim, et cetera. Make sure that at least once weekly you push your muscles to the point of strain or exhaustion. Press your limits.

6. Make sure your life doesn't get too comfortable and cushy. Do something each week that requires you to overcome your inner resistance to exerting your different strengths. That could mean getting up earlier than usual to finish a project or staying later to make sure that you did the best you could do. Apply discipline in order to build your male strength.

7. Try each week to do random acts of kindness—for others you care about or complete strangers. When an older person needs a seat, offer yours. While driving, when someone

needs to cut in, graciously slow down. Be magnanimous in your generosity.

When someone needs you and you feel like resting, make the effort to help them anyway. I am not saying that you should do this every time, but just occasionally.

8. When you are upset or angry, don't punish others. Instead, focus on your breathing. Count to five on the in breath and then count to five on the out breath. Count ten cycles of this process, and then start over until you are not upset.

9. Make a list of all the things you most enjoy doing. Make sure that you are creating time each week for your favorite hobby or hobbies. Do things that make you feel accomplished and in charge.

10. When something needs to be done that won't take a lot of time or energy, do it immediately. Repeatedly affirm inside, "Do it now!"

11. When you feel afraid to do something that would really be good to do, feel the fear and do it anyway. Take reasonable risks. It is better to have tried and failed than never to have tried.

12. Practice containing your anger. You can redirect it either through some physically constructive activity, or privately express your feelings in a journal. Look for other feelings underneath the anger. When you do express anger, ideally it should be without having to raise your voice, but in a firm, confident but centered, and nonintimidating manner.

Talk about feelings with male friends, or create a male support group. Don't rely primarily on women to heal or hear your feelings. It is very helpful for some men to experience gatherings of the "men's movement," reading poetry, telling and listening to the ancient myths, dancing, singing, or drumming.

Through these techniques, a man in a relationship can ensure that he doesn't swing too much to his female side. A single man can help strengthen his male side and attract a woman who will support his being both powerful and sensitive.

2. Change and Growth

Living with the same person can, over time, eventually become very boring if they are not regularly changing. Staying fresh is crucial for both partners in a marriage. Just as listening to a favorite song a hundred times in a row makes it grow stale, so also may our partners become boring if they do not grow and change. If husbands and wives do not continue to grow and change, they eventually lose interest in each other.

Don't Sacrifice Too Much

Change is automatic if a relationship is to nurture us in being true to ourselves. Just as physical growth is so obvious in our children, we must always continue to grow emotionally, mentally, and spiritually. We must be careful not to sacrifice or deny ourselves too much. When a relationship does not allow us to grow, the passion between two people begins to fade.

Change is automatic if a relationship is to nurture us
in being true to ourselves.

Spend Time Apart

Loving your partner does not mean spending all your time together. Too much time together can also make a relationship commonplace and devoid of mystery. Enjoying other friends and activities means that you can always bring back something new to the relationship. This applies to doing things separately from your partner and doing things with your partner and others. Having dinner with another couple on a regular basis is a good idea.

Good Communication

If a woman doesn't feel safe in talking about her feelings, she will eventually have nothing to say. Creating the safety for her to talk freely without her having to fear rejection, interruption, or ridicule allows a woman to thrive in a relationship. Over time, she can continue to trust and love her partner more if he is a good listener.

Men quite commonly grow bored when women tell them the details of their days. They are more interested in the bottom line. As a man begins to understand how to listen in an active way that his mate can appreciate, listening and sharing stops being a chore and becomes an important nurturing ritual. With open lines of communication, a woman will continue to grow.

Lots of Appreciation

When a man does not feel appreciated in a relationship, he also stops growing. He may not know why, but when he returns home he feels increasingly passive and disengaged from his partner. He stops initiating things to do. His routine becomes rigid and fixed.

What makes my relationship with my wife so uplifting is that she never expects me to do anything in the home. Almost every domestic responsibility I have doesn't feel like a chore that gets taken for granted, but is a gift that she appreciates as if I didn't have to do it. This makes me want to do it rather than feeling that I have to do it.

Creating Change

It is important to schedule special occasions. A man needs to remember that women tend to feel the weight of domestic responsibility and find it hard to take time off for themselves. If a man creates special times when she can get out of the routine, she is free to feel nurtured.

Celebrations, parties, presents, and cards also affirm the passage of time. They are particularly important for women. A woman greatly appreciates a man's special attention to her at these times. His remembering birthdays, anniversaries, Valentine's Day, and other holidays means a lot to a woman. Doing something special on those days for her frees her from feeling overwhelmed by life's repetitive responsibilities and assures her that she is loved.

Breaking the Routine

One of the chief passion assassins is routine. Even if you are comfortable in your rut, it is helpful to break out of it from time to time. Even doing silly things can help make a moment special and memorable. For example, on our last vacation, instead of just taking a picture of my family in front of the Washington Monument, I lay down on the sidewalk and shot a picture from a lying-down position. Everyone laughed, and as a result, that moment will be remembered. All of our little efforts to occasionally break the routine make a difference.

Ultimately, what keeps passion alive in a relationship is growing in love. When, as a result of living, laughing, crying, and learning together two people are able to love and trust each other more, the passion will continue.

3. Feelings, Needs, and Vulnerabilities

To continue feeling our love, we need to feel. When it is not safe to have feelings or sensitivities, we quickly lose touch with our passion. While women need to talk more about their feelings and be heard if they are to feel vibrant in a relationship, men need to be appreciated for their actions if they are to feel like doing things for their partners.

When a man stops feeling a tender desire to please his partner, his tender feelings are automatically repressed. When a woman stops feeling the safety to share her feelings, she also begins to close up by repressing emotions.

Building Walls Around Our Hearts

Over time, when a woman or man continues to repress feelings, they begin to build walls around their hearts. Each time a woman feels ignored, minimized, and unsupported, another brick is placed in her wall. Each time a man attempts to be there for her and he ends up feeling ignored, criticized, corrected, or taken for granted, another brick is placed in his wall.

In the beginning, we can continue to feel love because the wall of repressed feelings is not fully blocking our hearts. But once it does, it cuts us off from our loving emotions.

To bring back the passion, this wall has to be dismantled brick by brick. Every time we remove one by applying advanced relationship skills, a little light begins to shine through. We then suddenly become aware of the rest of the wall and again feel that we are shut off. Slowly but surely, by continuing to successfully communicate and appreciate each other, that wall can come down and feelings can be fully experienced again.

Feeling Pain

When we are not getting the love we need, but remain vulnerable to our partners, we feel pain. Many couples deal with this by numbing themselves. They might say to themselves "It doesn't matter, I don't care." They may begin to close up, saying "I can't really trust him to be there for me, so I won't rely on him."

The most painful and lonely feeling is lying next to someone you don't feel you can reach out and touch with love. At this point, you may turn to an addiction to avoid feeling the pain of not being loved. Such dependencies free us from the pain but kill the passion. Only by learning to reach out for love and ask for what we want in skillful ways can we really heal our pain.

Without having the skills to get the love we need, we may automatically begin to stop feeling our needs. When this happens, passion begins to disappear. By turning off our feelings, we lose touch with our inner passion. We may not even know what we actually need more of because we have stopped feeling.

Without having the skills to get the love we need, we may automatically begin to stop feeling our needs. When this happens, passion begins to disappear.

Working on Trust

The challenge women face in their relationships is to keep opening up when feeling disappointed or unloved. It is of paramount importance that they work on trusting their partners more and more and continue to be receptive. Otherwise, they will lose touch with their vulnerability and needs.

The secret to growing in trust is not to expect your partner to be perfect but to believe that you are growing in the skills that help you help him give you what you want. Through understanding how men are different, a woman enables herself to trust that he loves her even when he doesn't instinctively do the things *she* would do to demonstrate caring.

Over time, she can begin to see the ways in which he thinks he is loving her. Most important, she can apply advanced relationship skills to help him be more successful in supporting her.

Working on Caring

To take down the wall around his heart, a man must work on caring. To bring back the passion, he needs to remember that it will require hard work and effort. At times, it will be like lifting a heavy weight.

If there is no wall around his heart, doing things is easy. Once he is taken for granted, the wall begins to rise again. Each time he feels his efforts are not appreciated, another brick is added to the wall.

But as he consciously begins doing little things that she can appreciate, if only for brief moments, the wall building stops. When his determination frays, and the wall suddenly looks higher, he becomes weary and resistant once more. He craves only to spend a lot of time in his cave.

A man can eventually come out and overcome the inertia of not caring if he is aware of the effort required to open his heart again. As he does, he will see that he is truly becoming a stronger person. With this strength, his road ahead will be less rocky. Eventually, he will be energized as never before by pleasing his partner.

Feeling Our Needs

As we grow together in love and trust, open up and feel our mutual needs more strongly, our vulnerability increases too. Passion is most powerfully experienced when we know how much we need someone.

In the beginning of our marriage, securing Bonnie's appreciation was relatively unimportant to me. Over the years, I have grown to love receiving it. It brightens my day, and when we are having sex allows me to feel how deeply I need her in my life.

After years of my consistently trying to be there for her, she can freely feel her needs for my love as well. The more she can depend on my support, the more passion she can feel. Bonnie is also realistic. She knows that I am not perfect and that I cannot always be there for her.

Healthy Dependence

Bonnie's dependence on me is healthy because it is based on what I can really give her. This allows her to be more vulnerable, which in turn allows me to feel like I make a difference.

> Need and dependence become a turn-on when we are
> needing what our partner can give us.

It is unwise as well as naive to expect our partners always to give us the love we need. Sometimes they have none to share and yet we demand more (in a sense, it is as though we are saying to a person in a wheelchair, "If you love me, then you will stand up and walk"). Sometimes they just can't be there for us in the ways we mistakenly think they can or should. But once we begin to need our partners in ways that they can't or don't support us, we will not only turn them off but will disappoint ourselves as well. When we need our partners too much, we will eventually pull away our trust and caring.

The more successful we are in fulfilling each other, the more we can rely on that support. With this kind of trust, even when our partners let us down, we will know that they did the best they could and we can be much more forgiving.

4. Personal Responsibility and Self-Healing

As we continue to open up and have our emotional needs met in a relationship, our unresolved past feelings ultimately begin to surface. When they rise up, they don't say "Hi, I'm your anger with your dad"; instead, they are directed at our partners.

It is an irony that when we feel most loved, the unresolved feelings from past experiences of not being loved begin to affect our moods. One minute we are feeling passion, the next we are considering divorce. Such radical shifts we always justify by our partners' behavior, although it really isn't primarily about them.

For example, I come home in a great mood and my wife greets me at the door by saying, "You forgot to call and tell me you were late. I didn't know what had happened." Certainly, I don't like being greeted with such a negative mothering statement, but if I suddenly get really upset and go to my cave and even consider divorce over that one statement, I have to take responsibility for my strong reaction.

Whenever you feel you were fine until your partner did one thing that ruined your day, it is generally something deep inside you that needs to be healed. Blaming your partner is looking in the wrong direction and aggravates the wound.

Whenever you feel you were fine until your partner
did one thing that ruined your day, it is generally
something deep inside you that needs to be healed.

Symptoms of Regression

When past feelings begin to surface, they generally make us feel uncharacteristically negative. We may feel a lot of blame, criticism, doubt, resentment, confusion, ambivalence, judgment, and rejection. For a moment, we regress back to feeling and reacting the way we did as children when we didn't feel safe to freely react. When such feelings surface, it is vital for us to work on taking responsibility for being more loving and forgiving.

We should not expect our partners to be our loving parents. That, as we know, is a surefire passion killer. At those times, we need to parent ourselves, or work with a surrogate parent in a psychotherapeutic setting. It is up to us to re-parent ourselves, not our partners.

Re-Parenting Ourselves

When we start blaming our partners for our unhappiness, it is a clear signal that our own "old stuff" is coming up. Although we feel especially entitled to demand more from our mates, we should demand nothing. It is a time for self-healing. It is a time for us to give ourselves the comfort and understanding that our parents may have failed to give us.

Remember, to expect our partners to make us feel better is to put them in the role of parents. The more dependent we become on them to change before *we* can change, the more stuck we will be. By parenting ourselves, we are free to release them from being the targets of our blame.

Feeling Powerless

Another signal that we are dealing with the past is powerlessness. Whenever we feel out of control and therefore seek to control another, our childhood is generally affecting us.

Whenever we feel out of control and therefore seek to control another, our childhood is generally affecting us.

We *were* controlled as children. We were genuinely powerless to get what we wanted and needed. As adults we have many more choices and opportunities.

Even with advanced relationship skills you will at times feel like nothing is working and that you'll never get what you want. When this feeling emerges, we need to embrace it and sympathize with ourselves, but must also keep in mind that we are not really powerless. It is rather that our present assessment of the situation is definitely being clouded by old feelings seeking release. By applying self-healing techniques, a clearer vision of your abilities and opportunities will begin to come back into focus within minutes.

Impatience

When our hearts are open, we are patient toward our partners' limitations and our own. When strong feelings of impatience appear, they are another signal that childhood feelings are clouding our vision.

As adults we have learned how to wait patiently for desire to become reality. Patience is a skill and a part of maturity. When we suddenly begin to feel impatient, we lose our realistic perspective and immediately demand more than is possible.

Instead of feeling good that progress is being achieved, we feel frustrated that not enough is happening fast enough. With each setback, we negate our progress.

Quite commonly, after taking my seminar or reading my books, men will begin to make changes. Then, after a while, they stop. At that point, a woman may begin to feel "I knew it, he didn't care. He's just going back to the way he always was." Her negativity prevents her from assisting him to continue supporting her.

If he offers to do something, she withers him with "Well, I'll wait to see if you really do it before I get excited." There is no better way for him to lose his motivation.

When a woman becomes impatient, she will demand that her partner make his changes permanently instead of realizing that he is engaged in an ongoing process to give her the support she needs. Instead of giving up or demanding more, a woman needs to focus less on changing her partner and more on changing her own attitude.

How We Stop Loving

When we feel blame toward our partner, it is difficult to accept, understand, and forgive their limitations and imperfections. Only through learning to love them in stormy times can we grow together. Anybody can love somebody who's perfect.

The test of love is caring for a person even though we know them to be less than perfect and have experienced their daily limitations. We claim that we want to be loved for who we are. But can we really love our partners for who *they* are? When our hearts are open, love is automatic. When our hearts are closed, it is another matter.

When Our Hearts Are Closed

When our hearts are closed, we are responsible for opening up. We are no longer children. To have an adult relationship, we must shoulder responsibility.

The reemergence of our childhood feelings threatens that sense of responsibility. We always feel that it is the other person's fault. Although we feel blame, by committing ourselves to finding forgiveness, we can bring ourselves back to being adults and release ourselves from immature feelings. These are the six ways in which we stop loving our partners when we are in the grip of past feelings that cause our hearts to close up:

1. **Loss of Trust.** It is suddenly hard to trust that your mate is doing his or her best or that they care. Suddenly, you may begin to doubt their best intentions. This is the person who would risk death to save your life, yet you begin to judge them as if they do not care about you.

Women generally have to work harder than men to overcome this tendency. To re-parent herself at those times, a woman needs to open up again slowly by first being caring to herself. She needs temporarily to stop depending on her partner to nurture her female side. By taking responsibility for re-parenting herself even if she still blames her partner, she will release herself from the spell of past feelings and will remember that she is cared for by a partner who is doing his best. Each time this process happens, her ability to trust increases.

2. Loss of Caring. Suddenly, you feel as if you don't care at all about your partner's needs and feelings. Your justification is the mistreatment that you have suffered at their hands. Here is the person we would risk our life to save, and suddenly we don't care about them.

A man generally has to work harder to overcome this tendency. To re-parent himself at those times, he needs to slowly open up by trusting in himself to be successful in the future. He needs to stop depending on his partner's trust in him to feel successful.

At this time, a man should do something to nurture his male side. By taking responsibility to re-parent himself even if he is still blaming his mate, he is automatically released from the grip of negative feelings and will soon remember how much he cares for her. Each time this process happens, his ability to care increases.

3. Loss of Appreciation. In an instant, you begin to feel that this relationship gives you nothing, whereas at other times you were so very happy and grateful. You feel as if you're doing more, while they do zilch. With this sudden memory lapse, you suddenly begin to feel deprived and totally without appreciation for your partner.

A woman generally has to work harder to overcome this tendency. To re-parent herself at those times, she needs to slowly open up again by respecting and supporting herself and nurturing her female side.

Even if she is still blaming her partner, she will begin to remember the ways in which he respects and supports her. Each time this process happens, her ability to appreciate him increases.

4. Loss of Respect. Suddenly, you begin to feel like withholding love and punishing your partners when just a few minutes before you wanted only to love and support them. You genuinely feel that you want to make your partner happy, and then abruptly care only about yourself.

A man will work eight hours a day to earn the money to buy a present for his mate, then turn around and resent doing something small, like picking up his socks, to please her.

Men generally have to work harder to overcome this tendency. To re-parent himself at those times, he needs to slowly open up by appreciating himself for all he does, even when his partner doesn't. For the moment, he needs to stop depending on his partner's acknowledgment and appreciation of him.

Now he should nurture his male side. By taking responsibility for re-parenting himself even if he is still blaming her, he will begin to remember how much he respects her and wants to please her.

It is important that he not feel he has to surrender his sense of self in order to please her. Otherwise he would be weakened. Each time he is able to come back and be supportive of her after doing something for himself, he gradually learns that he can please her without giving up who he is. Making a small shift in our behavior does not mean that we can't be true to ourselves. This awareness gives a man the flexibility to create win/win solutions in a relationship so that everyone gets what they want.

5. Loss of Acceptance. Suddenly, you begin to notice all the things your partner does wrong or needs to change. This is the person that you have felt was perfect, and out of the blue comes the compulsion to change, improve, or even rehabilitate them.

One minute you love and accept them, the next they're in the doghouse for making a mistake. Under these circumstances, a woman begins to feel that a man should know better. She forgets that he is from Mars and doesn't readily understand her needs.

Women generally have to work harder to overcome this tendency. To re-parent herself at those times, she needs to slowly open up again by taking the time to understand and experience what she is feeling and validate her own needs. She must release her need to change him before she can feel better.

By taking responsibility for re-parenting herself even if she is still blaming her partner or demanding that he change, a woman will begin to remember the things her partner does right as well as his openness and willingness to respond to her needs when he can remember or when he is approached in a positive way. Each time this process happens, her ability to accept her partner's imperfection, along with her own, increases.

6. Loss of Understanding. Our partners may say something that makes us critical or judgmental of their feelings and reactions. We tend to minimize their pain as if it doesn't matter, and yet, if they were physically wounded, we would risk our lives to save them. We quickly become impatient or disinterested even when this is the person we care most about in our life. We easily become defensive and feel we are being attacked when they are just sharing their feelings.

Men generally have to work harder to overcome this tendency. To re-parent himself at those times, a man needs to slowly open up by appreciating himself for all that he does, even if his partner doesn't.

At such times, a man should graciously excuse himself, go into his cave, and do something that will nurture his male side. By taking responsibility for re-parenting himself even if he is still feeling defensive, he will be released from negativity and will eventually begin to think about what she was really saying or wanted to say. He will begin to understand her needs and consider how he can best support her.

It is important that he take the time to consider what her feelings are without feeling pressured to immediately respond or say something. One of the best things a woman can say to a man when he is having difficulty listening to her is to remind him that he doesn't have to say anything. A powerful phrase is: "I would just like you to consider what I am saying. You don't have to do or say anything."

Opening Our Hearts

If we feel we are not getting the love we need and are blaming our partners, it is a clear sign that we need something our partners simply cannot presently give us. Taking responsibility for supporting ourselves when our hearts are closed frees us from dwelling on our partners as the problem and allows us to examine the situation on a much more fundamental level. We are able to nurture ourselves and then come back to the relationship with more to give, not more to demand.

Instead of drowning in negativity and reacting in unloving ways when our hearts are closed, we can use this "downtime" for self-healing. Instead of looking to our partners to change when we are blaming them, we should focus on changing ourselves. When we are feeling open and forgiving, we can refocus and look for ways in which to solve or correct the problem that originally upset us.

The Feeling Letter Technique

A method I use to help release my negative feelings is called the feeling letter technique. By taking a few minutes to do this technique I can free myself from the grip of negative feelings and then feel more forgiving and agreeable.

For over twelve years I have used different versions of this technique and it still works dramatically for me at those times when I am not feeling very loving. It is a very powerful tool for both men and women.

Writing a feeling letter not only strengthens a man's ability to contain his feelings but is also helpful when he is on his female side and needs to be heard. Instead of dumping his negative feelings on his partner, he can write them out and achieve his goal more effectively than he could by talking.

A man can use this technique particularly when he needs to share his feelings but knows that this is not the time. As we have discussed, when a man displays more feeling or emotional vulnerability than a woman, it may push her to her male side. Rather than risk that, he should enact the following three steps.

This exercise is equally useful for a woman if she needs to share her feelings when her partner is in his cave and can't hear her. If she is feeling in the mood to blame or change her partner, it is also a good idea for her to practice this technique and get more centered before he returns.

We will briefly explore each stage. For more information on this technique, refer to my book, *What You Feel You Can Heal.*

Step One

Begin by writing out whatever you would have liked to say to your partner. It is perfectly OK to blame or sound critical.

Set down what makes you angry, sad, afraid, and sorry. Take a couple of minutes to dwell on each of these emotions. Even if you don't actually feel some of them, ask yourself what you would be experiencing if you did. For example, if you are not angry, write: "If I was the angry type, I would say . . ." Spend about two minutes on each of the emotions.

After taking a total of eight minutes to express your different emotions, take two more minutes to focus on writing out your wants, wishes, needs, or hopes, and then sign your name. In just ten minutes, you're done. Try not to spend more time than this unless, of course, you enjoy it and find an immediate release by writing out your feelings. With practice, this will automatically begin to happen.

Step Two

In step two, write a letter from your partner to you saying the things that you would want to hear him or her say. Pretend that you have shared your letter with your partner and that they have really heard you. Write out the words that would make you feel heard.

Have them first thank you for sharing your feelings. Then have them express an understanding of your feelings. Finally, have them apologize for their mistakes and make promises to support you better in the future. Even if your partner would not respond in such a positive way, use your imagination.

Take about three minutes to write this response letter. If it takes longer than that, it is certainly OK. Simply writing out the words you would want to hear will make you feel better. Even though your partner is not really saying these things, you will benefit by hearing them.

Step Three

In step three, take two minutes to respond back the way you probably would if your partner really did hear you and apologized for their mistakes. In this short forgiveness letter, be as specific as possible. Use the phrase "I forgive you for . . ."

If it is still hard to forgive, remember that you are not saying that what they did is OK. When you forgive, you are clearly pointing out their mistakes but at the same time are releasing your tendency to continue withholding your love, compassion, and understanding.

Forgiveness doesn't mean the problem went away. It means that you are not closing yourself up to dealing with it in a loving manner. By practicing this feeling letter exercise at those times when you are resentful or your partner won't talk, you will suddenly feel relieved. Then you can patiently wait for the right opportunity to share your feelings, thoughts, and desires in a way that works for you, your partner, and the relationship.

Finding Balance

Practicing the feeling letter technique is particularly useful when you find yourself in any of the three stages of role reversal. Sometimes you may feel that you are in all three stages at the same time.

A man may be consumed with work, stuck in his cave, and irritable all at once because he wants more. In this case he is experiencing all three stages of imbalance simultaneously. In this state he can also begin to experience the female stages of imbalance.

A woman may at the same time hunger for more food, feel overwhelmed with too much to do, and want her partner to be more emotionally available and talk about his feelings. In this state she may also begin to experience all the male stages of imbalance.

This tendency to go out of balance is similar to what happens when you are learning to walk a tightrope. When you start to lose your equilibrium, you reflexively begin weaving in a desperate attempt to regain balance. With practice, keeping your balance becomes less intimidating and more graceful.

Writing feeling letters over the last twelve years has been extremely helpful for me and thousands of others in getting back up and starting over again. Through repeatedly starting over from a more loving and balanced point of view I was able to discover and develop the various advanced relationship skills presented in this book. I cannot emphasize enough the usefulness of this feeling letter technique.

While advanced relationship skills in general can help you avoid falling over in the first place, until we master them we are bound to fall down many times. The feeling letter is an essential tool for picking yourself up when you are down. Through applying these different strategies and using the feeling letter at those times when you need to find forgiveness, you can and will keep the passion of love alive.

5. Love, Romance, and Monogamy

Through taking responsibility for our reactions and actions in a relationship, we can truly begin to give and receive love successfully. Without an awareness of how our partners specifically need love, we may be missing priceless opportunities.

Women primarily feel loved when they are receiving from their men the emotional and physical support they need. It does not matter as much what he provides but that he does it in a continuous way. A women feels loved when she feels that a man's love is consistent.

When a man doesn't understand a woman, he tends to focus on the big ways to fulfill her all at once but will then ignore her for weeks. While good communication provides a healthy basis for a loving relationship, romance is the dessert. The way to a woman's heart is through doing lots of little things for her on a consistent basis. Here is my "short list" of twenty "kitchen-tested" things a man can do to create romance.

1. Buy her cards or write her a note.
2. Bring her flowers.
3. Buy her chocolates.
4. Bring home little surprises that say you were thinking of her while you were away.
5. Give her random hugs.
6. Be affectionate at times when you are not wanting sex.
7. Light a candle at dinner or in the bedroom.
8. Put on her favorite music.
9. Notice what she is wearing and pay her a compliment.
10. Take notice of the foods and restaurants she likes.
11. Plan dates ahead of time.
12. Put the remote control on mute at the commercials and talk with her instead of scanning through the channels.
13. Look at her when she talks.
14. Don't interrupt her or finish her sentences.
15. Notice when she is upset and offer her a hug.
16. Help her when she is tired.
17. Help her with her domestic chores.
18. Call her when you are running late.
19. Call her just to say "I love you."
20. Plan little celebrations and do something different.

What Romance Says

When a man does little things that say, "I care, I understand what you feel, I know what you like, I am happy to do things for you, and you are not alone," he is directly fulfilling a woman's need for romance. When a man does things without a woman having to ask, she feels deeply loved. If he forgets to do them, though, a wise woman graciously persists in reminding him by asking in a nondemanding manner.

A man, however, receives love differently from a woman. He chiefly feels loved when she lets him know again and again that he is doing a good job of fulfilling her. Her good mood makes him feel loved. Even when she enjoys the weather, a part of him takes the credit. A man is happiest when a woman is fulfilled.

While a woman feels romanced by the flowers, chocolates, et cetera, a man's sense of romance is fueled by a woman's appreciation of him. When he does little things for her and she appreciates it a lot, then he feels more romantic.

Romantic Rituals

The basis of almost all romantic rituals is a male giving and a female receiving. Women generally do not realize that the kind of love a man needs most is her loving message that he has fulfilled her.

> The basis of almost all romantic rituals is a male giving and a female receiving.

When she is happy about the things he provides for her, he feels loved. When he can do something for her, he lets in her love. The most important skill for loving a man is to catch him when he is doing something right and notice and appreciate him for it. The most significant mistake is taking him for granted.

A man feels loved when he gets the message that he has made a difference, that he has been helpful in some way, and that his partner benefits from his presence. The other way to love a man is whenever possible to minimize his mistakes with statements like "It's no big deal" or "It's OK." Downplaying disappointments makes him much more open to future requests and needs.

Lighting the Fire of Passion

When a man does things for a woman and she is fulfilled, they both win. When I bring in the logs and build a fire, Bonnie feels special and cared for. Her romantic feelings begin to ignite. Knowing that, I am also quite pleased and confident.

However, when I sit on the couch and watch her bring in the

logs and build a fire, although I feel relaxed and grateful, our romantic feelings aren't being charged. It is a very different dynamic that occurs when a woman takes care of a man.

Passionate Monogamy

Although women need romance to feel loved, for passion to grow over time their most important intimacy requirement is monogamy. A man can make the romantic gestures, but if he is not monogamous, her passion cannot grow. Romance tells a woman that she is special. And there is nothing that makes a woman feel more special than a man in touch with his passions and wanting only her.

As a woman ages, her ability to feel and express passion increases if she feels she can fully trust her partner to be there for her. If she feels she is being compared to another woman or that she has to compete, she cannot continue to open up.

If she senses that he is having an affair or could have an affair, she shuts down. Like a delicate rose she needs the clear and clean water of monogamy to gradually unfold, one petal at a time. By clearly committing himself and assuring a woman that they are going to grow old together, her mate gives her the special support she needs to discover the fires of sexual passion deep within her soul.

By clearly committing himself and assuring a woman that they are going to grow old together, her mate gives her the special support she needs to discover the fires of sexual passion deep within her soul.

The Importance of Monogamy

As I described in the introduction, in the beginning of our marriage I promised to be monogamous because it was something Bonnie clearly needed. Over the years, I have discovered that each time I avoided the temptation, my own passion for Bonnie has grown stronger. Not only does she benefit from monogamy, but so do I.

As I continue to make Bonnie feel that she is special, she is able to make me more important to her. Not only does she trust me, but the people I work with trust me as well. I am very much aware of the fact that the phenomenal success of my books is because people feel that they can trust what I have to say. When a man is trusted by his wife and family, others sense something they can trust about him. Sexual monogamy strengthens a man and makes him worthy of the highest trust.

In the famous best-seller, *Think and Grow Rich,* Napoleon Hill interviewed five hundred of the most successful men in America about the qualities that created success. Remarkably, all of the men were sexually active in a passionate, monogamous relationship of over thirty years' duration.

These powerful, successful men had somehow learned to maintain passion with one woman for decades. Their sexual fire had not burned out, nor did they require the stimulation of an affair to be turned on. As they grew in passion through sharing their love in a sexual way with their wives, they grew in personal power and made a difference to the world.

Greater drive and success are waiting for those men who realize this simple secret of love. Through creating and sustaining a passionate monogamous relationship, not only can a woman grow in sexual passion but a man can be more powerful and effective in his work.

This study of only men was conducted many years ago. I am sure without a doubt that as women learn to master having careers in tandem with an ongoing passionate relationship, they too will be even more effective and influential in their work.

Knowing and sensing my ever-increasing sexual fulfillment with her and my clear commitment to our monogamous relationship, Bonnie is more satisfied, more centered. Even though she is not with me when I am away, she continues to feel the special sexual connection that only we share. I may share my mind and spirit with many, but only Bonnie gets my sexual energy.

Romance for Women, Sex for Men

Just as romance is important to a woman, sexual gratification is important to a man. He needs constant reassurance that his partner likes sex with him. Sexual rejection. is traumatic to a man's sense of self.

I'm not saying that a woman should feel obliged to have sex whenever her partner wants it. I am saying that she needs to work hard to be hypersensitive when sex is the subject under discussion. If he initiates sex and she's not into it, she shouldn't just say no. Instead, say "A part of me wants to have sex, but I think I would enjoy it more later." By considering his feelings, she frees him to continue initiating sex without feeling rejected.

Just as communication and romance are the primary means for a woman to experience love, sex is the primary way for a man to connect with love and passion on an ongoing basis.

6. *Friendship, Autonomy, and Fun*

Friendship is a breeze if we suppress our feelings. If one partner is willing to sacrifice who he or she is to the relationship, they will always get along—but the passion will die.

Make no mistake, although women quite commonly will "lose themselves" to accommodate their partners, men also surrender a major part of themselves. To avoid conflict, a man will also hold himself back. Without good communication skills, quite commonly a couple with a lot of love will choose to maintain the friendship and sacrifice their feelings. They do not realize that by suppressing negative feelings they are also suppressing their ability to feel in general.

When a woman cares for a man but doesn't use advanced skills to help him be successful in supporting her, she is actually hurting, not helping, the relationship. A man can only thrive in a relationship when he truly fulfills her needs. If she pretends to be fulfilled he will "think" he is fulfilled, but he doesn't even know what he is missing.

Balancing Dependence and Autonomy

To be really good friends in a relationship requires a balance of autonomy and dependence. As we have explored, needing our partners is the basis of passion. However, if we are not also autonomous, at those times when our partners have little to give to us, we will feel powerless to get what we need.

Through practicing personal responsibility and self-healing we can nurture ourselves at those times when our partners can't be our nurturers. The real test of love is when we can be our partner's friend, and give without any expectation of return. This becomes easier when we are not too dependent on them and when at other times we have repeatedly experienced that they can be there for us. When we are confident that we can get what we need at other times, then we are not so demanding at those times when our partners have little to give.

Lightness and Fun

A man is almost always annoyed when a woman wants to "work on the relationship." He doesn't want to work on it. He would rather just live in it.

A man needs to feel that sometimes he is on vacation in the relationship and, in a sense, can do no wrong. He wants to feel that he is fine the way he is and that he is not required to change. When a woman says "It's no big deal" or "It's OK,'" he tends to lighten up. When a woman can be lighthearted about her problems, a man feels like a success.

On the other hand, for a woman to feel friendship for a man it means that he can be relaxed about her getting upset. If he can just give her a little sympathy without taking the issue so personally, she can shift her feelings without making a scene.

Friendship for a woman means that her mate will, from time to time, go out of his way to support her or offer his help. Friendship for a man means that a woman will go out of her way not to be demanding or expect too much.

Being our partner's friend means never trying to change their mood or taking it personally when they are not feeling the way we want them to. Learning this lesson of detachment can totally transform a relationship.

In the next chapter, we will discuss the seventh secret of lasting passion: partnership and service to a higher purpose. Together we will explore dance steps for lasting intimacy through creating a win/win partnership which contributes not only to a more passionate relationship, but to a better and more loving world.

CHAPTER 13

Dance Steps for Lasting Intimacy

Practicing advanced relationship skills is like learning to dance. In the beginning, you feel awkward and confused and unnatural. Occasionally you will even step on your partner's feet. The last thing you feel is romantic. But once the steps are learned, you can begin to flow and dance to the music under the moonlight.

I always enjoy watching older couples dance. They seem so happy together. They know just what to do, he has all the moves down, and she trusts him to lead her exactly where she wants to go. She melts into his arms and he holds her charmingly and confidently. This trust and confidence can only come with years of practice.

When couples start out in love, they are always willing to do whatever it takes to make the relationship work. The problem, as we have discussed, is that the dance steps that worked for past generations don't work today. The music has changed, and new steps are required. Without an awareness of these new advanced skills, it is inevitable that the special light of love we feel in the beginning will grow dimmer.

A Woman's Influence

When a man is skilled in loving a woman, there is no question that his love can sweep her off her feet. In a similar way, a woman's love can help plant a man's feet firmly on the ground. By learning new skills to express her love, she can be a mirror to help him see and feel his greatness. She can be a motivating force that helps him succeed in expressing his most competent and loving self.

Gentle and Fierce Love

The support I have experienced through my wife's gentle and sometimes fierce love for me has dramatically influenced my ability to relax and feel good about myself. It has allowed the real and loving person to come out of me.

For example, instead of being critical when I would forget things, she was accepting and patient. This was the gentle love. But instead of giving up and doing things for herself without my help, she persisted in a nondemanding way. This was her fierce love. She didn't give up like so many women do. She kept on practicing the dance steps.

The Well-Earned Gift of Love

Although Bonnie's love is a gift that I have earned, it is also given freely. Through her willingness to "pause and postpone" her immediate needs, "prepare me" to listen and respond to her requests, and "persist" in asking for my support in a nondemanding way, I gradually discovered how important love was and how to get it.

The growth we have experienced together has been the result of hard work. Now it is much easier. Life always has its difficult challenges, but with new skills for relating we are able to grow closer instead of farther apart in our journey together. We are able to support each other in our ongoing process of living, growing, and sharing ourselves in the world.

As I have focused on developing my masculine side to improve communication by learning to duck, dodge, disarm, and deliver, she has focused on developing her female side to assist me in being successful in fulfilling her. Through her learning to pause, prepare, postpone, and persist, it has made a world of difference.

Nobody Is Perfect

Although neither of us is perfect in these skills, each day we get better. They are no longer difficult to practice because we know they work, and we know how painful it is when we don't use them. Sometimes she is the more supportive, while at other times she has little to give. Even when both of us are empty, just knowing how to start giving again to get the support we need is a tremendous source of strength.

When I am in my cave and Bonnie is not getting what she needs, instead of panicking or feeling responsible, she knows how to pause and give me space. She practices preparing me to do more by asking for support in easy ways and then appreciating me.

Instead of trying to change me or improve the relationship, she focuses on using her feminine skills to give me space and gradually draw me out of the cave with her patient love.

Two Steps Forward and Then Back Again

Just like dance partners, when a woman takes two steps back, the man can take two steps forward. When he takes two steps back, she can take two steps forward. This give-and-take is the basic rhythm of relationships.

At other times, they both pull back and then come back together. Every relationship has those times when both partners have little to give and so they pull back to recharge.

When couples work together in the same office or business each day, it is even more important that they create time each week when they are apart. This separation gives them a chance to come back to the partnership. It is this movement that keeps a relationship fresh.

While dancing, a woman gracefully swings into the man's arms, then spins away. In a successful relationship, this same pattern is expressed. A woman is happy to see her partner, she moves into his arms, and then after pausing and preparing him, she spins out of his arms and shares her feelings in a circular manner.

At other times, he will hold her in his arms as she swings back and dips. In a similar way, as a woman shares her feelings she may dip. With his sympathetic support she is able to go almost all the way down to the dance floor and then experience the joy of coming back up.

In dance, a woman naturally spins around while the man stays steady. In a similar manner, when a woman can share her feelings without a man reacting with his, she can feel heard. Certainly, there are also times when they both spin, but as in dance they need to pull away to do the movement before again making contact.

While dancing, a man gets to feel his sense of independence and autonomy by leading, and a woman gets to feel her need for cooperation and relationship through supporting him as he supports her in the moves she wants to make.

Teamwork and Practice

This kind of teamwork is ideal for intimacy to thrive. With an awareness of these new skills and plenty of practice as we learn the new steps for making relationships work, the intimacy we share in the beginning of a relationship can continue to grow. By learning to change with the music and learn new steps, our relationships can become graceful and fluid.

When we dance together to the music of romance, life becomes a grand ball where the coaches don't turn into pumpkins at midnight, the flowers never fade, and the chandeliers sparkle like an infinity of diamonds through the decades.

Although many of our parents couldn't dance the dance of

lasting intimacy and increasing passion, we can and, in turn, as our children grow up they will be able to as well. Ours is indeed the transformational generation whose task it is to forge ahead to create new and better relationships between men and women.

The Care and Feeding of Partnerships

In our journey we must remember to nurture and respect our differences. Differences create passion. We start relationships because we are drawn to another person who is different but complements us.

In the beginning, Bonnie and I had no idea how different we were. We were so focused on the ways in which we were similar. We were both very spiritual, we both enjoyed sex, we both liked to go for walks, we both liked tennis, we both liked movies, we had many friends in common, we were both easygoing, we were both interested in psychology. The list of commonalities was delightfully long.

Once we were married, we began to notice the differences. I was detached, she was emotional. I was goal oriented, she was relationship oriented. She liked discussing problems, I wanted to solve or postpone them. Besides these and other standard gender differences that create the inherent attraction between the sexes, there were many other differences as well that are not necessarily gender based.

She liked the bedroom temperature cool, and I liked it warm. She liked antiques, and I liked high tech and modern. She liked to balance her checkbook to the last penny, and I would round it off and get a vague running total in my mind. She liked to get up early, and I liked to stay up late. She liked eating at home, and I liked going out. She drove the speed limit, and I liked to drive fast. She liked to save money, and I liked to spend it. She made decisions slowly, and I liked to make them fast. She held on to old relationships, and I quickly moved on. I have big ambitions, and she is quite content with her life the way it is. I like electric gadgets, and she likes the garden and other "real" things of the earth. She likes to visit museums, and I like elegant hotels. I like new, modern homes, and she likes older, more charming homes. I like views with a vista, and she likes being in the woods.

Although each of these differences creates a possible conflict, they also create the opportunity to grow together as well. In relationships, we are generally attracted to a person with certain qualities that, in a sense, are either dormant within or yet to come out of us. When we are one way and our partner is another way, we are instinctively attracted to them to help us find balance with ourselves. Finding this balance creates passion and attraction.

Shopping for a New TV

After about a year of being married, I confronted my first big challenge relating to our differences. I wanted to buy a larger-screen TV. I love new technology and gadgets. Bonnie wasn't in favor of the idea. She said that she didn't like the idea of having to see it looming in the living room every day.

This was a very difficult moment for me. I began to feel that to make her happy, I had to give up something that would make me happy. At that point I was just beginning to understand how we could resolve our differences by working out a win/win solution.

Internally, I was furious. All kinds of buttons were being pushed, but I contained myself by remaining focused on finding a solution. As long as I kept thinking that we could both some-how get what we wanted, the frustration did not turn to anger at her.

"I want to respect your wishes," I finally told her. "And I really want to get a bigger TV. I've waited a long time to be able to afford one. I also really want you to have a beautiful home. What do you think we can do?"

Bonnie answered, "I wouldn't mind a big TV if it was in a cabinet that closed in the front. Then when you weren't watch-ing it, I could close it and not always have to see it."

I immediately said great, and we went together to buy a cabinet. I thought it was going to be an easy solution. We soon found that we had completely different tastes in furniture.

The Win/Win Solution

The cabinet I picked out was high tech and would hold all my stereo equipment. The cabinet she wanted had glass-backed shelves with lights for displaying china and crystals, but it didn't have a big enough space for the TV that I wanted.

For weeks we looked for something that would accommodate our differing needs. During this process, I felt like I wanted to explode, but I did everything I could to contain my frustration. It was a very difficult time. I thought that she was so stubborn and resistant, and I became very judgmental of her. In my darkest moments I thought, I'm getting a divorce!

Hindsight helps us to see how we tend to blow things out of proportion. Although I thought she was being stubborn, I was being just as stubborn. I wanted my big-screen TV, and she wanted it covered. I wanted a cabinet to hold my stereo, and she wanted something to hold her crystal and beautiful things.

We teetered on the brink of hating each other, and then came the day when we finally found a cabinet we both agreed on. It was a miracle. Except that we had to wait another three months for it to be shipped to us. The whole ordeal couldn't have been more frustrating, but once the cabinet arrived, we were both very satisfied with it.

Building Relationship Muscles

What we ended up getting together was much better than what I would have gotten if I'd gone shopping on my own. By stretching myself to include and respect Bonnie's tastes and wishes, I had achieved an end result far greater than anything I alone could have created. Through exercising our patience and flexibility we were both able to strengthen our relationship.

This experience became a strong metaphor for all our future conflicts. I realized that even when it seemed that I could not get what I wanted, with persistence and a willingness to fulfill both our wishes, we would always end up with more. Although I didn't initially care much for the display shelves, I love and greatly appreciate them now. And Bonnie greatly enjoys the thirty-six-inch TV.

Once we had worked through this problem successfully, I realized that we were much closer than we had been before. Our trust level had gone up. The strength, patience, faith, and flexibility it took to find a win/win solution made other challenges much easier.

The Challenge of Relationships

The challenge in a relationship is to overcome conflict and merge our differences into a workable alliance. In each area of difference, there is a tremendous opportunity for conflict or growth. In very practical terms, each difference is an opportunity to strengthen our ability to create loving relationships through creating solutions in which we are both supported.

Partnership and Service to a Higher Purpose

Partnership is the seventh secret to creating a lasting and passionate relationship. To create a mutually fulfilling partnership, it is helpful to understand how men and women experience partnership differently.

A woman feels partnership when she and her partner are doing things together in a cooperative manner toward the same goal. There is no hierarchy or boss. They make all decisions together, sharing their input equally.

A man experiences partnership very differently. He likes to have his department, where he is in control, and he is happy for her to have her department, where she is in control. He doesn't want her telling him what to do, nor does he feel he has to be involved with what she is doing. Together, doing different jobs with different responsibilities, they are a partnership teaming up to get the job done.

With an awareness of this difference, both men and women can create the partnership they want. Using sexual intercourse as a metaphor, we can easily see the solution. In sex, a man leaves his world and enters hers. This brings them both great pleasure. Then, quite naturally, he pulls back into his world (or department), leaving her alone in her world (or department). Then again, back and forth, he moves in and out of her world. In a similar way, to create a win/win partnership, a couple can have more or less clear departments, and the man can occasionally move into hers and help her as an equal.

As he gets better and better at working and cooperating with her in her departments, then slowly but surely he will begin to invite her into his departments. Using this as a general guideline can be very helpful, particularly when couples work together.

Serving Something Beyond Ourselves

For a partnership to thrive and not be self-serving, it must have a purpose beyond itself. For the passion to grow, partners must share a common interest and work toward that end.

We all come into this world with gifts to share and purposes to fulfill beyond our personal happiness. They may not be earth-shattering, but they are there. For a relationship to grow in love and passion, the love we share with another needs to be directed in some loftier way.

Having children is a natural fulfillment of this need. As a team, parents give to each other so that they can more successfully give to the children.

Once children grow up and leave home, couples need to find a new goal or purpose. When as a partnership we are serving the highest good of the family, community, or world, our love can continue to grow without limit.

The Power of Forgiveness

To fully open our hearts to each other and enjoy a lifetime of love, the most important skill of all is forgiveness. Forgiving your partner for their mistakes not only frees you to love again but allows you to forgive yourself for not being perfect.

When we don't forgive in one relationship, our love is, to various degrees, restricted in all our life relationships. We can still love others, but not as much. When a heart is blocked in one relationship, it beats more weakly in them all.

Let's say a person who is very important to you makes a big mistake. As a result, you feel hurt or wounded. You decided that what they did was so wrong, you can't forgive them. This decision blocks your ability to love and shuts down a big part of your heart.

Even though you may try to forget that person, as long as you don't forgive them you are giving them the power to continue hurting you. Forgiving means letting go of hurt.

Forgiveness allows us to give our love again and helps us to open up both to give and also to receive love. When we are closed, we lose on two counts.

Not Forgiving Is Painful

The more you love someone, the more *you* suffer when you don't forgive them. Many people are driven to suicide by the agonizing pain of not forgiving a loved one. The greatest pain we can ever feel is the pain of not loving someone we love.

This agony drives people mad and is responsible for all the violence and craziness in our world and in our relationships. It is this pain of holding back our love that moves many people to addictive behaviors, substance abuse, and random violence.

We stubbornly hold on to bitterness and resentment not because we are not loving, but because we do not know how to forgive. If we were not loving, then ceasing to love someone would not be painful at all. The more loving we are, the more painful it is to not forgive.

How We Learn to Forgive

If when we were children our parents had asked for our forgiveness when they made mistakes, we would know how to forgive. If we had watched them forgive each other, we would better know how to forgive. If we had experienced being forgiven for our own mistakes again and again, we would not only know how to forgive but would have experienced firsthand the power of forgiveness to transform others.

Because our parents did not know how to forgive, we easily misunderstand what it means. Emotionally, we associate forgiving someone with the realization that what they did was not so bad after all.

For example, let's say that I am late and that you are upset with me. If I give you a great reason or excuse, you are more inclined to forgive me. I tell you, for instance, that my car blew up on the way over. That's why I am late. Surely, you would be more inclined to forgive me. Better yet, let's say a car blew up next to me and I stopped to save a child from dying. With such a "good" reason for being late, I would immediately be forgiven. But real forgiveness is needed when something really bad or hurtful happens and there is no good reason for it.

Real Forgiveness

Real forgiveness acknowledges that a real mistake has been made and then affirms that the person who made it still deserves to be loved and respected. It does not mean that their behavior was condoned or agreed with in any way.

If forgiveness is required, the implication is that you are acknowledging that a mistake was made that you want corrected or at least not repeated.

Forgiveness contains many of the sixteen messages listed below. Before reading down the list, take just a moment to think about a situation in which you found it almost impossible to forgive. As you verbally or mentally read these phrases, imagine the person who wounded you standing before you.

1. What you did was all your fault and not mine.
2. I am not responsible for what you did.
3. What you did was wrong. I did not deserve to be treated this way.
4. There is no good reason for what you did.
5. There is no excuse, and I am not willing to be subjected to that treatment ever again.
6. It is not OK with me.
7. It was very painful.

AND

8. I do not want to spend the rest of my life punishing you for this.
9. I can reach within my heart and see that even though what you did was "bad," you are still a good person deep inside.
10. I am willing to find the innocent part of you that is doing your best. No one is perfect.
11. I will not withhold my love from you.
12. I will freely give my love, but I will also protect myself from this happening again.
13. It will take time to rebuild trust, but I am willing to give you another chance.
14. It may be that I am not willing to give you another chance with me, but I do wish you well with others.
15. I release my hurt. You are no longer responsible for how I feel. I forgive you and wish you well.
16. I am responsible for how I feel. I am a loving person, and I can be loved just the way I am.

When forgiveness is learned and expressed, a huge weight is lifted. Through saying those three simple words, "I forgive you," lives and relationships have been dramatically saved again and again.

Practicing Forgiveness

The power to forgive is within us all, but like any other skill we must practice it. In the beginning, it takes time. We work at forgiving our partner, and then suddenly, the next day we are blaming them again. This is par for the course. Mastering the advanced relationship skill of forgiveness takes time, but with practice, it becomes a natural response.

In the beginning, a helpful phrase you can write out or think is: "Nobody's perfect, I forgive you for being imperfect. What you did was wrong. Nobody deserves to be treated the way you treated me. What you did was wrong and I forgive you. I forgive you for not being perfect. I forgive you for not giving me the love and respect that I deserve. I forgive you for not knowing better. I wish for you the decency and respect that every human being deserves. I forgive you for making a mistake."

The Message of Forgiveness

Christ's message to humanity from the cross was one of forgiveness. To rise above death, beyond pain, one has to forgive. His words were: "Father, forgive them; for they know not what they do." In this simple phrase is contained the secret of how to forgive.

We can begin to forgive our partners and others who hurt us when we can recognize that they really don't know what they are doing.

I remember when I first experienced pure forgiveness. It was when my daughter Lauren was two years old. She was playing with her food. I kept telling her not to, but she went ahead anyway. Within a few moments she was holding the spaghetti in her hands, then dropping it all over our carpet.

I was furious inside because she made a mess and I had to clean it up. At the same time, however, I was completely forgiving of her. I was angry with her, but my heart was completely open and filled with love.

I wondered how this could be and then remembered Christ's words, "Father, forgive them; for they know not what they do."

In that moment it was easy to forgive her because she clearly didn't know what she was doing when she dropped the spaghetti. I suppose she thought she was creating a work of art! What she didn't realize was that she was causing a problem for me.

Why People Don't Forgive

As a counselor I have repeatedly experienced that people act and react in nonloving ways when they don't know better. People bear grudges out of ignorance and innocence. When they can experience a better way, they go for it. No one in their heart of hearts really wants to withhold and punish. It is merely the only way he or she knows to react when another person disrespects them.

The ideas in this book and my other books about male and female differences have been helpful to people because these insights are based on forgiveness.

No one is being blamed. Your mother and father are not blamed because they didn't anticipate what you would need to know to make your relationships work. Men are not blamed because they are "from Mars"—and don't understand women. Women are not blamed because they are "from Venus"—and don't understand men. We have problems because "we know not what we do." Once we bear this truth in mind and heart, our mistakes and our partners' mistakes are more forgivable.

The Angels in Heaven Rejoice

The angels in heaven rejoice each time you forgive. When you choose to love instead of closing your heart, you bring a little spark of divinity into our dark world of struggle. You lighten the load of others and help them to forgive as well.

When men and women fail in relationships, it is not because they are not loving. We are all born with love in our hearts and a purpose to fulfill. We experience pain in our relationships because we do not know how to share our love in ways that work. We are missing the skills.

Sometimes love is not expressed because it is buried deep inside or locked within the fortress of our hearts. Hiding behind a wall, we are safe from hurt but barred from love.

So many people are imprisoned in themselves. They do not know how to find love so that they can share it. Infinities of love are wasted in a lifetime when we are not taught the basic skills for communicating and relating in a loving manner.

A Time for Hope

Perhaps for the first time in history, we are entering a phase when love can be mastered. This millennial time is one of great hope for relationships and the world. Previously on our planet "survival" was the guiding purpose. Slowly but surely, in the last several thousand years love has become increasingly important. It can become a guiding force within us all. The widespread dissatisfaction between men and women in relationships is a symptom that the world wants more. The pain of nations is the pain we feel when we can't share our love.

We can no longer turn our heads away from our deeper feelings. We hunger deep in our hearts to love. This shift has already taken place. The love is already there.

With this new understanding of what our mothers could not tell us and our fathers did not know, we're now much better prepared to love our partners. With practice, this new, open-ended love can dramatically improve relationships.

It is my hope that in applying the different skills for improving relationships you not only can forgive your partner when he or she forgets to use these skills, but you can also forgive your parents and yourself.

Remember, even if our parents could have taught us more, we still wouldn't have perfect relationships. The most intelligent and successful people around are having problems in their intimate and family relationships. There is no shame in needing to learn and practice.

We all need to practice. Although we are born with the ability to love, it is a skill and must be learned. Mastering any new skill requires infinite rehearsal time. Give yourself and your partner or potential partner as much as possible. Through being easy on your relationship, you are being easy on yourself. You and your partner deserve that.

Making a Difference in the World

Through mastering the secrets of passion and practicing forgiveness, we are not only creating a lifetime of love for ourselves, but we are making a difference in the world.

Practicing advanced relationship skills and learning to harmonize dissonant values is not only the prerequisite for creating more passionate relationships, but directly contributes to a more peaceful world.

Imagine a world where families are not shattered by divorce or neighbors are not hating each other. This kind of world is possible. Each step you take in your relationship helps actualize that possibility. Peace and prosperity for the world become a reality each time it approaches being your daily reality.

It is naive to assume that we can create peace in the world when we cannot make peace with the people we love. When our leaders are capable of having loving and mutually nurturing family relationships, then they will have acquired the skills to negotiate world peace.

By learning to resolve the differences between men and women, we are, in effect, easing global tensions and allowing ourselves and others to effectively embrace and connect different cultures and races.

As we realize through our relationships that our differences are really superficial and that deep within we are all one, we can transcend conflict and war and approach our problems with a new awareness that respects and harmonizes differences.

As in male/female relationships, the solution is not in denying that differences exist. The potential for conflict is resolved solely through honoring and respecting each other and finding creative ways in which to fulfill our differing needs.

Each time we take the sometimes painful or difficult step to positive resolution in our personal relationships, we are paving the way for harmony in the world. Your every effort and attempt makes it easier for others to follow you. If you cannot make it work, what hope is there for others? But if you can, who among us cannot succeed? I hope you cherish this new information as much as I do and continue to share it with others.

Thank you for letting me be a part of your journey in this world. May you and your loved ones experience a lifetime of love, and in our lives may we also share the experience of a world filled with love.

Audiotapes and Videos by John Gray

Audiotapes

The Secrets of Successful Relationships Series (12 audiotapes)
Enjoy John Gray's humor, compassion, and simple wisdom as he presents his complete relationship seminar on tape. In this insightful and entertaining series for both couples and singles, John shares powerful secrets for creating and sustaining passionate relationships as well as practical tools for improving communication in all your relationships. In addition to creating lasting intimacy you will discover in the last two tapes the secrets of great sex.

Healing the Heart (12 audiotapes)
John Gray shares seven powerful techniques and visualization exercises to master your emotions, overcome fear, increase self-esteem, and harness the power of forgiveness.

Men Are from Mars, Women Are from Venus: A Practical Guide for Improving Communication and Getting What You Want in Your Relationships (1 60-minute audiotape)

What Your Mother Couldn't Tell You and Your Father Didn't Know: Advanced Relationship Skills for Better Communication and Lasting Intimacy (2 60-minute audiotapes)

Videos

The Secrets of Successful Relationships
Advanced Relationship Skills
Secrets of Great Sex (Viewer discretion advised)

To order any of John Gray's audiotapes, and videos please call:
1-800-834-2110

FREE VIDEO OFFER

Dr. John Gray introduces a special video, available for the first time, featuring excerpts from his exciting seminars, plus information on his latest seminar audio and video series, at a special discount price.

You'll experience special moments from Dr. John Gray's fascinating seminar programs, with excerpts that will help you enrich your relationship.

To enjoy this preview video and the featured programs, just send $5.85 to cover the costs of shipping and handling, and it's yours free. Make your check payable to John Gray Video and mail it to:

John Gray Video Processing Center
5959 Triumph Street
Commerce, CA 90040

Please include your name, address, and telephone number with your order.

To order by phone using your credit card, please call **1-800-791-3900**. Allow 2 to 3 weeks for delivery.